COMMUNICATION AND ENERGY IN
CHANGING URBAN ENVIRONMENTS

Published in the United States of America
by
ARCHON BOOKS
The Shoe String Press, Inc.
995 Sherman Avenue,
Hamden,
Connecticut 06514

1971

Made and Printed in Great Britain by
J. W. Arrowsmith Ltd., Bristol, BS3 2NT

COMMUNICATION
AND ENERGY IN CHANGING
URBAN ENVIRONMENTS

Edited by

DOUGLAS JONES

R.W.A. Professor of Architecture
The University of Bristol

Proceedings of the
Twenty-first Symposium of the Colston Research Society
held in the University of Bristol
March 24th to 28th, 1969

ARCHON BOOKS
1971

series:

This book is Volume XXI of the Colston Papers. Permission must be obtained from the Colston Research Society, 71 Winterstoke Road, Bristol 3, England, and from the Publishers, before any part of the contents may be reproduced.

Foreword

THE name of Edward Colston, the great seventeenth-century philanthropist and educationalist, is associated in Bristol with a number of scholastic and charitable institutions. It was adopted by a group of public-spirited citizens when, in 1899, they established the 'University College Colston Society', with the aim of fostering the young and struggling University College. For a decade it played a part in the movement which culminated in the institution of the University of Bristol in 1909.

The Society then changed its name and made its object more precise: it became the 'Colston Research Society' and devoted itself to the encouragement of original work in the University. It made grants for the purchase of apparatus and for other expenses of research. As resources increased activities expanded and, notably in the later 'thirties, the Society financed a full-scale Social Survey of Bristol.

After the war a new reconsideration of policy led to the decision to devote the major part of the Society's efforts to the promotion of an annual symposium, the first being held in 1948. The rapid growth of the symposium as a means for the advancement of knowledge is one of the remarkable features of the intellectual life of recent years. Usually such meetings are fostered by bodies interested in one particular field of learning. As the list of titles (on the page opposite) shows, no such limitation applies to the symposia of the Colston Research Society. That the subject should be one at an interesting and active stage of development is the main factor in making a choice. The fact that the symposium is held in one of the younger seats of learning, with its home in an historic city, is a stimulus not only to the University but also, we believe, to the visiting guests who have come from many countries. The publication of the proceedings ensures the communication of the papers and discussions to wider circles.

It was my privilege to be President of the Colston Research Society for the year 1968/69, during which the twenty-first symposium was promoted by the Society. The subject was 'Communication and Energy in Changing Urban Environments' and the proceedings are printed here as the twenty-first volume of the Colston Papers.

J. E. C. CLARKE

Preface

THERE is a growing realisation that those who are responsible for the development of our towns and cities cannot think and work in isolation if they hope to achieve integrated answers. The days have gone when building was catered for by simple technical means master minded by a few men and when growth was slow and, because of it, answers were direct.

Now the opposite is true.

The technology of building is vastly complicated and needs the capacity of many men of different disciplines to sustain it and growth is so rapid that we no longer have points of reference from which to orientate our thoughts.

So here was an opportunity offered by the Colston Research Society to get together a group of people, like minded and of different disciplines, each of whom was interested and involved in the problems of the Urban Environment.

To do this successfully a framework is needed which must be of common interest to a number of disciplines, it must give ample scope for discussion and prognostication, and it must be capable of offering intellectual rewards. Urban Communication, which concerns the needs of people to converse and meet, seemed to fulfill all these conditions. Energy, in the sense of Environmental control, also seemed to fit. And so the title arose— 'Communication and energy in changing urban environments'. The introduction of the word 'changing' needs no explanation. So most of our time was divided between these two things and in looking at some of the design tools that are becoming available. We did not allow ourselves to forget that the purpose of technology is to serve our needs, as can be seen both from the papers and from the discussion, although the beauty of technology was often very seductive.

For the purpose of this book, we are beginning with a short summary of the proceedings and this has been prepared by my colleague Peter Burberry. He has been a tower of strength throughout. He contributed so much to the initial thinking about the subject matter of the Symposium, to the names of those we should invite to give papers, and to the Symposium itself, and without him its shape would have been completely different.

Of my other colleagues within the Department of Architecture I must single out for special thanks my Secretary Joan Waldock who gave a background of support one always hopes for but rarely gets, and Graham Holland who coped so calmly yet efficiently with those essential but boring and mundane things which, as far as I am aware of, were the cause of not one single criticism of organisation. It is impossible to thank everyone who helped us whether they were members of the Department, or of the University, or beyond; but I must make special mention of the great help that was given by the G.P.O. and by Plessey. The equipment they delivered, set up, manned and then collected, and which was used as background to two of the papers, showed great openhandedness by both organisations and provided a deal of interest and pleasure.

Lastly I want to thank the Colston Research Society and its honorary officers for the help they gave and for making this Symposium possible. They entrusted the 1969 Conference to a new University Department—as is our Department of Architecture—and for this confidence they showed we are deeply appreciative.

DOUGLAS JONES

List of members

ALEXANDRE, A., Organisation for Economic Co-operation & Development, Paris.
ARSCHAVIR, A., School of Architecture, Hull.
BAILEY, Dr. P. B., British Medical Association, Bristol.
BAYLISS, D., Centre for Environmental Studies, London.
BEGG, R. C., Lawrence Williams & Co., Bristol.
BENNETT, Sir H., Greater London Council.
BENTHAM, D. S., South Western Electricity Board, Bristol.
BOND, D., Clarke, Nicholls & Marcel, Bristol.
BONES, J. A., University of Bristol.
BOYNE, D. A. C. A., The Architects' Journal, London.
BROWN, P., University of Bristol.
BURBERRY, P. J., University of Bristol.
BURROUGH, T. H. B., University of Bristol.
BURTON, M., University of Bristol.
CAMACHO, O. O., Public Institute of Venezuela.
CARTER, B., University of Bristol.
CHERRY, Professor Colin, Imperial College of Science & Technology, London.
CLARKE, D. E., University of Bristol.
CLARKE, T. F. W., Ministry of Housing & Local Government, London.
COBLENTZ, Dr. A., University of Paris.
COLLINS, N. R., Gloucestershire County Planning Department.
CRESSWELL, R. W., University of Nottingham.
CULLIMORE, Dr. M. S. G., University of Bristol.
DAKIN, Professor A. J., University of Toronto, Canada.
DE BARRA, F., University College, Dublin.
DOVELL, Professor P., University of Manchester.
FARMER, M., University of Bristol.
FINDLAY, C. M. P., University of Bristol.
FLOYD, P. J., Bristol Corporation City Engineer & Planning Officer's Department.
GEESON, T. A., Birmingham City Engineer, Surveyor & Planning Officer's Department.
GEOGHEGAN, P. F., Ministry of Public Building & Works, Newcastle upon Tyne.
GILL, Dr. R., University of Bristol.
GREY, L. L., Post Office Telecommunications Headquarters, London.
HARTLEY, Dr. M. G., University of Manchester Institute of Science & Technology.
HILLIER, W. R. D., Royal Institute of British Architects.
HILLS, P. J., Imperial College of Science & Technology, London.
HOLLAND, G. E., University of Bristol.
HOPKINSON, Professor R. G., University College, London.
HORN, D. F., South Western Electricity Board, Bristol.
HUTCHINSON, Professor B. G., University of Waterloo, Ontario, Canada.

IRELAND, J. C., Plessey Telecommunications Ltd., Liverpool.
IRENS, A. N., South Western Electricity Board, Bristol.
JONES Dr., B. W., University of Bristol.
JONES, Professor Douglas, University of Bristol.
LANGDON, Dr. J., Building Research Station.
LAWRENCE, R. H., Ministry of Transport, Bristol.
LAWSON, T. V., University of Bristol.
LEES, F. G., Sir John Burnet, Tait, Powell & Partners, Bristol.
LOTEN, A. W., Ministry of Public Building & Works, London.
MACARA, Dr. A. W., British Medical Association, Bristol.
MEDHURST, F., Planning Consultant for Teesside.
MELVILLE, I., University of Newcastle.
MITCHELL, C., University of Bristol.
MOXLEY, R., Moxley, Jenner & Partners, Bristol.
MULCAHY, S., Varming Mulcahy Reilly Associates, Dublin.
NEALON, K., Kenneth Nealon, Tanner & Partners, Bristol.
NEWALL, A. D., Shankland, Cox & Associates, Liverpool.
ODELL, Professor P., Nederlandse Economische Hogeschool, Rotterdam.
O'FLAHERTY, Professor C. A., University of Leeds.
PARSONS, F. B., South Western Regional Hospital Board, Bristol.
PHILLIPS, R. O., University of New South Wales, Australia.
PRIEST, E. G., University of Bristol.
RAFFLE, Dr. P. A. B., London Transport.
REDFERN, G., Cwmbran Development Corporation.
ROBINSON, V. J., Bristol Corporation City Engineer & Planning Officer's Department.
SANDERSON, J., Northern Polytechnic, London.
SCHATZ, P., Eidgenossische Technische Hochschule, Zurich.
SCHLAFFENBERG, B., London Borough of Camden Planning Office.
SCOTT, Dr. D. R., National College for Heating, Ventilating, Refrigeration & Fan
    Engineering, Borough Polytechnic, London.
SHOUL, M. L., Royal Institute of British Architects.
SIMS, D. R., Bristol Corporation City Engineer & Planning Officer's Department.
SMART, D. H., South Western Electricity Board, Bristol.
SMITH, D. W., South Western Electricity Board, Bristol.
STANTON, G. R. T., University of Bath.
STEEN, E. J. L. C., Bristol Corporation City Engineer & Planning Officer's Department.
STEWART, R. H., Sir Robert Matthew, Johnson-Marshall & Partners, Welwyn Garden
    City.
STONE, Dr. P. A., Greater London Council.
STUTCHBURY, Dr. H. E., City Architect & Planning Office, Bath.
THOMAS, H. D., Oxford College of Technology.
THRING, Professor M. W., Queen Mary College, London.
WHITING, Miss P., London.
WHYTE, J. S., G.P.O. Telecommunications Headquarters, London.
WILSON, W. L., Ministry of Public Building & Works, London.
WOOD ROBINSON, M., South Western Electricity Board, Bristol.

Contents

Summary of papers

by

PETER BURBERRY

THERE IS a number of aspects of our theme which impinge very acutely on technical design considerations. It is to be hoped the symposium proceedings will greatly clarify many of them.

The need to exchange information has been one of the critical influences in urban design and buildings. In the past we had to go to somebody in order to communicate with him, or if we did not go ourselves, we had to send some physical object. This has changed. It is no longer necessary to go and if we credit the claims of electronic communication, as obviously we must, it does seem that information is no longer a restraining influence upon the concepts that we may have of urban building form. Wires are relatively small and flexible and, in relation to roads and sewers, comparatively cheap. Information is no longer a constraint on what we do. A remarkable change from the situation which has existed for the whole of recorded history when it has been necessary to make personal physical contact of one sort or another. There is a bewildering range of possibilities and it is up to the professions concerned with design and communication to exercise imagination to take advantage of the new possibilities. This symposium gives us a collective opportunity.

Transport has also clearly been a major problem for designers throughout history. Nowadays we all express pious horror at the traffic congestion, but this horror does not in fact seem to be shared by the rest of the population, who still use their cars and apparently enjoy it. I suppose it was 40 years ago that Bernard Shaw said 'What Englishman will give his mind to politics as long as he can afford to keep a motor car' and, perhaps, if he were to come to this symposium, he would say 'What Englishman will give his mind to planning if he can still continue to park his car'. I mean are motor cars as horrifying to everybody as we, perhaps, think they are? The main point to make about this aspect of the field to be considered, is that the wealth of mechanical invention that we enjoy in the transport field is not matched by the same wealth of invention in the fields of building and planning. We move about with twentieth century means of locomotion which must fit into a Rennaisance lay-out of roads and buildings and even the Rennaisance is, perhaps, in this context too advanced a period. This does seem to be a very fundamental area to be considered.

The environment field is one in which, the changes due to electrical and mechanical influences seem most clear. For the whole of recorded history the form of buildings has been governed by natural lighting and natural ventilation and this seems so natural that we do not regard them as limitations. It seems to be the natural law, but obviously it is not and the future and the past will be quite quite different. The constraints which

1

have been inevitable in virtually every building throughout the whole of recorded history are now no longer inevitable and the implications of this, for building and urban form are enormous. I do not suggest that all, or even many, buildings should be artificially ventilated and lit but it is now a problem on which a decision can and in many cases must be taken whereas in the past no decision was possible since the solution was inevitable. This development is obviously one of the key things which should enable us to postulate ranges of building solutions to match the electrical and mechanical fields. On the other hand, it is essential to take great care when we do. The history of high buildings is a warning. They were advocated and in many cases built in the hope of achieving better environment conditions. In fact mechanical ventilation had to be employed to overcome stack effect and wind problems. Noise from distant streets grew in volume as local noise decreased. Intolerable glare came from the unshaded sun and sky. All these things were predictable at the time the erection of high buildings began. The intolerable draughts that whistle round the bottom of them have been observed in other countries, but no notice was taken and designers in this country were amazed when these results emerged. It seemed from experience near the ground that advantages would result from high buildings but although experience is a vital guide to design, it must not be relied upon outside its scope of validity.

Another aspect of environment is, of course, the medical one, and many people have been concerned about this mental, social and psychological aspects. People worry about degradation of human values. It seems important to take the physical environment and the mental environment together. Many people deplore the motor car as a source of intolerable noise, but, on the other hand, the same motor car that is producing this sort of noise, is vastly extending the environment of people who are using it and if many of us were to be put to a test where we had either to endure a certain amount of noise, or give up our motor cars, I think it would be very surprising how much noise we would in fact endure rather than sacrifice this other dimension of the environment that the motor car makes available to us.

Some people are worried by the apparently mechanistic view of people which must emerge from these technical considerations. Objections on the grounds of human values are raised against calculating what people are going to do and calculating how big the provisions for people must be. The motives of this are unexceptional, but the result of avoiding this problem is likely to give rise to conditions which are extremely inhumane where numbers of people are crushed into conditions of congestion which might have been minimised, or avoided had we been prepared to look at the flows of people as akin to other mechanical processes.

It is not, after all, romantic to be forced to queue unnecessarily.

One of the other problems in human values does seem to be that of taking away the opportunity of people making decisions. I came across an example in the Midlands a year or two ago, where some automatic equipment had been installed which eliminated people taking decisions. This was not very satisfactory, the workers became distressed and unsatisfied. As a result of this people were employed, not to do anything, but simply to be about and smile at the workers and this, though it seems on the face of it to be wasteful, solved the problem. But after all why not have the mechanical processes which can be done by machines, and have the human beings to make the whole process more pleasant.

The question of economics can never be forgotten but it is not at all certain that economics is such a prime consideration in many of the decisions in building and towns. It is almost certainly cheaper to have candles and go to bed at dusk, than it is to have electric lighting. It is horrifying to consider how expensive motor cars are. Although obviously one will think about alternatives in economic terms, it certainly does not seem to me that we do things basically because they are economic. We do them because we wish to and probably the only thing that governs us in economic terms is the degree to which we do them; how much of them we have. Not usually whether we do them or not, although there are tragic examples of families who cannot afford to turn on the heating and the environmental advances that most of us enjoy are denied to them on economic grounds.

Another fundamental consideration is the concept of the city. There are many interesting new ways of thinking about cities, not in terms of bricks and mortar, but in terms of information flow and in terms of movement. But, the whole validity of the city and particularly the centrality of the city may be fundamentally questioned and this is one of the critical issues of the moment. Are we going to go on concentrating central functions into new central areas? Are we going to take advantage of the vast possibilities of electrical communications and personal transport to produce something which is better than the central city concept. It seems quite clear that the central city concept as we see it, at the moment, has emerged from constraints of communication and safety as well. Getting together in order to build a wall around ourselves for protection is quite outdated. Safety tells us to scatter as far as we can, and in terms of communications and transport we can scatter if we wish.

Essential to a solution of all these problems, is the relative time scales of the technologies involved. Many Engineers in the transport field cannot foresee the year 2000, and one can easily accept this. Of the vehicles that are on the road today there will be very few still on the road in the year 2000. We shall be operating probably, with quite different bits of equipment, in a different way. But, in the building field, it is possible to foresee what is going to be there in the year 2000. We can look at it already. There are not many buildings designed by living architects which will not be there in the year 2000. Whilst we have this gross disparity in the time scale of development in the various technologies, it seems that there is very little real possibility of any fundamental solution to our problems. By the time we implement Buchanan's proposals the mechanical transport systems for which they were produced will almost certainly have gone and we shall be in precisely the same situation with new transport methods but outdated roads. It does seem vital that we bring the various technologies which together frame our environment into some sort of time correspondence and until this happens no practical solution is likely to emerge.

These are some of the points that seem to me to be fundamental for consideration during the proceedings.

The last theme is that of feed back. It is often suggested that we can get feed back from existing building and actual urban conditions. I suggest that, in fact, we cannot do this effectively, because even against the background of comparatively slowly developing building technology, by the time a design has been conceived, planned, built and been occupied and used for long enough to get any feed back, the basic conditions have changed and we have new problems and new technical resources and methods of solving them. We shall find it very difficult to base our decisions on feed back type of information. We shall need to make decisions, however, we shall need criteria for them, we shall need to be able to postulate ideas and, we shall need to be able to test and appraise these ideas in rational ways before taking action. Traditionally in planning and building, one appraised ideas by looking at drawings and that was all. In many ways in the past this was perfectly adequate because the only thing that one could influence was the physical shape and size. The environmental conditions were fixed by the inevitable form and fabric of the building and there was little mechanical opportunity of altering them. There was a limited range of constructional possibilities available. When the weather got bad the occupants sent for their overcoats; nowadays when the weather gets bad and the building environment follows suit occupants may send for their solicitors and sue the man responsible. The appraisal technique of visual inspection of drawings or models of buildings is no longer adequate in the modern world of design. We have to be able to appraise abstract things which cannot be looked at. We have to have some methods of modelling these in order to render them intelligible, and it is to be hoped that the symposium will cast some light on this critical aspect.

Thamesmead

by

HUBERT BENNETT

I AM GOING to talk about one of the responsibilities that lies with the Architect of the Greater London Council in respect of civic design and the visual aspect of highways in Greater London. The Greater London Council is responsible for all Metropolitan roads within the Greater London area and the major road problems arising in the next 25 years are estimated to cost more than 1000 million pounds. This field of work is one of the most difficult I undertake for the Council.

With regard to the kind of organisation we have the most brilliant work can be of little avail without the full consideration of all the professional and other resources involved in planning, civic design and execution.

By way of example, the precincts of the Tower of London form a comprehensive development and one where segregation of urban transport, the motor car and the pedestrian, are all important.

This is the kind of proposal we require for almost every action area, where most careful studies are undertaken. Other schemes show the motor road system as part of the Greater London Development Plan.

The Department of Architecture and Civic Design at County Hall is a large organisation and as well as collaboration in our own establishment we collaborate with some 200 private Consultants—Architects, Structural Engineers and Quantity Surveyors. In fact, the private Consultants assisting the Department at the present time are undertaking about £40 million of work. The responsibilities of the Department are comprehensive in that they cover three dimensional town planning work, architectural work, social and civil engineering, quantity surveying, management, building legislation in the form of administrating the London Building Acts, historic buildings, structural engineering, housing, ambulance stations, courts, fire stations, and schools and colleges for the Inner London Education Authority and expansion work in some sixteen towns anywhere between the Wash and Cornwall. In addition we have the improvement and maintenance of the Council's buildings, and we have to manage our finance, establishment and administration. We have seventeen integrated divisions, fully co-ordinated with the Director of Highways and Transportation in all his development work and in all the services of the Council.

THAMESMEAD

A good example of these skills working together is the new development at Thamesmead for 60,000 people; an ideal exercise in environmental planning, traffic and pedestrian movement.

5

The site area is $1\frac{1}{2}$ thousand acres with some three miles of river frontage; seven miles from the centre of London. The site during the last century was part of Woolwich Arsenal and the ground is made up of 30 ft of peat. All the buildings, drainage and roads require piles to a depth of 35 to 40 ft. The site was purchased by the Government at a very low figure to offset the cost of foundation work. In preparing the master plan for this town, we had previous experience in designing a new town in Hampshire although that project went no further than publication. We sold some 5000 copies of the book, The Hook Book, which illustrates our planning methods and design. The Thamesmead scheme was designed as one model by a small number of staff who could hardly work side by side on the drawing board over such a large proposal. Having decided the main elements of the scheme which included a spine road cutting through the site from Woolwich to Erith, and a large inter-section passing under the Thames to form the C Ring road of London, we then designed the proposal in some detail and in nine weeks completed the first model.

With this model technique we virtually designed the town three dimensionally as a piece of sculpture.

The model of the centre of the scheme shows the possibility of a monorail, the station for commuters, the shopping centre—which may be covered—and a yachting basin for 160 ocean going yachts.

The site is between the spine road and a large sewer bank which is used for a new factory that is producing the concrete panels for the building of the town. The housing generally is of a density of 100 people per acre, and half the people get a garden; 25% an outside terrace and 25% are in two room flats. There is provision of one car space for every house.

Because of the levels of the site, nobody can sleep within seven feet of the existing ground level because of possible flooding of the Thames. Segregation from traffic is provided at first floor level for people to walk around the area and to visit the town centre. Public bus services circulate on all main routes in the town.

Road traffic seriously affects the environment and the quality of the areas developed, and although these are difficult to measure they are real and must be identified and considered carefully. The road system is not merely a permanent way for the movement of motor vehicles but serves many other urban activities, particularly pedestrian movement, and it forms an integral part of the built environment. The problem is to achieve maximum vehicle accessibility, whilst maintaining or improving the quality of urban life. The motor vehicle has multiplied in variety and numbers on a road system originally developed for the pedestrian and the horse and cart.

Widespread awareness of the effects of traffic was first crystallized in the Buchanan Report of 1963. The Wilson Report of the same year had shown that the problem of noise in urban areas is bound up with the needs of transport.

Road traffic and aircraft give rise to the most noise complaints.

Despite the impetus given to studies by these reports, the amount of relevant data and research remains limited. Experience suggests that there are five types of environmental problem caused by traffic.

1. Conflict with pedestrian movement
2. Noise

FIGURE 1. Greater London Council, Thamesmead. Model of General Planning Proposals.

3. Fumes, vibration and dirt.
4. Visual impact
5. Psychological impact

Conflict can be illustrated by the Metropolitan Police District figures for 1966—when 453 pedestrians were killed, 3995 seriously injured and 13,910 slightly injured. The cost of these casualties is estimated at some £2 million by the Road Research Laboratory. This figure takes into account loss of output and medical costs only.

Noise has been measured in London at 540 points over an area of 44 square miles.

Rail traffic was the dominant source of noise at only 22 of the 540 points partly because tunnels and cuttings are excellent noise barriers. A third of the resident population lived in streets where day-time kerb-side noise levels exceeded the standards suggested by the Wilson Committee. Night-time conditions were worse over the whole area.

Petrol and diesel-vehicle engines produce fumes containing carbon monoxide which is toxic at high concentration; old structures are affected by vibration, although we have little evidence to date; and litter and oil stains accumulate where cars are parked at kerbs.

Traffic sometimes forms a visual barrier between people and the things they wish to see, although in contrast, traffic has its own visual qualities in colour, form and texture which can add vitality to townscapes.

However, there is evidence that traffic flow is having a detrimental effect especially in areas of architectural and historic interest, and on small gardens and squares.

From the psychological point of view heavy traffic can create a barrier across communities when new or widened roads cut through them, but for many, the possession of a car represents a major advance to a better way of life with the increased freedom of movement and range of activities that the car can provide.

The aim must be, therefore, to take account of the repurcussions on land arising from road proposals, and to make the insertion of new roads into the built-up area acceptable environmentally.

And now let me consider how we approach our responsibilities as they affect planning and three dimensional design? While it is easy to criticise, it is less easy to produce work of quality.

There are four conditions which should affect our outlook. Firstly, we must assume a dual responsibility—social and personal. Secondly, we must accept the philosophy of preservation and change. Thirdly, we cannot work alone.

We have to organise a whole range of skills, assistants and consultants, and preserve the integrity of the scheme throughout the whole design process and during construction.

Finally, we have to ensure that our successors carry on and improve the values and methods we have adopted.

In design there is an inseparable relationship between material and shape, structure and form, and the desire to express the potential characteristics of the materials we employ.

In the past structures have been essentially formed in compression, in stone or in brick, and with one element placed upon another, and the problems of weight and mass limited architecture. With two materials of great strength—steel and reinforced concrete—the ability to become economic in tension as well as in compression became possible. Thus, with greater flexibility and with less visible effort we can now achieve greater heights and spans and enclose more space.

In comparison with the linear nature of steel, reinforced concrete is a plastic material that can change in shape and in which the enclosure of space and structure can be one.

Today we have great diversity of new materials and new methods of building and of these, pre-cast concrete gives precision and speed of erection, systems of tensioning for greater strength, and improved methods of formwork for better finishes. All of these things expand the possibilities of this responsive material.

We live in a world of growth and change but it is important to distinguish between what is new and what is merely fashionable.

The design process must respect the complexity of our scientific potential and relate to the type of world we see in the future.

In his presidential address to the British Association in 1964, Lord Brain said:

'The important division between people is not between the classical and scientific outlook on life, but between those who have been educated to see the world in terms of the rapidly changing environment which science is creating, with all its potentialities and those who see it in the terms of the static environment and frozen emotional attitudes of the past . . . we must prepare all our people for a new world which will be quite unlike the old.'

Architects and engineers have produced many brilliant individual structures, but this has often been at the expense of comprehensive planning and unity that cannot be ignored in a civilized environment. With an isolated commission it is easy to overlook the limited role that a building or structure can play in an area of high-density development.

Planning conditions establish a framework, not a strait-jacket of uniformity. Without planning we can only have chaos.

A hundred years ago we had an industrial technology that was the most advanced in in the world, but faced with 'the machine' we found emotional security in the craft movement of people like William Morris. So we turned our back on the new technology and on people like Joseph Paxton and others whose early Victorian works were without precedent.

Some people regard the efforts of the architects today as the 'end of the road', but perhaps it is just the beginning, and when our time is over there will always be something new.

Great things are never easy. They are as difficult as they are rare.

Introductory address

by

A. J. DAKIN

I WOULD LIKE to start by putting on record what I would choose, for the purpose of this Conference, as significant elements of our cultural situation. They are: an enormous growth of communications capacity both for physical objects and pieces of information; a large actual and potential increase in energy; the heavy impact of extending the human nervous system by electronic devices; changes in the production system resulting in enormously enhanced output with greatly reduced human labour; a macro movement of growing populations migrating into the world's major metropolitan areas combined with a micro movement out from them into new style exurbanite regions; deterioration in the quality of cities; for some countries there is the reality of civil disorder. On the positive side we should add a growing concern for the quality of living in the city, and a new stress on human beings as more important than the apparatus of society.

Many perspectives of concern for the future of our society seem to come to a simultaneous focus in the city. The very rapid growth of this concern for the city in its planning and the life lived in it must be regarded as a major phenomenon of our time. The wide variety of interest displayed in the papers of this Conference is a reflection of this and it is an indication of the complexity with which we must deal.

I would like to make clear three elements with which I had difficulty when compiling this paper. First is the ability to conceptualize what the city is—the city in the largest sense, meaning our urban kind of life. We have contributions from various disciplines; the economist has some kind of a model of the city which he subscribes to; the sociologist a model of a city which he subscribes to, and the political science scholar has also his. The planners have not yet succeeded in synthetising these three, or any others, so there is not, in fact, an overall view of the city which allows us to say that we will provisionally regard the city in this or that particular light: that we will describe it like this, or will categorize it like that. This may seem unimportant, but the real question is: If we are going to intervene in the life of the city by altering something by taking an old piece out and putting a new piece in then, according to the way in which we see the city, so we shall decide what we shall do. In other words, there is necessary to the question of intervention and renewal the *concept* of the city. How can we do something to this entity if we have not some concept of it? In amongst this is that important question, which of all things seems so vital in planning circles the other side of the Atlantic—the question of values. What is it that we are doing? Why are we doing it? So, at this stage we ought to bear in mind these three things: that there is the need for some conceptualisation of what the city is, some need to understand what our values are and, therefore, what is it that we are doing when we plan, and lastly to examine *how* we are intervening.

As it would be quite impossible to attempt to cover all three of these, I thought it best to try and give three aspects that belong to the first group (conceptualisation) on the grounds that if we have some ideas of what we think the city is, then we might more intelligently be able to talk about the values we are concerned with, the reasons why we should intervene in it and the rationale of our techniques. So I will leave the question of values and the techniques of intervention for discussion.

The first aspect that I would like to suggest to you, is the thinking of Richard L. Meier of the University of Michigan.[1] Richard Meier is a man of great imagination. On a recent expedition to India, when he was considering Bombays and Calcuttas to the tune of 100,000,000 inhabitants each, he came to the conclusion that water was the key item for planning and the multiple uses of water in India could not be organized without entirely reconstructing the total Indian social structure.

As a result of his research Meier came to see the city essentially as the originator, conserver and transmitter of information. He thought that if the city is to remain viable as an open system, its function will be to conserve negative entropy, if it does not do this it cannot survive. He believes that the city does not have the option of whether to increase the rate of information handling. If it does not do this it will expire. It is not a choice. We cannot stand where we are. We have constantly to increase the speed of communication if the city is to remain viable.

Meier is not much concerned with the movement of bodies and freight: he is essentially talking about quanta of information. He believes that indicators derived from the study of information flows can tell us much more about the nature of the life of cities than can the traditional models of the economist and the sociologist and others. The chief conclusion, when we come to this part of his theory, is that it is the increase in the *rate of communication that is the prerequisite of socio-economic growth*. Growth of the society's capacity to generate wealth is dependent upon increasing the rate of information flow, and per contra, if the rate of information flow increases, then there will follow economic growth. It does not really take a great deal of imagination to see that this has all kinds of possibilities and ramifications for our gross national products.

In the early 1960's Meier thought that the increases in the flow of information that were already present in society must indicate that there would be an explosion of economic growth. He concluded: 'Cities face some unprecedented crisis in the not-too-distant future'.

Obviously, much communication is now virtually instant, and the rate may not be increased. But where it is slower there is a drive to shorten it. Hence, the threat of crisis. Hence, also perhaps, in part, the social troubles of the 1960's. We live in a world demanding to be instantly satisfied, as foreseen by Aldous Huxley in *Brave New World*. The key indicator of cultural shifts, says Meier, is information. He predicts that the present explosion of information will 'lift humanity into a new dimension of mass interaction'. If this is correct we should regard information as a basic dimension of our thinking about the city along with mass, energy, and space.

Meir's, then, is the first theoretical concept: the notion that the rate of information flow determines the rate of economic growth; and that if you have the one speeded up, the other will also be increased.

The second concept is based on the idea of energy and derives from the research of the physical ecologists and certain concepts of biology. Specific sources are the writings of H. T. Odum, and E. P. Odum [2].

The idea is that the city may be conceived as a system through which energy flows. The urban system is characterized by a faster flow—i.e. it has a more rapid metabolic rate than does the non-urban system or the rural region.

The ecosystem, so envisaged, has the additional characteristics that its edges are imprecise and liable to change, that its total is greater than the sum of its parts, and that it strives constantly to come to a state of 'balance', although perhaps never achieving equilibrium because the elements change before a position of rest can be achieved. The system is regarded as being in an open steady state.

Applied to cities the concept would suggest that an element of major importance is the rate of metabolism, or the speed with which the energy passes through the system or is degraded. Conceivably a change in the metabolic rate would be as important a prerequisite and indicator of cultural shift as Meier's change in the communication rate. So I am here suggesting that we have probably two elements that have increased their rate and that, in increasing their rate, they will, in fact, cause increases in other things, chiefly in terms of our capacity to produce, our capacity to become wealthier, and so on.

The metabolic rate of cities increased enormously in the nineteenth century when they invented heat engines. Our own time is seeing another rapid acceleration because of the use of more refined technology and atomic energy.

If we are right in concluding that the acceleration in rates of communication and metabolism is crucial to urbanised life, Le Corbusier's dictum, made in the early 1920's, that 'The City that achieves speed will achieve success' takes on a new significance. The insight of the late 1960's might, however, put this more pessimistically, by saying that the city which does *not* maintain continuous acceleration of its communication and metabolic rates will die. The reason for suggesting this is the fact that the urban mass of people, cars, and spatial spread, constantly increasing may rule out the possibility of survival on the basis of the status quo in communication and metabolic rates.

So much for two purely theoretical approaches; the third is theory plus some practice. I would now like to talk about the movement of bodies and goods. This we are familiar with in transportation engineering. While this rate has increased rapidly for some movements in the city, for others it has remained the same, or has actually declined. The rate of movement in the centres of cities is often no better than it was thirty years ago, and in many cities it is effectively worse. The idea that the extensive use of electronic techniques, by substitution, will reduce physical movement has been well aired and, generally is now only thought to be a partial solution to our problems. Current thinking tends to play this down on the grounds that although some movements are eliminated our cultural situation is constantly demanding higher physical mobility and an increasing supply of goods. This is a controversial statement, because there are planners who are already thinking about trying to reverse this trend. The plan of New York State actually envisages in its third phase (about the year 2000) that the planning that will have gone on in phases one and two will make it possible to reduce the physical movements necessary in the urban centres themselves—places like Buffalo and Albany, and between the urban centres. This, as far as I know, is the first overall state plan to admit that kind of thinking. But we are dealing, not with a static situation, nor with a situation that can be persuaded to be static, as far as the amount of information and people and goods to be moved is concerned. What we have is an accelerating condition which feeds upon itself. The better the facilities and the better the standard of living, the more we shuttle bodies and goods about. We do not substitute, in a straightforward one for one kind of way; we take the benefits of the information system, we pass more information, and we also move ourselves around more. This condition is a product of our human value system which, stressing relatives and not absolutes, sweeps us upwards in an ascending spiral of wants and desires which in our affluence we experience as realisable.

We have to consider, therefore, whether the Achilles' heel of the city is its internal physical communication system, despite what Meier may say. It may be that successful control of the city's inexorable tendency towards entropy must primarily be achieved by ensuring an adequate level of movement of goods and people. The rates of information and energy flows, although obviously related to the rate of physical movement, are not perhaps as crucial as this latter.

It would therefore seem reasonable to give an important place to the research carried out during the last 15 years concerning the way in which the physical movements in cities can be conceptualized as systems. I would like here to use as example[3] the planning and research that has been done in the Metropolitan Toronto area. Around 1956, the Metropolitan Toronto planners decided to try to develop a mathematical model which would simulate the movement of goods and people throughout the urban area over a period of years.

This model is well worth looking at because of the things that it discovered and the originality of its techniques at the time. It was set up to permit the simulation of the generation and attraction of movement trips, by both private and public vehicle and to show the way in which these trips would accommodate themselves to existing or hypothetical transportation road and rail links. There were two things that made such a simulation possible at that time. The first was the commercial use of the computer. The other was that there was emerging in the mind of the planners the idea that some systematic simulation of urban movement could be achieved.

The intellectual insight on which the model technique was based was the discovery that Newton's law of the attraction of masses* can be applied to areas of ground on which people perform various functions. So it is possible to simulate what goes on by assuming that here we have one piece of land, and here we have another piece of land connected by transportation links (roads, rapid transit etc.) along which people move at certain times of the day in various kinds of vehicles. The pieces of land will generate and attract travelers. The Newtonian formula is not used cold; it is modified, particularly in regard to the exponent. Newton used the square; in using a gravity formula for traffic the square is modified on the basis of empirical work done in observing how people move between two areas of a city, in terms of their activity patterns. One of the most important people in North America, whose name I am sure you will know, is Alan Voorhees. He has been a pioneer in developing formulae for simulation of this kind, and he has now reached the stage where if he is given certain indications about a city, he does not need to do any empirical research on it at all. He can gauge what the factors necessary to modify the formula would be in that particular instance.

Very briefly, the procedure of the model consisted of dividing the metropolitan area into 600 zones, smaller at the centre, larger toward the periphery reflecting population

---

* Newton: Any two bodies attract one another with a force proportional to the product of their masses and inversely proportional to the square of their distance apart.

density. Next, an assumed transportation system was set up and each zone assigned a node at which trips were assumed to begin or end. The land use data of each zone, such as population, number of dwelling units, number of cars, work opportunities, etc., was given. Similarly, for the transportation links, data was assumed: the number of traffic lanes, lengths, capacity function, transit vehicles per hour, and fare structure.

A trip generation program was next developed to calculate for each zone the number of 'person trips' leaving and entering each zone. Trip generation equations were used to calculate the number of trips originating in, and being attracted by, each zone.

A difficulty arose because when the model was set up in the late 1950's, calculations were made so that the move by car was roughly comparable in cost with that of public transport. Since then the rate of increase in cost of movement by public vehicle has been much greater than the rate of increase of cost by private car. So there is now an imbalance between the two. In 1969 the fare is two and a half times more. The cost of running a car over the same distance had not increased two and a half times, because of the proportion of the car's costs which are fixed. This leads to the conclusion that public transport must be heavily subsidized, in the same sort of way as we subsidize roads or water supplies. If economic viability is insisted upon it will drive out the reasonable use of public transportation.

The next stage was to develop equations expressing travel characteristics. The basic material was obtained from surveys, and one of the most interesting of these was the home interview survey. People were visited and asked what they did as work, how often they changed it, why they did or did not go on public transport. A profile was built up of what people's 'needs' were, what they expected of transportation, and what kinds of preferences, traditions and prejudices they had. Here was a psychological-social element which the researchers tried to get and were, I believe, successful in incorporating.

This leads to the question of travel decision choice. The planners wanted to know, assuming an individual had the choice of different forms of travel, why he selected such and such a mode, such and such a route, or such and such a combination of modes?

The main program consisted of 6 program blocks used sequentially and in iteration until traffic settled on the given facilities. The blocks were: route operation, travel factors (choice of destination, travel mode and route), trip origin-destination interchange factors, mode and route proportional split, route assignment, and travel time.

The diagram which looks like the inside of a grandfather clock shows the sequence of running the model.

1. A series of routes was constructed between each pair of zones, each with the shortest possible travel time.
2. The travel factors block estimated the effects of those times on the person's inclination to travel, to use one mode of travel, to go one route rather than another.
3. The trip origin-destination block used the conclusions of 2 to estimate how many people in total would travel from one zone to another.
4. The mode and route proportional split block used the total interchange volumes and modal split factors of 2 to calculate how many people would travel via each mode (car, public transit, etc.) and via each alternative route.
5. The route assignment block assigned these split-trip figures to pertinent routes and gave traffic flows on the links.

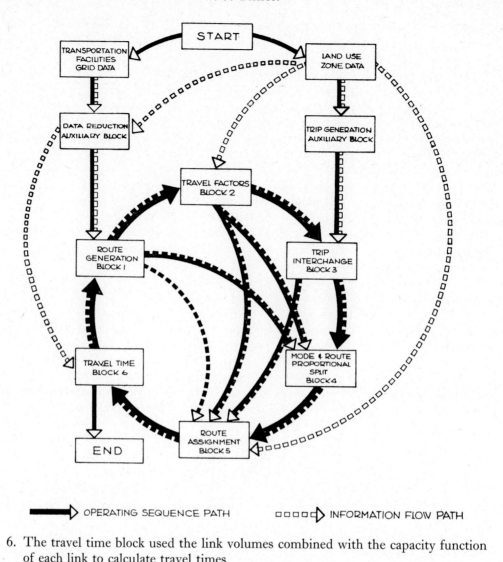

OPERATING SEQUENCE PATH   INFORMATION FLOW PATH

6. The travel time block used the link volumes combined with the capacity function of each link to calculate travel times.

On running the model, once round, the link time will be different from that of the previous run. This produces a variable which enables the model to be rerun until the iteration produces a condition when no more significant change takes place.

By using different assumptions about land use and the transportation links, different traffic flows and travel times can be produced. The Toronto model explored particularly the effects of varying the road and public transit links, trying varied transportation systems lying between the extremes of maximum public transportation facilities—and maximum facilities for the use of the private vehicle.

These studies produced important finding of general applicability to cities. The chief discovery was that a total transportation system which has a 'balanced' mix of public and private transportation will give certain benefits over an 'extreme' system.

It is a criticism of the use of the model that the position of the point of balance between the two extremes was guessed rather than scientifically calculated. At that time there were no techniques for doing this more precisely. A research project at present being carried out in the University of Toronto is attempting to remedy this lack.

The balanced plan gave the following benefits:

1. Higher average trip speeds (in Toronto 8 m.p.h. higher on the expressway network).
2. Reduction in time spent in travel (in Toronto 15% for the average trip).
3. Longer trips are possible (i.e. acceptable and therefore greater mobility is achieved).
4. A wider choice of trip destinations is available.
5. Street congestion is moderated.

The Toronto model for the first time gave insight into the way the balancing system works. It is an oscillation across the point of division between trips by private vehicle and trips by public transportation. Thus if the division (called the modal split) is 30% public transportation and 70% private vehicle the 'balance' is an oscillation across the 30–70% position.

The study of the operation of the modal split gives, in theory, the hope of planning it. The working of the Toronto model, however, circumscribed that hope since it showed quite clearly that the modal split, at any rate in Toronto, was not as amenable to being manipulated as some planners had thought.

Further study showed that the attempt to move the modal-split meets great resistance. This is, of course, partly a physical and partly a cultural matter. Suppose that the modal-split is in a certain position and hopefully the planner tries to move it, perhaps because of congestion downtown. He has to try to persuade some of the car travellers to leave their cars at home and ride on a public vehicle. But what happens is that as movement is made away from the position of balance, the resistance to movement very rapidly becomes serious, so much so, that to move a little in either direction would incur costs in expressways or subways that would be excessive. Specifically, what happens is that one mode is underused. Even supposing subsidized underground railways were put in extensively with trains at the rate of one a minute, the percentage of trips that would be saved on the roads would not be significant. That is why study of the social-psychological element is so important in this kind of research.

In other words, we cannot solve our transportation problems by arbitrarily saying that more trips must be made by public transportation. The model showed clearly that the system would manifest rapidly increasing resistance to forcing the use of public vehicles, and would not reduce the use of the motorcar for central and mid-town trips.

The implication of this research is that, assuming we agree the increase in the rate of physical communication in our cities to be of prime importance, the rate will not automatically be improved by providing more public transit facilities. The rate can only be increased by producing increased higher average speeds. The Toronto research indicated that this can be done by discovering a better position of balance between the two modes.

Our cultural situation is that a constantly higher level of mobility and accessibility is not merely desired but is actively sought by the public. The planning problem is to provide for this enhanced opportunity for choice while avoiding the resultant nullifying congestion. We are in the paradoxical situation in regard to physical communications that we must give the individual the expressways and rapid transit lines which make possible higher mobility but we must discourage him from using them!

It seems likely that although electronic communications will carry an increasing amount of data the key communications-energy problem of the city is that our kind of culture demands an ever-increasing amount of physical movement. This cannot be accommodated on the basis of supplying a simple manifest 'demand' or 'needs' for to do this is too expensive financially and is quantitatively very difficult in terms of land.

The experience of the Toronto model shows that the attitudes, values and behavioural patterns of the population for whom we plan are an integral part of a whole system. They manifest cultural lags and inertias which are part of the framework within which the planning must be done. Hence, there is need for theoretical concepts of the kind represented by Meier's communications theory and the ecological theory of the city to be assisted by empirical-simulation research of the Toronto kind since we must understand the ways in which our values affect the physical arrangements for communication.

Our cultural values lead us to use our communication facilities and energy resources in certain ways, but in using them new value emphases develop. So, in turn, the facilities themselves come to influence the values. Thus the city is made to the pattern of our values, but in turn, its accelerating rate of communications and metabolism of energy modifies and remakes the pattern of our culture. Communications are not therefore to be seen as serving our environment; they are an integral part of it.

The well-known theorist of the cultural meaning of communications, Marshall McLuhan, is famous for his aphorism: 'The medium is the message'. By this he means that the important thing about communications is not the material communicated, but the fact that the mode of communication has certain characteristics, for example, it is instantaneous, all-pervasive, and demands the spectator's involvement.

The message of this conference might well be that in our kind of society *communications and energy are the environment*.

REFERENCES

1. MEIER, R. L. (1962). *A Communications Theory of Urban Growth*. Joint Centre for Urban Studies, Massachusetts Institute of Technology and Harvard University, Cambridge.
2. ODUM, H. T. (Oct. 1962). 'Ecological Tools and Their Use: Man and the Ecosystem' in *Proceedings of the Lockwood Conference on the Suburban Forest and Ecology*. Connecticut Agricultural Experimental Station. Bulletin 652.
   ODUM, E. P. (1963). *Ecology*. Holt, Rinehart, and Winston, New York.
3. METROPOLITAN TORONTO PLANNING BOARD. (1964). *Report on the Metropolitan Toronto Transportation Plan*, Toronto.

Discussion

Moxley: Is there a tendency for the traditional city centre functions to move to the outskirts in Toronto?

Dakin: Yes. The central business functions have moved to the places where the sub-way stations and the intersections of the arterial roads coincide.

Langdon: In the model which Dr. Dakin demonstrated, I wonder how one would alter the variables if one of the variables is the answers to the social survey enquiries.

Dakin: As far as I know there are no techniques.

Collar: Dr. Dakin said that the number of people wishing to make a journey is inversely proportional to a power of the length of the journey. As it happens, I have recently been looking into the question of the number of people who might wish to take very long journeys—in excess of 6000 miles, or a quarter of the circumference of the globe. This question is complicated by the effect of the curvature of the Earth's surface; but available statistics indicate that for long air journeys, the number of people is inversely proportional to the fifth power of the distance travelled. Can Dr. Dakin give an index for suburban travel?

Dakin: The negative power is greater than two; but only by a decimal point or so. It is not of the order of five.

Collar: This is not surprising; the conditions under which people want to travel thousands of miles must be totally different from those relating to thousands of yards.

The planning context

by

FRANKLIN MEDHURST

MY TOPIC IS TO outline the planning context and this I interpret as the physical framework for all systems of communication in cities in the next 30 years.

The amount of urban development that there will be in Britain at the end of the twentieth century has been variously estimated in terms of figures for population growth, which have constantly been revised, and always upwards. The current estimate of growth in population by the end of the century is an increase of about 30% or 17 million more people than we have now. But because of rising standards for space in all parts of towns, and the need to rebuild worn out areas, the amount of land required for urban purposes will be in the order of twice what we use now.

In this sense we view a Britain today that is no more than half developed; only half way to the physical form of urban organisation that will exist in thirty years. Population growth beyond the end of the century is very difficult to forecast, but if we assume population stability, and project the needs for urban land to 100 years from now, then the Britain we see now is no more than one third developed, probably only one quarter.

A similar prediction of growth might have been made in 1869 and it would, in many parts of the country, have been short of reality. The conflict which faces all nations undergoing rapid expansion or change, is that between current problems and long range vision. Most of that which goes under the name of planning is not planning at all, but corrective measures applied to repair an urban machine that is on the point of seizure. This is not planning. It is urban maintenance. It absorbs almost our entire resources in this field and leaves little for the proper business of assessing and accommodating the needs of the future.

In all spheres of study, scientific, social and artistic there are lines of thought which continue through centuries of application. These arise from the basic theories of a study. Its practitioners will, when faced with new problems, return to first principles of perhaps mass, gravity or magnetism, colour or texture or religious ethic. In the practice of town planning here and elsewhere there is no accepted basic foundation of this kind but there is a host of second tier consequential subjects which have become the basis of planning evaluations. These are factors such as land values, population density, traffic volumes, employment rates, shopping floor space, and so on. The standards set for these factors are derived by empirical means. We refer to what the situation has been before, or what it is in other places where we have observed the consequences, and we propose remedial action in the light of this information.

The application of empirical rules in planning has led us to build motorways where there is the greatest congestion, that is, in order to rectify the past errors of building towns in the wrong places. The real problem is to prepare a broad strategy that would accommodate a four fold growth of cities in this country over the next one hundred years rather than ossify what occurred over the last hundred. If the problem had been examined from basic elements of communication and energy, it is possible that the motorways might have been built elsewhere. Similarly the selection of sites for new towns to accommodate the overcrowded populations of cities reflect the nineteenth-century approach of the industrial philanthropists; an approach which these worthy men devised for very different circumstances. In under-developed Britain the attitude that is required is that of the colonisers and the settlers. In developing territories they had to take into account the means of transport and the power sources available, whether it be man power, wind or water power or mule power. They were thrown back on to the primary elements necessary for development; communications and energy. The success of political and military strategy and social and economic control depended upon these fundamentals.

These principles we have forgotten since the first wave of urban industrialisation was completed about a century ago. Since then we have step by step through bye-laws, health acts, and planning acts frozen the whole urban structure of towns and cities and the national communications network. We have assumed that the pattern of land values, of shopping habits, of population densities, and in this country even travel patterns, was approximately right some time in the latter part of the nineteenth century, and we now have a plethora of complex statutes, the most recent and obscure of which was passed by Act of Parliament only a few months ago (The Town and Country Planning Act 1968) to ensure that the urban structure is not changed. Thus the Roman or mediaeval foundation of a city remains its centre. Slums, even modern ones, occupy the sites upon which the Victorians first built them. Congested places grow more congested. Larger roads generate more traffic, until as the Americans have discovered, there are not sufficient resources to continue pouring money into this particular bottomless bucket.

It is a stimulating and sobering exercise to imagine Britain to be a newly found un-populated island where it is intended to settle a population of 70 millions in a manner which could create a viable economy in the twenty-first century. The first consideration in surveying this land of fields, forests, hills, and rivers, is where would we build the cities. Have we any need for a Birmingham? and would the capital be located on the Thames? would the first motorways run the length of the land but not across it, and would we settle a quarter of the population in the south east corner?

Under twentieth century conditions of an import/export trade economy, of high living standards, and increasing demands for leisure activities, it is likely that we would design a Britain very different from the one we have. Bearing in mind that we have to undertake almost as much development in this country in the next thirty years, as has been accomplished in its past history, must we not question the continued acceptance of the existing pattern of town and city developments of roads, ports, airfields, energy production and agriculture?

This becomes even more vital with the long term view of development in the twenty-first century. The philosophy of planning should be akin to the attitude of the eighteenth century property developers of country parks. The avenues of oaks and elms they planted we enjoy today. Blenheim and Hampton Court, Castle Howard and Seaton

Delaval; these country houses were created and occupied by their owners, but the land-scaped estates which now enshrine these mansions were concepts not to be fully realised in the lifetimes of their creators. So it is with planning; we are now preparing the ground for posterity. That is our duty.

What I have outlined is the broad planning context against which the subject of this symposium can be set. I go on to describe an approach to planning which would permit this country to prepare progressive and adaptable policies for its future, rather than to be bound by the strait jacket of the development plan system. Under the planning machinery of this country it has been customary to prepare plans for periods of five years at a time. Because of the established nature of the structures of towns and their proposed growth a new five year plan is often no more than a review incorporating minor adjustments. It tends to be a negative document because it cannot ensure that proposals will be implemented. If for instance land is allocated for industry, the planning authority will direct factory development to it, should it arise. But if no-one wishes to build factories the land will remain unused for this purpose. It is interesting to note that in a review of development plans of County Boroughs a few years ago, the Ministry of Housing pointed out that twice as much land was in total allocated as the combined labour resources of these cities could sustain.

In fact, the five year plan is useless for any purpose other than that of administrative control of the existing structure. In a study of Teesside begun in 1965 it was found that so many decisions had been taken relating to town centre expansion, the line of new roads, the locations of schools and houses etc., that no fresh constructive planning could be operative in the succeeding ten years. The original aim of preparing a twenty-five year plan for that area was subsequently modified to a ten year plan which was largely a tidying up operation, or remedial measures, followed by a fifteen year plan of purpose-ful growth.

In this study it was found that whilst estimates and assumptions became increasingly unreliable the further ahead one planned, it was nevertheless essential to look at the period beyond 25 years in order to consider the possibilities and effects of continued growth. A town cannot cease to expand when a plan period expires, there must be a space for continuity of all programmes. The Teesside Survey adopted a long-range 45 years for this purpose. The planning processes then became:

first 10 years	remedial action
following 15 years	the plan
following 29 years	continuity.

Immediately it is realized that little in the way of constructive planning can be done in the first ten years, many of the day to day problems of maintaining a town's physical fabric are seen, in perspective to be less important; and the opportunity to change policies is very much greater. The next breakthrough which the Teesside Survey initiated was to take advantage of the now widely available computer services. The method by which the computer was applied to planning was simple in concept but extremely difficult in practice.

The surveys, which employed almost 100 people over nine months involved ques-tioning nearly one quarter of the population of almost half-a-million. The information was coded and subsequently transferred to magnetic tape as a permanent store of base material. From time to time this material is to be revised and updated without destroying the base record. The information for revision will be obtained from the normal operations of the various departments—planning, health, housing, roads, rating, treasurers etc.

The plan proposals are recorded on tape in similar terms so that at any time there is available, at a few hours notice, a comprehensive record, up to date within three or four months, of the present structure and the planned development of the entire County Borough. When, as is inevitable, there is a perturbation which would upset the plan, such as more money being made available for roads, or less for schools, or a closure which would throw 10,000 people out of work, or a windfall which would require an employment force of 20,000—for instance a new car factory—the new data is incorporated in a computer program. This data is compared against the stored information, the plan is adjusted to the new situation and the machine will print out information on any aspect, e.g. housing, communications etc., on which planning data is sought.

More than this, a number of variables can be introduced so that a range of alternative plan amendments can be obtained to take account of new possibilities which were not foreseen originally. This approach to planning is flexible, fast, and is likely to engender confidence in planning decisions. Indeed we should think not so much of a plan being an orthographic document, that is a fixed and finite drawing on paper, but more as a continuously operated flexible process in a machine which computes a continuous flow of data.

One of the factors which mitigates against any fundamental change in the pattern of urban structure, is the amount of existing investment in towns. This is considerable compared with the amount that might be expected in a period of 5 or 10 years, so there does not appear to be a justification for moving a shopping centre or for building a road where there is no immediate need, in order to avoid a foreseen but long term problem.

The influence of investment can be observed in those towns which have been deprived of it, chiefly some of the less prosperous industrial towns of the north. Here the fabric of towns has decayed, the shopping centres may be out-of-date, the road system inadequate and the industrial structure declining. The extent of decay in these towns is the very opportunity for them to recast their pattern completely. Unlike some of the prosperous cities of the south where continuous capital expenditure, in the years since the war, has consolidated the pattern of the former urban industrial and communications structure for the next fifty years; the older cities should be able to re-equip themselves. Indeed it would appear that a recurring cycle of industrial growth, prosperity, decline and decay is indispensable, and is a function of industrial renaissance. The other opportunity for recasting the pattern of urban structure is in those underdeveloped areas selected for their considerable growth potential.

Arising partly from a need to disperse population from the conurbations and particularly from the south east; and partly to develop deep water port facilities together with industrial and commercial expansion, a few locations have been selected for study by the Government.

The first of these areas was Teesside, the report of which was published in 1969. Three more studies are under way, Tayside in Scotland (Perth/Dundee), Humberside and Severnside. It seems probable that by the end of the century these four will be the first of the new style conurbations. All of them have towns grouped around estuaries but they are distinct geographically and in time from the existing conurbations of London, the Midlands, Merseyside, Tyneside and Clydeside.

The industrial re-equipment of these exploitable areas is likely to contain some or all of the basic ingredients of the future national economy; steel manufacture, oil-refining, chemicals and petro-chemicals, energy production and comprehensive communications. A wide range of manufacturing industries will be required to back up the capital intensive industries, and the employment that these generate will lead to a fast but steady growth in population. Energy is likely to be generated from nuclear power and gas producing installations. Add to this the construction of deep-water berths, ore stocking grounds, container services, new road crossings of the estuaries and a rapidly accelerated rate of town growth and we have the modern equivalent of a potential which inspired the Merchant Adventurers nearly five centuries ago.

The Teesside Study has been completed and the future of this area would seem to be assured. Of the others, the most advanced study is for the area which includes Bristol. No information about the course of the study or its conclusions have been released, and I have no knowledge of what these might be so what I have to say is largely conjecture.

The object of the study is to consider whether it would be feasible to locate a very substantial increase in population in the Severnside area by the end of the century.

The area stretches from Newport, through Gloucester and Cheltenham around to Bristol and Weston. The present population is about 1·6 millions. How a study of this kind can be carried out without including Cardiff I don't know. For my purpose today I am considering it a part of Severnside with a total population of almost 2·0 millions.

The pattern of population growth in this area in recent years is one where the amount of net immigration has equalled the natural increase. It is estimated that the effects of natural increase and migration will increase the population of the South West Planning Region as a whole by 20% by 1981 and 40% by the year 2000. The Severnside area would expect to receive a greater proportion than these averages. But accepting these figures and applying them to the sub-region, the existing two millions population would increase to 2·4 millions by 1981 and 2·8 millions by the year 2000. This does not allow for a redistribution of the national population, that is planned overspill.

The projected population growth for the U.K. indicates an increase of some 20 millions by the end of the century. A sizeable section of this, moving away from the conurbations, would move to new developing regions. On the assumption that two thirds of this growth is accommodated in the existing conurbations and one third of this is moved to the three study areas (Teeside has been informed that it will not receive any planned overspill) then the Severnside sub-region could expect an additional 2·3 million people. This added to the projected 2·8 millions would give a total population of over five millions by the end of the century.

For the purpose of this symposium the actual population does not matter, it is sufficient to state that the population of Severnside is likely to be doubled and the land required for urban use will possibly be trebled in the next thirty years. In this context it is high time to rethink the whole basis of urban growth, it may even be too late when you consider that many decisions affecting the next ten years or so of growth have already been taken.

There are various ways in which an urban complex can expand, once it is clear that the necessary basis of communications and energy can be provided. In the Teesside study we devised and developed seven unique strategies, each designed around a characteristic or a series of characteristics important to growth. One was based upon a metropolitan concept of a mother city and a ring of smaller towns, another on linear expansion of the existing city, and another upon the principle of making use of the finest landscape by building a number of smaller towns in the foothills of the Cleveland Hills. One strategy was aimed at minimizing traffic flow across the river, and so on.

Each of these strategies was applied across seventy zones each of 10,000 population. To each was attached secondary factors of socio-economic groups, traffic flows out of the zone, potential rateable values, accessibility to employment and shopping centres etc., and computer programmes were prepared and run.

After a study of the results an eighth strategy was prepared. This was divided into a fine grain of 220 zones, and likewise evaluated. In terms of the criteria which we had selected it proved to be the most efficient plan. This was in terms of investment in roads, vehicle mileage, accessibility etc. This became the plan for Teesside.

Extending the experience of this work to Severnside, I would expect various forms of growth to present themselves (Figure 1). Three such strategies are illustrated. One is that of the metropolitan city where Bristol, Gloucester and Cardiff each approximately double in size, fulfil this role, surrounded by a number of smaller towns. Many of these would be existing towns expanded in size. Some would be new towns (Figure 2). The second is a dispersed pattern of settlements, new and expanded towns, with populations of between 100,000 and 200,000. Fifteen of these would be required outside the three cities and this becomes difficult to provide within economic travelling distance of the centres of employment (Figure 3).

The third diagram is that of the linear city where each of the existing cities expands along the lines of communication taking in, and expanding, other towns within its system (Figure 4).

Each community remains physically distinct and separate, like beads on a string, but the city is administered as a unit, its roads, transport planning, education, trade and employment, managed by agencies with knowledge of and executive powers over the entire region.

In all these strategies, the three cities that would be within the Severnside city region of some 2000 square miles would have distinct functions. The industrial centre would be the Cardiff/Newport complex with its steel mills and refineries. Bristol/Bath with its emphasis on manufacturing industry, would be the commercial centre, and Gloucester and Cheltenhan the centre for administration, arts and services.

I have selected linear growth as the preferred pattern because I believe it is the nearest approach to a form of building which is reasonably efficient and which will not subject unduly large areas of countryside to urban, or near urban invasion. That is, it will permit future generations to find their own solutions to growth whilst most reasonably satisfying ours. In the linear city travel times are minimal, the use of public transport is maximised, the concentration of populations of one and a half million to two million people, permits a highly specialised culture to develop, and the opportunity for social interaction is greater.

The linear city is not new, it now has a very respectable history throughout Europe but it has been ignored in this country. Some years ago I carried out some studies in

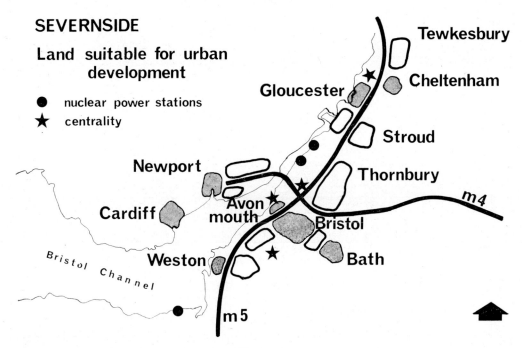

FIGURE 1.

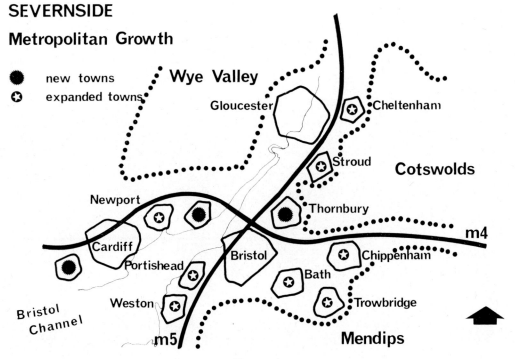

FIGURE 2.

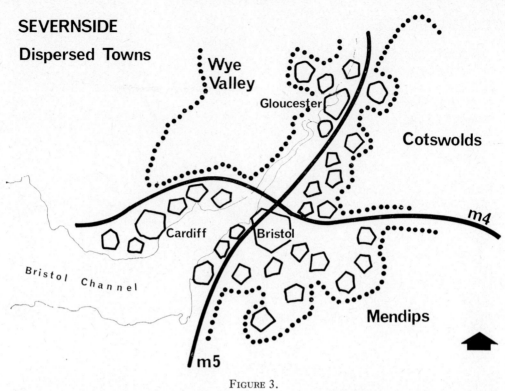

FIGURE 3.

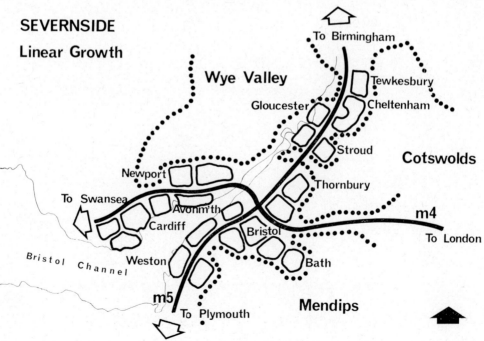

FIGURE 4.

which half-a-million people could be served entirely by a public transport system. It was based upon a directional grid eight miles by three miles.

The form of this city would permit a high degree of concentration of activities at its centre, and would permit the functions to be linked by mechanical public transport of the cable, rail or belt type. The slow moving methods, the cable and the belt, require long straight runs for efficiency, but can be designed to transport in any direction at the junctions of straight runs. High speed transport such as the monorail, is not able to change direction easily, and must have long straight runs with only gentle curves in direction. The general principle of efficiency in movement of belts, cables and rails is that they should run from point to point in straight lines. The buildings of the city centre are, therefore, most suitably placed along the line of communication in a linear form.

There is no reason why towns designed for modern systems of transport should conform to a radial pattern. The radial arrived by the historical evolution of centrality, poor transport methods and growth. Because of its ever widening catchment are for passengers between the routes of the radials, it is a most inefficient form for a public transport system. The ideal form is that where the system has a regular catchment area for the whole length of its route. The system requires, therefore, a series of parallel routes running from the centre, rather than radiating from it like spokes from the hub of a wheel.

The pattern of use arising, is one which is consistent along the length of the city but which changes across its width. The implication being that the longer and faster journeys are made on straight runs with few stops, whilst the shorter cross town journeys, with frequent stopping points for pedestrians, are made by the slower belt system; and interchanges are located where rail and belt routes cross. This would give the linear city a similar time scale in both directions. The radial city had this uniform time scale when most travel was by foot; it was inherent in its design, that all parts should be equally accessible.

With a system of communications involving eight parallel lines of rails and about twenty cross routes of belts, no one in a city of half-a million people would be living more than some 300 yards from access to the system and the longest journey from the furthest part of the city centre to the remotest residence would take about twenty minutes door to door. Most citizens would be within ten or fifteen minutes journey from work or centre. With such a system other influences would arise. The space consuming elements such as schools and their playing fields, cemeteries, sewage works, institutions and open space could be placed outside the city proper at the terminals of the cross town routes. A substantial saving would also arise from the limited road widths and parking areas required for service traffic. Householders cars would not be garaged at the house, but in large parks on the fringe of the city with direct access to the national routes. Thus vehicles would be used principally for intercity journeys, collected and brought to the dwelling only for specific purposes or loading.

More recently the south Hampshire study has come out in favour of a directional grid. The proposal is to link the towns of Southampton, Gosport and Portsmouth. The structure of this plan contains the elements of all urban activities, and such a linear city, in this case 8 miles wide by 25 miles long, may be expected to be the prototype for the kind of growth that might be expected on both sides of the River Severn.

The principle applies not only to the large city region but also to country districts. The South West Economic Planning Region is used to illustrate this (Figure 5). Apart

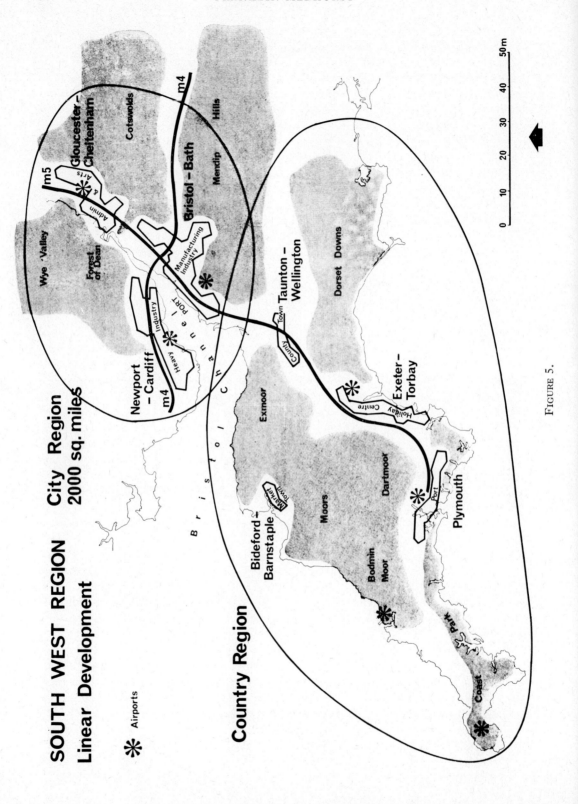

SOUTH WEST REGION   City Region
Linear Development   2000 sq. miles

Airports

Gloucester – Cheltenham

Cotswolds

m4

Bristol – Bath

Mendip Hills

m5

Arts

Admin

Manufacturing Industry

Wye Valley

Forest of Dean

Heavy Industry

Canal PORT

Dorset Downs

Taunton – Wellington

Town

County

Newport – Cardiff

m4

Bristol   Channel

Exeter – Torbay

Holiday Centre

Exmoor

Bideford – Barnstaple

Market Town

Moors

Dartmoor

Port

Plymouth

Bodmin Moor

Coast

Country Region

0   10   20   30   40   50 m

FIGURE 5.

from the area around the Severn this region has largely been by-passed by the industrial upheavals of the last 130 years, and its growth has been very slow. Now in the age of of leisure and greater wealth it is experiencing development pressures. Growth is more by migration of people into the area than by natural change and we may expect to see twice as much urban development in this area by the year 2000.

The diagram indicates what form it might take. Three population concentrations are shown. The first is Taunton Vale where urban growth may be expected to take place along the valley of the Tone creating a linear city of about 100,000 people from Wellington, through Taunton towards Langport on the east. Its function would remain predominantly a marketing centre but with greater amounts of service and manufacturing industry.

The second concentration is the Exeter/Torbay line of development. Already the framework of this is seen in travelling from Exeter to Torquay and Brixham via Starcross. The incentive comes from the attraction of this area as a place to retire to and from the holiday industry generally. In a string of urban towns around the coast it may be expected to accommodate a population of three quarters of a million or more.

The third city would develop along the coast plain to the east and west of Plymouth. Here the function of the naval port is becoming increasingly modified by commercial uses and this, backed by the growth of the manufacturing industries, would increase its population to about 600,000.

Another centre which may expect considerable growth is the Bideford/Barnstaple location in north Devon. The estuarial plain between these towns is the natural area for new urban growth and these twin towns may be expected to at least double in size to a total population of between 50,000 and 60,000.

In all these conjectural essays the phenomenon centrality plays a dominating part. The conjunction of the crossing of motorways and the port at Severnside, creates one of the strongest incentives for development that we have in this country. The lesser towns have it too. Taunton Vale is the accessible centre of a wide and prosperous farming region. The pulling powers of the Exeter/Torbay area are the road communications which centre, like webs, on Exeter, Newton Abbot and Totnes and the coast attraction of the towns around the bay. Plymouth's comparative difficulty with landward communications is compensated by its magnificent port.

The final part of this paper is devoted to a growing concept of an aspect of urban communications; that is total energy production and transmission. The concept embraces a means of providing and conserving energy for the various activities within a town in such a manner that it permits a greater efficiency in communications. At present a town's energy is obtained from various sources; coal, gas, electricity, oil and tidal or water power. The loss of energy in its various forms in a town must be considerable. The efficiency of most fuels is normally below 40% and transmission losses reduce this further. In using fuels to drive reciprocating engines in congested areas, or to heat inadequately insulated buildings, the total efficiency of all fuels consumed must be very very low. For the function of the end product I wonder if we get as much as a 10% return.

To illustrate this, a house has recently been designed from components already available on the market but with an insulation value of its outer walls some nine times that of conventional brick walls. No central heating is installed because for most of the year the body heat of the occupants would be sufficient to maintain a room temperature of 70°F. For really cold weather two 3 kw fan heaters are incorporated in ducts. The energy input to such a building would be used almost to its maximum efficiency. Not only can this principle be applied to a complete town but the energy input can be rationalised. So that instead of obtaining power and heat from a number of different fuels, it is obtained from one such as oil or gas. This is delivered to the town by pipeline and there converted to the various forms required; electricity, steam heat, hydraulic power, refrigeration, vacuum or whatever form is needed.

If natural gas is the input fuel, the efficiency in energy production at the point of use is almost twice that of producing electricity from coal in power stations. This principle, the total energy concept, has been used in the United States for small complexes of buildings. The application of this principle to a complete town may be expected to affect the physical form of the town fundamentally, and its system of communications. That is its mass and time components.

In analysing a town in these constituent parts—mass, energy and time (or in planning terms, morphology, power constituents and communications) we may begin to develop a core of planning theory.

The impact of total energy upon a town may arise in four ways. First because of its economy, efficiency and availability, it can be used to provide a great many more amenities such as heated, air conditioned and automatically cleaned buildings and complexes of buildings throughout the town. Equally it may be applied to the field of vacuum powered communications whereby household refuse is disposed, goods delivered and people travel in containers in tubes. Secondly through ground, road and pavement heating, for increased crop production and snow and ice clearing purposes, and in using energy for pollution dispersion etc., the ecology of the area would be modified. Thirdly the layout of services to buildings imposes a discipline in their arrangement to avoid transmission losses. Groups or tight clusters of buildings would be likely to be an efficient method of reducing capital and running costs of the installation and this characteristic would be reflected at each scale of development, neighbourhood, town, and city. Fourthly the economics of operating with such a power source might tip the commercial scales sufficiently to attract a wide range of industries to the town.

Some of the most interesting technical developments that might be made possible are vacuum powered communications. The simplest of these is the disposal of refuse, whereby hoppers are installed in all buildings. The hoppers are connected by a vacuum pipeline system to a central incinerating plant. The household refuse is dumped in the hopper as and when it accumulates. Such a system, which is a Swedish patent, is in operation in that country.

An advance on this is the use of a vacuum system for the delivery of household goods. Shopping purchased at the town centre or by telephone is packed into a nine inch diameter container. This is programmed for delivery and put into the vacuum system. Very quickly it arrives at its destination, is unloaded and the container returned by the same method. An installation of this kind has been designed for a suburb in Prague.

The next step is the use of passenger carrying cars in a vacuum tube. A system of this kind was first patented by my namesake—George Medhurst—in 1810. The idea was to propel a train by the pressure of atmosphere acting upon a piston travelling in a tube. About the middle of that century atmospheric railways were built by Brunel and the powerhouse of one can still be seen at Starcross in South Devon. At the time it was not a roaring success. However the time is now more opportune for a modern development of this principle.

SUMMARY

In all parts of Britain we are experiencing a population explosion and in some selected locations this will increase and will be considerable. The demand for land for urban purposes will be greater than the proportionate growth of population. In the new connurbations it may amount to land fever.

Our pedestrian approach to planning legislation cannot adequately cope with this. But we have a tool in the computer which enables us to comprehend a situation of rapidly changing events. The plan then becomes a constantly manipulated and adjusted process directed by broad guidelines.

Selecting the guidelines becomes the critical function of planning. The criteria we chose for the Teesside Survey and Plan were largely value judgements made whilst we were trying to obtain some consensus of public opinion. They were made early in the preparation of the plan and, once formed, the planning process followed systematically. If they were the wrong criteria the plan is wrong, but the ability to feed in new data as soon as it is understood, allows for this. However there is no doubt in my mind that the creative process in planning takes place in a comparatively short period of time when the planning team is making its value judgements, selecting its performance standards and arriving at its assumptions. This is a field of study in which we have very little information.

We have the incentive and the technical means to prepare the kind of long term planning policies that the scale of development require.

Broadly that is the planning context, but I have mentioned the planning implications and consequences of linear cities and some of the effects which total energy might have upon towns, because it is my opinion, as a planner, that these are developments of form and energy which will become increasingly relevant in influencing the pattern and type of communications.

Discussion

FOLLOWING PAPER BY F. MEDHURST

Cresswell: Mr. Medhurst mentioned that planning legislation led to a lack of dynamic growth particularly in this country, but I wonder if the real problem is not our planning legislation, which in some ways is the finest in the world, but the framework of Local Government within which planners are working. Planning has meant to many planners the filling up of the spaces in urban areas and immediately outside the urban boundaries. It is only with the setting up of the various regional studies, and perhaps with the sub-regional studies and with the new towns, that we began to see new expressions of urban form which has been impossible within the Local Government structure. With the Maud Committee proposals for the reform of Local Government, and the setting up of regional structures throughout the country, we may be able to create new urban forms on a much larger canvas than that on which planners have been able to plan. In this country we are building about 350,000 houses a year and if this figure is multiplied by the average number of people per house, we are building the equivalent number to rehouse Birmingham every year, but this development is so split up, partly because of the framework of Local Government. One would hope to see more concentrated development instead of it being spread around in various little bits and pieces.

Medhurst: Legislation has been a restrictive element in looking at new forms of growth and has tended to ossify the existing land use structure. Where, for instance, there has been shopping there must continue to be shops. We have reached a stage in the middle of this century when our planning legislation will not accommodate the sort of growth we shall need in the next thirty years.

Grey: The vacuum powered delivery system, though it seemed rather far-fetched, does have considerable possibilities. Has any form of study been carried out into the Engineering and costing of a project such as this?

Medhurst: There is a proposal to instal it in a suburb of Prague, but I do not know of any other study. It is little more than the laying on of a drainage system. When water first became available to housing this was something that seemed far-fetched. But in time we will have a great number of total energy services of this kind laid on in which underground ducts will carry the electronic power, sewage and water supplies together with a delivery system of some kind.

Dakin: At least one study has been made on the eastern seaboard of the United States on the movement of people and goods, and the broad economics are that the costs of duplicating major airports compared with the cost of constructing vacuum pipes that would do, say, 500 miles an hour are comparable. In other words, the pipe idea built from Boston to Washington is not economically impossible in comparison with the duplication of say New York airport. In the case of New York airport, certain things that go wrong there may push the mishap back about 1000 miles into the continent. So that all this must be considered in a cost estimate.

Cherry: We are predicting to the end of the century which is impossible. Prediction, based on the extension of existing technology and existing models, seems to be dangerous, for example, people keep on saying that the population is going to explode, but we do not know that this will be so. We may have to assume this to guard against the worst.

But what is going to be the influence of telecommunication on people's lives? It may have a major effect on the need for the public to move about. Shopping centres were mentioned but they may disappear. Even going to school may be something quite different in another 20 years.

Medhurst: The computer enables us to modify, day by day, the effects of predictions. If predictions are wrong they can be modified and this is an important element in planning today. The plan is no longer something static in which certain things have to be done at certain times. The plan provides an overall strategy that can be modified and it is, therefore, constantly changing.

Langdon: Planning seems to me to be based on the present habits, present technologies, and the present procedures which relate to them. We multiply these, make a forecast, and then see what bits of hardware we can pull out to satisfy them. This is possibly the wrong way round. This seems to me to be a permanent communication system for producing wrong answers, because what we are putting in each time is a backcloth of what people were doing yesterday and then we predict from this what they will probably want tomorrow which will, of course, be more of yesterday, and then we dream up the technology to produce it for them. This seems to me to be rather unconvincing. Do we take seriously the belief of Professor Harrington that in 1980–1985 there will be a world food crisis? If this is correct our real object will not be landing in space, but just getting something to eat. We may then have to sweep aside all these plans and all these marvellous technologies because we shall just be sweating our guts out in order to put something into our mouths.

Medhurst: On one side there are trend patterns and on the other aim patterns. Trend patterns include land use, population distribution, climate, pollution, and things of that kind, and on the other side—aim patterns include the sort of society we are trying to build. This is based on value judgments and opinions. There are principles, aims and ideas, which should be clarified and amplified by study and research. The idea of planning is not just to project what is happening *now* in terms of desires, population, growth, and things of that kind, but also to consider our ideas of what a city will and should be in 20 to 30 years' time modified, of course, by the resources available. In my field of planning we cannot ignore population trends and expect a decline in population.

Dakin: The statistics both for the United States and for Ontario show that the birth-rate is now below that in the 1930 depression. The Ontario birth-rate has fallen for the last few years from approximately 28 per thousand to 18 per thousand. Actually the population does not fall; the rate of growth continues because of migration.

Steen: From my own experience I know that is very difficult to forecast longer than about ten years ahead, and most of the theories that have been put forward are for new cities. In designing a new city on a virgin site all the options are open but in dealing with an existing city and with the pressures and problems that come about daily is no easy matter. After producing a development plan all sorts of things which one never imagined could happen, suddenly happen, and policy has to be completely redesigned. So, planning for 30 years hence frightens me. You may be making decisions which might well put the people who are coming after you into difficulties and you may have made decisions that they cannot go back on. This is why options should always be kept open.

Bayliss: Our expected population of the year 2000 has recently been revised from 72 million to 66 million, which means something like $\frac{1}{2}\%$ per annum compound growth rate. Kahn suggests that the population in this country at the end of the century be estimated at 55 million, which is at no change, so that the words 'population explosion' are probably misleading. Secondly, as to the possibility of substituting electronic means of communication for physical communication, I understand that where there is increased electronic communication, physical communication has also gone up. Finally, I understand you produced several alternative plans for Teesside, each directed to a different sort of goal. How does one compare the plan that is orientated towards a maximisation of say, the quality of landscape with one which is orientated towards the minimisation of traffic? These are so diverse, are they comparable?

Medhurst: Population growth: 9 millions at the beginning of the nineteenth century; 27 millions at the beginning of this century; something like 70 millions at the beginning of the next century; that is the sort of growth. But it is not just a question of population growth, it is also a matter of the amount of land required. A survey of Bolton in Lancashire, made about six years ago showed that although the population was going to fall considerably in ten years the amount of land required in those ten years would be 10% more. Even when the population is falling the town is expanding because of new standards. On the Teesside study, we devised seven different strategies. We tested them by comparing them with the same factors of rateable value, travel times and things of that kind. We could not evaluate abstract qualities such as the attractive natural landscape of one scheme which was set in the foothills. This is intangible and although we tried to find some method of measuring these qualities we could not.

Some economic restraints
on building and town development

by

P. A. STONE

INTRODUCTION

THERE IS A considerable gap between the creation of imaginative solutions to urban needs and the development of functional urban facilities. The gap between the technical and the economic solution is often even greater. Many imaginative urban solutions are never realised, because their use would create an unacceptable number of technical disadvantages. Many solutions, although technically acceptable, are often available for several decades before they are utilised, or never are utilised, because the necessary economic conditions cannot be met. Often solutions which are economic in one country are not economic in others, because the supply and demand prices for the facility differ fundamentally from one country to another.

Both individuals and society wish to obtain the maximum benefit from the resources available to them. Basically, the resources consist of land and other natural endowments, the man-made stock of produced goods and human effort. From these man obtains all his requirements, both material and spiritual. In the long run satisfactions, what the economist calls utilities, decline as the quantity of a particular type of goods or services increases. In a rough and ready way, man tries to adjust the use of his resources so as to obtain equal marginal returns in each direction. Man is thus, not seeking perfection, but compromise, and he may well reject technically satisfying solutions because he values some other type of goods or services more highly. The community which rejects a tidy, handsome, hygienic form of settlement for a dirty and disordered one, may, of course, lack the technical and economic organization to obtain anything better, but on the other hand, it may simply value leisure more highly.

Thus, the scale, standard, and form of buildings and town development will depend on the resources that are available, on the relative values placed upon them, and on the machinery available for reaching and executing decisions on the provision of urban facilities.

RESOURCES FOR THE BUILT ENVIRONMENT

A considerable proportion of national resources are required to develop, improve and maintain the built environment. The proportion depends on the scale, standards and forms of built facility, on the condition of the stock, and on the size of the national

37

resources. In this country, this work uses about an eighth of the gross national product.[1] New construction currently uses about three quarters of these resources, that is something under a tenth of our gross national product.[2] This proportion is not high compared with other European countries, most of which spend a greater proportion of national resources on new construction, some 50% more, and one country, Switzerland, about 100% more. The United States also spends a greater proportion. Generally, the proportions of expenditure are tending to rise, Thus, there is little doubt that the built environment is an important consumer of national resources. The scale of provision, standards and forms, can only be raised either if more resources are produced, or if the community is prepared to devote less resources to the provision of other goods and services, and to leisure. In either case, if standards are to be raised and more expensive forms used for the built environment, more resources need to be devoted to construction work, and more capital and labour is needed in the construction industry to design, build, service, manage and administrate built facilities, and to manufacture the materials required. The movement of resources into construction will not, of course, occur if sufficient finance is not provided to attract resources in this direction and away from other uses. The rate at which standards can be raised tends to be slow, because the resources required to replace the stock of built facilities are very large in relation to current output.

COSTS, VALUES AND CHOICE

The problem of choice of standard and form of built facilities is difficult. About a half of the built environment is in the public sector and hence not fully subject to market influences. Moreover, the amenities of the built environment which are enjoyed by the individual, depend not only on facilities bought or rented by him and on publicly provided facilities but also on the side effects of facilities created primarily for others. The community needs to be able to compare the range of policies for the built environment which are open to it and to be able to consider whether more or less expenditure on this aspect of living would increase the overall sum of satisfactions. In practise, of course, clear cut choices of this form are rarely made. The decision to spend on the built environment is taken, in fact, by many different people in many different sectors of the economy; their decisions depending on the criteria appropriate to their situation. Broadly there are three sectors to be considered, the business, personal and public sectors of the economy.

In the business sector, decisions are taken by the entrepreneur. He is concerned with the purchase of factors of production and with their use to produce goods and services for sale to the personal and public sectors of the economy. A building is one of these factors of production; it has no value to the entrepreneur of itself but it is of value only in so far as it facilitates his business. He is concerned with the difference between revenue and expenditure, and with its relationship to the capital employed. Thus he is prepared to meet the costs of constructing and operating built facilities only in so far as they enable expenditure in other directions to be reduced, or because by meeting the requirements of his customers, they lead to a greater revenue. Of course, entrepreneurs are not entirely motivated by the profit motive but the extent to which they can depart from it, is limited by the need to supply goods and services in a competitive market. Customers will not, generally, be prepared to pay extra for the entrepreneur's services in order to finance a standard or form of building much above the currently accepted level. The less competitive the situation, and the lower the costs of providing space in relation to turnover, the easier it is to meet relatively high costs for building space. The costs to which reference is made is, of course, the total costs-in-use, that is, the annual equivalent construction costs, maintenance, heating, lighting, cleaning and other service costs.

Thus, by and large, expenditure on buildings in the business sector is determined in some broad sense by the community's level of acceptance of standard and form. If buildings are erected at standards substantially above this level, costs will tend to be more than the market can bear and in the long run buildings will remain on the market until prices drop below the level of economic cost. If, on the other hand, standards are too low, some entrepreneurs will create a demand for better quality buildings. As a result of a gradual process of filtering up, the poorest buildings will be abandoned. However, because the range of turnovers per unit of building area vary widely, both from trade, to trade, and from one entrepreneur to another, the range of standards and forms which the market can support will always be very wide.

The personal sector of the economy consists of private persons who purchase or rent buildings for consumption. The value of a building to them arises not from a money revenue but from the satisfactions they enjoy in using it. The price they are prepared to pay depends on the satisfaction obtained and on the other costs which arise from occupying the building. Often, of course, the user will not be aware of all the costs which arise, or perhaps of all the satisfactions obtained. Again, national standards and forms will depend in the long run on the generally accepted level of values placed on buildings in relation to the resources which need to be spent.

The level of expenditure on built facilities and, hence, the standards and forms obtained is also, of course, affected by financial and fiscal constraints. The former are partly, and the latter completely, under the control of governments. Capital is often restricted so that less can be spent on construction than might otherwise be desirable. Again, the higher the rate of interest, the higher the annual cost of capital and the less can be afforded on construction. In some countries, of which this is an example, taxation bears more heavily on construction costs than on running costs and, as a result, construction standards are reduced, frequently at the expense of higher running costs. Again, as in this country, taxation levied on the scale and standard of buildings raises costs in relation to the values obtained, as compared with those obtained from other goods and services. Thus in various ways government action may depress the standards of built facilities and the demand for built space. Equally well it could set financial and fiscal controls to provide incentives to the adoption of higher standards. Governments can set minimum standards by regulation but the higher these are set, the smaller the demand for built space may be.

The public sector broadly consists of two markets for building and built facilities, that of nationalised industries and public authority trading services, and that of public authorities built facilities for consumption services and public use. The nationalised industries and public authority trading services are generally expected to provide something near a commercial return on the capital they employ. Hence, their criteria for built facilities will not be dissimilar to those of business organisations. In the public sector the user generally does not have any direct control over either the costs or the level of satisfactions provided. Generally, the choice is made on his behalf by administrators who neither directly enjoy the services provided nor themselves meet the cost. The amount of resources available for the creation and improvement of building construction is limited by the resources available to the public sector and by the amount which can be made available from it for construction work. Generally, the more money which is spent on each unit of construction, the fewer the units which can be constructed.

It will have been appreciated that in each sector of the economy the decisions about the scale, standards and forms of built environment are made in relation to the interests of the decision takers operating in that sector. That is decisions are taken in relation to the internal economies as seen by the person taking the decision. It is not in his interests to take account of the external economies, that is the economic consequences of each set of decisions on the rest of the community. The satisfactions obtained by members of the community arise, partly from buildings and developments provided for their use by the public service, and partly from the external economies which arise as a consequence of buildings and developments provided by the business and personal sectors for their own use. Such buildings and developments often result in a loss rather than a gain in amenity to the public at large, for example, loss created by traffic congestion, by noise and fumes and by disfigurement of towns and landscape. The public interest is safe-guarded partly by the public spirit shown by those taking decisions, although frequently they cannot know of the diseconomies they produce, and partly by financial, fiscal and physical controls which set constraints, in the public interest, on the activities of persons and organisations. Such constraints can only, in the main be negative. Thus, there can be no guarantee that the sum of even the best individual decisions will produce the best balance between the standards and forms of urban facility and the resources needed for their creation.

BUILDING FORM, COSTS AND VALUES

Although the proportion of gross national product spent on the construction, improvement and maintenance of the built environment, current in this country, about an eighth may appear substantial, in fact, the total impact of built environment on the use of resources is much greater. For most types of building other service costs, broadly heating, lighting and cleaning, tend to add another quarter to a half to the equivalent costs of construction and maintenance.[3] As higher and higher standards of environment are demanded, the costs rise, so that the proportion of the national product spent in this field tends to be nearer a sixth than an eighth.

The real initial costs of a building in relation to floor area tend to be rising. This is to a large extent because of an increase in the amount of engineering services now considered necessary. The capital costs rise, not only because of the costs of the engineering equipment and its installation, but because of the building work necessary to accommodate the services. This adds both to the cubic contents of the building and to the loads which it has to carry.

The increased capital costs will, of course, be reflected in the annual costs of the building. The running costs will be increased even more because engineering services usually need to be replaced more frequently than most of the building components and additionally use considerable quantities of fuel. For example, in this country, whereas the annual costs-in-use (the annual equivalent of construction costs and running costs) for an office building would currently be about an eighth greater if mechanical ventilation, rather than just heating, were installed, the costs would be increased by nearly a third if air conditioning were installed.[4] The costs-in-use for a typical office building per 1000 square feet of floor area were estimated, in 1967 to be increased by £70 for heating, £140 for heating and mechanical ventilation, and £280 for full air conditioning. These figures were based on the use of oil and electricity for the fuel.

Lighting systems also add to the capital and running costs of buildings. A really high quality lighting system in a factory building, could add about a quarter to the total annual costs-in-use.[5] The costs would rise, not only because the installation and running costs would be high, but also because the hours of using the lighting system would be increased, since, unless the amount of glazing were greatly increased, the hours during which natural lighting would provide an adequate standard would fall.

The costs of lighting and heating are, of course, both dependent on the amount and arrangement of the glazing. Other things being equal, the costs of heating rise and the costs of lighting fall as the amount of glazing is increased. The overall effect on the costs-in-use of a building in relation to the amount of glazing varies with the situation. Currently, in this country, the lowest costs-in-use are usually obtained with a moderate degree of glazing. Generally, as the area of glazing is increased beyond a moderate level, the annual equivalent costs for fabric construction, maintenance and cleaning and the costs of fuel for heating rise substantially, while the saving in fuel and tube costs for lighting fall only moderately. As a result the costs-in-use rise. The extent to which they rise depends on the various levels of cost, the way in which the building is used and the natural environment in which the building is situated. Broadly, the higher the standard of lighting required, the longer the hours the building is used and the closer the outside temperature is, on average, to the required internal temperature, the higher level of glazing at which costs-in-use are minimised.[5] Of course, in some buildings, process heat is so excessive that fabric heat losses are of no importance and even an advantage.

Glazing, of course, brings other problems, problems of glare, problems of unwanted solar heat gain and problems of noise. The solution to these problems usually adds in some way to the costs-in-use. However, while excessive glazing tends to add to the costs-in-use, reductions in the amount of glazing beyond a moderate level do not necessarily reduce the costs-in-use. There comes a point, when the natural light provided by glazing falls to such a low level that artificial light is necessary throughout the hours of use. Usually, the levels of lighting which are considered satisfactory for working during hours of darkness are considered unsuitable for rooms largely or entirely dependent on artificial lighting. Where there is little or no glazing, levels of the order of 40 lumens per square foot are frequently suggested. The additional costs of installing and operating lighting at that level tends to raise the costs-in-use, in this country, above those obtained with a moderate degree of glazing.

These conclusions about the level of glazing tend to be reinforced when full air conditioning is provided, so that the spread of air conditioning would not, under current conditions in this country, appear to lead to a situation in which either large glazed areas or unglazed (windowless) buildings would result in lower costs-in-use.[4] In fact, it has been argued that air conditioning is only necessary in modern buildings, in this country, because of the need to combat the excessive swings in temperature which result from the solar gain inevitable in buildings with large areas of glass.[6] The need for air conditioning, or at least mechanical ventilation is not, however, confined to buildings with excessive glazing. It also tends to be necessary for tall buildings, because of the excessive air currents which are created and which result in open windows being unpleasant, and also for buildings in noisy situations.

The intensity of noise, and the duration of high noise levels, along roads with a high traffic density, near railways and some industrial plants, and near large airports is quite unacceptable. Often the nose level is as much as 90 decibels.[7] Even the traffic flow along a two lane road can reach nearly this level at peak capacity.[8] With traditional types of wall construction the window is the sensitive point for the entrance of noise. Openable windows only give a comparatively small reduction in noise level, although the reduction increases with the distance from the windows. To obtain a substantial reduction the glazing needs to be sealed; sealed single glazing gives about 20 decibels reduction and double glazing with about a six inch cavity gives about 40 decibels reduction. Since it is almost impossible to hear the telephone when the noise level is above 50 decibels, there are a large number of situations for which sealed glazing is necessary. (It is possible to obtain a 20 decibel reduction with a six inch cavity double window with baffle ventilation in which case natural ventilation is feasible.) In such cases mechanical ventilation needs to be provided, although not necessarily full air conditioning.

While the problem of noise incidental to the site cannot be avoided, it may be possible to avoid some of the cost consequences which result. One method is to use the buildings on the site to shield each other from external noise. For example, if continuous terraces were constructed along the major traffic streets, these would shield the areas lying behind from traffic noise, although, at the cost of greater noise intensity along the traffic street. If the rooms along the traffic streets were to be used for purposes for which relative freedom from noise was necessary, they would need to be insulated from noise and would generally need at least mechanical ventilation, if not air conditioning. An alternative solution, which might be economic in the case of buildings of several storeys, would be to roof in the traffic street. This would, of course, have the incidental benefit of transferring costs from the private to the public sector. If such solutions were adopted the rooms facing into the court, whether in the same or in another building, would probably not need any special protection. The greater the scale on which areas were developed in this way, the greater the proportion of space for which natural ventilation would be adequate and the greater the saving in resources. The forms of development do not, of course, protect the users of the buildings from aircraft noise but generally, except near airports, aircraft noise is only intermittent. Such protection can only be provided by the use of sealed glazing and mechanical ventilation or air conditioning.

However, the ability to develop in this way is restricted in this country by the system of planning control, particularly that part intended to protect daylighting standards. The distance of the external walls from the boundaries of the site are regulated, so that sufficient light can fall on the face of the walls of the building being tested and its neighbours, to provide adequate lighting within the building in average conditions.[9] In practise the level of adequacy of internal daylighting depends on a number of factors, in particular, on the way the building is glazed, on its depth and on floor to ceiling heights Despite the use of daylighting indicators, many commercial buildings have an inadequate level of daylighting throughout their depth and supplementary artificial lighting becomes necessary throughout the day and as a result there is an increase in their costs-in-use.

The operation of such daylighting controls, particularly on expensive city sites, tends to result in free-standing slabs and towers, often on a podium. Since the traffic and other external noise can circulate freely around them, and since the noise level is little reduced by the height of the room above the pavement, noise levels tend to be much the same all over the building. Thus, in noisy situations, sealed glazing is likely to be necessary for all windows and mechanical ventilation or air conditioning is likely to be necessary for every room. The need for sealed windows is likely to be reinforced, particularly for the higher storeys, both by normal wind conditions and conditions created by the form of buildings themselves. Thus a paradoxical position is reached, in which partly because of design fashion, planning controls intended to improve standards, not only fail to achieve this objective, but indirectly result in a form of building and town development, which uses far more resources and which creates other difficulties which result in reduced standards.

The feasibility of using high buildings also depends on the development of high speed lifts. Without lifts the practical height of a building is limited as a result of the fatigue and time taken to climb stairs. The higher the building the more important it is to provide high speed lifts to convey people to the upper floors. Even so, there is an economic limit to the height and number of floors which it is worthwhile to provide. While the cost of a lift, to install and operate, does not increase proportionately to the height of the building, the amount of floor space it takes up and the journey time, does tend to rise proportionately. As a building becomes taller and contains more floors, it is necessary, other things being equal, to increase lift operation speeds and the number of lifts. Both increase the costs-in-use of lifts; increasing the number of lifts reduces the net floor space available for economic use. Because the capacity of lifts tends to be small in relation to the number of potential users, their operation in peak periods tends to lead to queuing and to time costs; the greater the number of floors, the greater these will tend to be and the greater will be the costs of operating in the building. While escalators have a greater capacity than lifts, they are much more expensive to install and operate and consume a much larger amount of floor space.

The costs-in-use of floor space tend to rise in tall buildings also because the costs of construction, maintenance and servicing tends to rise with the height and number of storeys in the building. The way these costs rise tends to depend on the type of building and on its form of construction. In this country the price of constructing dwellings rises steeply per unit area as the form of construction changes from the house to the flatted block. The price per unit area continues to rise as the number of storeys is increased but at a declining rate. Whereas eight storey blocks are about 50% more expensive than those at two storeys, fifteen storey blocks are only 70% more expensive.[10] Maintenance and management costs are also about 50% greater for flatted blocks than for two storey houses.[11] The cost of constructing factory buildings is also increased sharply per unit area as the form of construction changes from a light weight shed building to a concrete framed two storey building. For such deep buildings costs rise less than for narrow buildings, such as housing; between two and seven storeys the rise is only about 20%.[5] The amount of rise in cost is also affected by the amount of vertical transport which needs to be provided. Of course, whereas, the single storey building can be lit through the

roof, the multi-storey building can only be side lit and normally is dependent on artificial lighting, this further increases the costs. Operation costs are also frequently higher
where production has to be spread over several floors, partly because internal transport
and supervision become more expensive.

It will have been noticed that the form of building with the most favourable costs-
in-use depends to a large extent on the interaction between the form of the building and
the costs of installing and operating the mechanical and electrical services. Their costs
vary with the type of fuel and with the costs of different types of fuel relative to other
costs. The price of electricity is clearly particularly important. A substantial fall in its
price might greatly reduce the costs of lighting, heating and ventilation, and reduce
the economic importance of the right balance of glazing and the reliance on natural
lighting and ventilation.

As was pointed out earlier, the increasing use of mechanical and electrical equipment
in buildings tends to result in substantial increases in both the real costs of construction
and operation. If this occurs on a large scale, it will tend to lead either to a greater real
expenditure per head on built space or to a decline in floor area per head or in other
building standards. A decline in building standards may make itself manifest not only
in the standards of new buildings but also in the standards of existing buildings. There
is no shortage of evidence of the extent to which the standards of the stock, particularly
of housing, are being depressed by inadequate maintenance and by an inadequate rate of
replacing obsolete components and of installing modern equipment. This is true not
only in this country. Since generally new construction represents less than 2% of the
stock, the standards of the stock of buildings as a whole can be raised far more rapidly
by raising the standards of existing buildings than by raising the standards of new
buildings.[12]

Moreover, because, in this country, of the scale of work necessary to rebuild and to
raise the existing stock of buildings up to current standards, and of the work necessary
to add to the stock to meet new needs and the needs of additional population, it appears
unlikely that it will be possible to achieve any substantial shortening of the lives of
building in the foreseeable future unless, of course, revolutionary new methods are
found which produce considerable economies in construction.[12] In particular, it appears
unlikely to be possible to replace buildings erected since the war during the course of
this century. Buildings, therefore, need to be constructed to be sufficiently adaptable to
meet changes in use and standard likely to occur in the next four or five decades, and in
particular, to be able to house any new forms of mechanical and electrical equipment
which is likely to be developed.

Again, since the proportion of the costs of a building, both in the case of initial costs
and costs-in-use, which is due to mechanical and electrical equipment is increasing and
appears likely to increase substantially, the search for economies in building costs is
likely to become more fruitful, if it is applied to services than if it is applied to building
structure.

BUILDING FORMS AND TOWN FORMS

The form for a settlement depends partly on the form of the buildings of which it is
composed and partly on the way the buildings are disposed over the settlement. Land

is required both to provide a base for the buildings and to provide a space for the performance of various outdoor activities. In a conventional settlement, in which most buildings are only of two or three storeys, about an eighth of the land is used for the base of buildings, a further eighth is used for private access, storage and parking, about a sixth for roads and three-fifths for gardens and open space.[13] Except exceptionally, these proportions would not be changed dramatically by changes in building form.

Piling one building upon another, or even using multi-level decking for parking and storage, would not reduce the proportion of land covered by buildings very much, as long as such a large proportion of the land continued to be used for roads, gardens and open space. Large savings in land could only be achieved if internal and external space standards were appreciably reduced, for example, to the levels provided in Asia. If such standards were not reduced, and with a rising level of affluence, it is more likely that they will be increased,[14] no substantial increase in densities would be achieved by making a greater use of artificial internal environments, since the space about buildings would still be required to accommodate such external uses of space as access, parking and amenity areas.

Nevertheless, by using different building forms, urban form itself could be radically changed. If, for example, buildings were much taller and much larger, their numbers would fall and there would be fewer but much larger spaces. Technically, it would be possible to provide accommodation for a large group of people in a single large, tall building. As long as the spaces in the building were to be lit and ventilated naturally, the building could not be very deep. But technically it is feasible to provide adequate lighting and ventilation artificially, although as shown earlier this currently increases, in this country the costs-in-use. In fact, even in a deep building the rooms along the periphery could still be lit and ventilated naturally. While it is generally accepted that living rooms should be lit naturally, in unfavourable climates they are frequently ventilated mechanically, if not provided with full air conditioning. This practise might be more general if it did not use so many resources. A completely artificial environment with little or no views out is generally acceptable already for a large variety of building uses, for example, for large shops, restaurants, places of entertainment, various types of public building, and in many cases for offices and factories. If such floor spaces were provided in the interior of large buildings, the buildings could be very deep and the exterior of the building could be used for living rooms and other spaces for which external views and a natural environment were required.

However, the greater the complex of spaces under one roof, the greater would need to be the proportion of space provided for circulation and storage within the building. Such space would be far more expensive to provide and service than space outside. Even open shopping decks cost about five times as much per unit area to build as those on the ground, while multi-storey car parks cost about ten times as much as those on the ground. Internal transport would need to be electrically powered in order to overcome the problems of fire, polution and noise. The flexibility of such a settlement would tend to be far less than that of a conventional one and hence change would be more costly. Thus the difficulties of housing a city in a single building are economic rather than technical.

Housing a city in a single building is not the only imaginative suggestion which has been made recently. Other ideas which have been suggested include running the roads on the roofs of the buildings, roofing the city over, using the city roof as the site for open space and building the city underground. While all these suggestions raise various technical problems, all of them could probably be solved on the basis of current knowledge. The real problems are, again, economic rather than technical.

Clearly, it is quite impossible to predict the economic consequences of such far reaching new solutions without first examining the technical problems in some detail.

If the road networks were constructed on the roofs of buildings, considerable costs would arise in creating frames strong enough to carry the heavy live loads that would result in bridging between buildings and in creating the ramps at the terminals of the buildings. Roads at roof level would be very exposed to wind and frost, and extra costs would arise in meeting the difficulties thus created. The problems of noise and fumes would also need to be met.

Roofing over a city would have even greater consequences. It could take either the form of a roof over the whole city, or roofing between buildings. Either buildings would need to be strengthened or columns would need to be set up to carry the roof frames and cladding. If the roof covered the whole city, much more storm water would need to be handled than in a normal city. Even if the roof were glazed, and any other solution would be difficult to imagine, some natural light would be lost and lighting costs would be increased, especially if the glass were not kept clean, itself an expensive operation. Natural light would also be lost when the glass was covered with snow and ice, as it would in some climates. Provision would have to be made for ventilation, in particular for dealing with solar gain and with fumes; the problems of reflected noise would also need consideration. Probably all energy consumption would need to be in the form of electricity. On the other hand, the roofed city would have a dry climate and would be warmer than the traditional city. In a cold wet climate there should be savings in heating costs, in a warm climate ventilation costs might be higher. Cladding costs might be lower and a greater proportion of activities might be carried on outside the buildings, thus reducing the need for covered space. If the city roof was used for open space the construction costs would be greater and artificial lighting would be required permanently unless the area between the building was glazed.

Most of the problems described above would arise in the case of a city constructed underground. Additional costs would arise for the provision and servicing of a permanent artificial environment. These would be only partly offset by savings in heating costs. In addition, costs would arise for tanking the floor, roof and walls of the city.

Such cities would be far more integrated than conventional ones, they would be far less easy to phase, and would tend to have far more resources under-used during the early stages of construction. They would be far less adaptable, or at least far more expensive to adapt to changing needs. While people might eventually adapt to such cities and there must be some doubts about the effects on physical and mental health, there would be at least some loss of satisfactions, if only during the period of adaptation.

Clearly, in the absence of details, it is not possible to estimate costs but some idea of their scale can be gauged by examining the costs of some comparable structures Roofing over a city would probably add something of the order of upwards of £50,000 per acre to the costs. Elevated motorways cost about eight to nine times as much as a similar road on the ground, while motorways in bored tunnels cost fifty to sixty times as much.[15] On that basis, space for an underground city might cost something over £4 million per acre. If it were built by the cut and cover method costs might only be a quarter as much. Of course, in the future new systems of engineering might enable such costs to be considerably reduced. As indicated earlier, the possibility of being able to meet scales of costs of this order, other than exceptionally, appears to be rather remote within the foreseeable future. Again, the more integrated the construction of a city, usually the greater the need for its construction to become a public enterprise, and if its costs were greatly in excess of those of competing cities, the more likely that it could only be provided as a public service.

Some of these town forms would, of course, save land. As pointed out earlier, building tall multi-storey blocks and the multi-use of space saves only a small proportion of town land. Even less land is saved by building transport networks within the buildings, since the buildings need to be larger to accommodate them. Land would be saved if roads were developed on the roofs of buildings, or if open space were provided there. Space for outdoor recreation would hardly be provided at conventional standards in a roofed or enclosed city; most of it would undoubtedly be provided outside the city, or in the case of an underground city, partly on top of it. Thus, the net saving of land would probably not be proportionally very great. The largest savings of land would be obtained be reclaiming land from the sea. This has been suggested not only for cities, but also for airports and ports. Given favourable circumstances this is probably commercially the cheapest way of obtaining sites without using existing land. Estimates for reclaiming suitable land have been put as low as £5,000 per acre. Since a developer would generally have to pay as much as this and frequently much more for land for town development, it would be worth his while in some cases to reclaim land. The position from the point of view of the national economy would, of course, be rather different. In the final account the land saved would be farmland, the capitalised value of which would only be a few hundreds of pounds.

Despite the density of population in Great Britain, it is not possible to say that nationally land for urban development is in short supply, although it is in some areas. Estimates suggest,[10] that over the rest of the century, about 5% of the current arable and permanent grassland is likely to be required for development. The output of agricultural land is increasing as husbandry improves, as better use is made of land available, and as a higher proportion of land is used for the more valuable types of product. Although over the last decade, yields rose only 1 or 2% per annum, the total value of net output per acre rose over 3% per annum. The output lost from farmland taken for development over the rest of the century could probably be replaced within three or four years. If the rate of productivity only rose by $1\frac{1}{4}$% per annum over the rest of the century, output would be nearly 50% greater on the reduced land by the end of that time.

COMMUNICATIONS AND REGIONAL STRUCTURE

There is no lack of awareness of the dominance of the systems of communications on regional structure. Large groups of people could not live in one locality, until systems had been developed which were capable of transporting sufficient food, water and other necessities of life and of disposing of waste at an acceptable cost. As the capacity of such systems increased, so did the possibility of developing large scale settlements. The large settlement has many advantages to offer over the small one. It can support a greater range or urban facilities and permit a much greater degree of industrial specialisation.

The need for a large number of people to live in close proximity in order to enjoy the advantages of scale is, however, less a need for physical proximity than for proximity in time. Hence, as the speed with which the communications network can operate increases, people have less need to be physically close together. Whereas in the days of the pack-horse and the hand-cart production generally needed to take place in close physical proximity to its source of supply and its market, today the production process itself can be spread over hundreds of miles, the different production units being linked by fast and economic mechanical road, rail and air transport. Similarly, the development of electronic communication reduces the need for face to face contacts. The telephone already provides an instant and economic system of oral communication. The development of television may soon provide an equally satisfactory visual system. If mass production reduces costs sufficiently, universal closed circuit television might eliminate the need for face to face conferences and make it economically feasible for people to examine goods and documents without moving from their place of work or home. Linkages to computers may similarly provide rapid and economic reference to information of all types.

Such changes could have a far reaching effect on regional structure and on the structure of settlements. Firms and other organisations could operate economically in smaller units, particularly those which operate on the basis of information. Private and public administration could be located locally. Much of the process of learning could be carried out in small local units, perhaps even in the home. Shopping could be centred on specialist units which displayed its goods to the purchaser in his home by television and dispatched orders from warehouses. Savings would arise in storage and display costs; the need for shops, large central offices and large specialized educational institutes would be reduced, there would be less need for travelling for non-social reasons and hence less need for transport facilities for these needs, but there would be faster services when travelling was necessary. People could live in smaller settlements, and people and settlements could be more dispersed. On the other hand, the amount of social travelling appears likely to increase considerably.

Development is already moving in this direction. First the railway unified distant places. The tram, bus and to a less extent the railway dispersed the larger settlement, increased their size and reduced their densities. The aeroplane and now the railway are further unifying settlements to the point where in Great Britain soon no important settlements will be more than a few hours journey apart. The possibility of being able to fly to most places of importance in the world within a day is probably not far distant. The need for self-sufficiency is declining.

Thus, while at first the growth of fast and economic communications allowed cities to grow larger, the mechanical and electronic development of communications in the future appears likely to erode the importance of cities and to allow people a much greater freedom in deciding their location. A dispersed network of relatively small settlements might well prove to be quite economic. Of course, the possibility of such regional structures is constrained by the availability of space and by the existence of the present stock of urban facilities. It appears to be most unlikely that sufficient resources would be available, at least in this country, to allow more than about half of the urban stock to be replaced over the balance of the century.[16] Because the urban facilities and communication networks in an existing settlement have such differing future potentials, it is difficult to find a point in time when it is not more economic to replace and improve existing facilities than to start a new settlement to replace it. The technical, social and economic problems of closing and clearing large settlements do not yet appear to have been studied on an adequate scale. Thus, any new dispersed regional settlement structure appears likely to take place in relation to the existing patters of settlements.

COMMUNICATIONS AND TOWN STRUCTURE

The structure of towns tends to be dominated by the form of transport. The amount of space given up to the transport system depends on its form. Human transport is the most economic of space and both enables and requires a high density of development. The amount of space required increases as the size of vehicle and its incidence increases. The congestion caused by the car is less a result of its size than of its incidence. If the horse-drawn carriage had been used as universally as the car, congestion would have been far greater than it is today.

The car is not just a means of town transport but equally a means of inter-city and recreational transport, as well as something of a symbol of prestige. While for the journey to work systems of mass transport are generally more efficient, they are not necessarily more convenient or more economic. Any additional costs of the private car are often thought worthwhile. Once people possess personal transport and this appears likely to be universal in the future, they will compare its marginal costs, against charges for public transport. These will be based on average costs and these tend to be inflated as a result of the peakiness of demand. As the extent of personal transport increases, it will be all the more difficult for public transport to compete on an equal footing. On the other hand, complete reliance on personal transport is unlikely to be acceptable for both social and planning reasons; without public transport many people would be deprived of any convenient transport at all.

Studies at the National Institute have indicated that it is physically and economically feasible to construct settlements, certainly up to the size of a quarter of a million, with road networks capable of accommodating journey to work movements by car for 80% of the working population. Restricting the use of the car for such journeys would not appear to be economic. The greater the use of public transport for the journey to work, the peakier the loading would be and the more it would tend to be uneconomic. The situation in existing towns, of course, would be very different. There the construction of suitable roads would be much more expensive because of the need to replace built facilities with a remaining useful life but which would need to be destroyed in order to develop the roads.

The importance of a universal vehicle will be appreciated. A special town car, as is sometimes suggested, would need to be extremely cheap to justify itself. The comparison with public transport costs would then be in terms of average costs and unless the town car was extremely cheap, its use would not be justified. Thus, the battery driven vehicle, unless it is far cheaper, than appears likely, needs to be suitable for all types of journeys.

As pointed out earlier, unless a much greater proportion of national resources are devoted to construction work than in the past, it is unlikely that it will be possible to rebuild our cities during this century, either to provide roads capable of handling potential traffic, or to provide new forms of transport. Changes in transport appear more likely to take the form of making a better use of existing facilities, for example, developments of existing railway systems to provide much greater speed, and on commuter lines, capacity, and the development of vehicle control systems which would increase the capacity of existing roads.

If the high speed possibilities of railways were realised, they should have a large part to play in internal transport. In a country as geographically small as Great Britain, the railways would probably be able to compete on speed and price with aircraft for practically any internal journey. In terms of total journey time, door to door, greater aircraft speeds would produce only at best small time advantages over railways. Larger planes would be likely to bring price advantages. On the other hand, vertical take-off aircraft, if economic in operation, might again restore the cost and speed advantages to the plane.

For international traffic and internal journeys in geographically large countries, aircraft appear likely to have economic and speed advantages, at least for passengers and valuable small cargo, over other forms of transport. On sea routes, the large bulk carriers and the large container ships appear likely to keep shipping competitive for most cargo traffic.

These changes in transport forms appear likely to have important consequences for town form. The rationalisation of railways and the concentration of goods handling in large depots appears likely to lead to the release of land for other uses. The growth of size in goods handling depots will, however, tend to generate large amounts of traffic in their vicinity and increase the length of road haulage journeys. The increase in size of ships and container traffic tends to push the port facilities down river to where there is deep water and ample land for cargo handling and so to release land in the cities for other uses and to remove traffic generation points out of the congested parts of cities with port facilities. On the other hand, the growth in the carrying capacity of planes will enable airports to handle much more traffic and, as a result, will generate far more road and perhaps rail traffic, both in the vicinity of the airport and in the cities they serve. The use of vertical take-off aircraft would redistribute air generated traffic back into the built-up areas.

As was mentioned earlier, the level of noise has a considerable impact on building and town form. Industrial noise, while often considerable at its source, tends to be confined to limited areas of a town. It is probably more of a nuisance to those who have to work with it, than to the public at large. In contrast, noise generated by transport tends to be widespread. Methods of developing built form which would limit the impact of traffic noise and reduce the costs of insulation against it have already been discussed. Clearly however, it would be unwise to re-orientate the form of urban development, or to go to the considerable expense of insulating against noise, if a universal vehicle with a quiet form of propulsion is likely to be viable in a few years time. The problem of air pollution might be solved at the same time. Aircraft noise is, however, much more universal and much more difficult to insulate against. The insulation of buildings (including providing and operating the necessary mechanical ventilation) has been estimated to have a capitalised costs-in-use for the central areas of large cities of as much as £90 million per square mile and would clearly be far too expensive to be carried out generally.[7] Control of noise at source, might be less expensive. Of course, if it was necessary to develop buildings insulated against a high noise intensity and consequently to provide mechanical ventilation, it might be that some of the building forms requiring an artificial environment, would be found to be economic.

CONCLUSIONS

Building and town development require a substantial use of the resources of both individuals and nations. In the past the resources used have not been adequate to provide a built environment of an acceptable standard, although the range in standards has been very wide. If minimum standards are to be raised to acceptable levels, it would appear that a much greater proportion of resources would need to be spent on improving the existing stock. Unless revolutionary new forms of building with substantially lower resource costs are developed, the life of buildings is unlikely to be substantially shortened in the foreseeable future.

Thus the opportunity to introduce new mechanical and electronic developments on a large scale, unless their introduction results in savings in operation costs sufficient to offset any additional initial and running costs, may be limited. As a result it would appear that mechanical and electronic developments which increase productivity substantially in relation to costs have a much greater chance of being adopted than those which only provide greater comfort or a new way of meeting existing needs.

Generally in this country the provision of artificial environments appears to be expensive in relation to natural environments. While the use of artificial environment would remove many of the restraints of building form and could lead to substantial changes in town form, there would not appear to be adequate economies in other directions to offset the increases in direct costs. If the relative price of electricity was to be substantially reduced the relative costs of artificial environments would thereby be greatly reduced. On the other hand, many of the developments in mechanical and electronic communications appear likely to result in overall economies, particularly where they can be employed without drastic rebuilding of existing settlements. Such improvements in communications appear in the long run likely to lead to a much more dispersed type of settlement pattern.

Perhaps the most dominant force operating on building and town form is the internal combustion engine. Employed in road vehicles it tends to be a greedy user of town space and one of the most potent sources of noise and polution. Used in the aeroplane it is an even more effective distributor of noise. Unless economic methods of increasing the efficiency with which road vehicles use roads can be developed, either their use in existing towns will need to be restricted or much redevelopment will be necessary. Unless the noise output of internal combusion engines can be considerably reduced at source, or a substitute found, or their use in and over towns prohibited, it may be necessary in future to insulate buildings against noise and as a result economic to use artificial environments. Nevertheless this would greatly increase the costs-in-use of buildings and might result in the need for undesirable economies in other directions. However, the acceptance of buildings with artificial environments from both a physical and economic standpoint would remove the restraints which would otherwise exist against the employment of the more revolutionary forms of building and towns.

REFERENCES

1. National income and expenditure—Central Statistical Office. London: HMSO. Annually.
2. Bulletin of Housing and Building Statistics for Europe. Geneva: United Nations. Annually.
3. STONE, P. A. (1967). Building design evaluation—costs-in-use. London: Spons.
4. STONE, P. A. (1968). Thermal environment—Some economic considerations. Thermal environment in modern buildings—Institute of Heating & Ventilating Engineers/Building Research Station Symposium. London.
5. STONE, P. A. (1962). The economics of factory buildings. *Factory building studies*, No. 12. London: HMSO.
6. Thermal environment in modern buildings—Institute of Heating and Ventilating Engineers/Building Research Station Synposium. London (1968).
7. PARKER, J. W. (1960). Noise problems in buildings. Royal Society of Health—Sessional Meeting. 9th November. London.
8. The Greater London Council.
9. WATTS, K. (1963). Functional control and town design. *Architects' Journal*, Vol. 138. 23rd October. London.
10. STONE, P. A. (April 1970). Urban development in Britain—Standards, costs and resources 1964–2004, Vol. 1. *Population and Housing*. Cambridge: Cambridge University Press.
11. STONE, P. A. (1963). Housing, town development, land and costs. *The Estates Gazette Ltd.* London.
12. STONE, P. A. (1966). Building standards and costs. Royal Institute of British Architects Annual Conference 1966, London.
13. STONE, P. A. (1961). The Impact of urban development on the use of land and other resources. *Journal of the Town Planning Institute*, Vol. 47, No. 5. London.
14. Growing space needs in the urbanised regions. Conference of the International Federation of Housing and Planning. Sweden 1965.
15. GOLDSTEIN, A. (1966). Motorway route location studies. Town and Country Planning Summer School, Institute of Town Planners, London.
16. STONE, P. A. (1969). Resources and the economic framework. *Urban Studies*, Vol. 6, No. 3. November.

Discussion

Melville: Dr. Stone has been talking about the possibility of quite small units of settlement. So far we have been talking about cities, and about large urban settlements, but the time may be approaching when urban settlement may not be at all what we are expecting. If it is economical to have small units of settlement, and this seems to be possible, then major changes will come about in the urban pattern. I wonder if we can define the size of a small urban settlement? What form will the diffusion of settlements take? Are settlements going to be so similar that there is not going to be any recognisable differentiation between one settlement and another?

Stone: During the past 20 or 30 years the big cities have grown at their fastest. If one accepts that, what are the reasons for it? Perhaps we have only seen one side of the coin. I think that you may discover that this relates in part to the planning regulations which are thought of in terms of existing Local Authority Areas. The fact that there have been attempts to keep certain parts of the country free of building and the fact that planning is not unified and has been concerned more with what goes on in individual Local Authority Areas, has been the result of people pushing against this.

Bayliss: While agreeing with what Dr. Stone says, this sort of phenomena of urbanisation seems to be world-wide, surely there must be some behavioural ethos in the development of these agglomorations.

Odell: Peoples inclinations to live further apart are made possible as a result of technicological developments in communication. When one compares an Indian City with a North American city we see the opposite extremes of technical inovation on society. In the one a large number of unfortunates are still herded together, while in the other a large number of suburbanites and ex-urbanites move over extensive regions, but in doing so they are still in the same sort of functional relationship with each other and with the city.

Landgon: I understand the question to be a comparison of different schools of urban development. In order to explain change one must bring into the picture the different phases through which technological development passes, and take into account the fact that the different patterns of motivation and different social habits change at different rates. So, in the first place, the effect of the mass march, the effect of mass production, the effect of industrialisation is produced by large urban agglomerations. Smaller centres might have become possible in the future because of increased communications technology, by private transport, by the telephone and so on, but this to produce any effect and to have any real mass significance, means a deep seated change in personal habits and

53

expectations of how people want to live. I would have thought that this will only occur at a much later stage and it is this later stage that we are thinking about now when we raise the question of whether smaller settlements will become more generally typical of urban development than large cities have been so far. I would have thought that we are now only at phase one of technological development. What makes it more difficult is that we seem to be at the edge of phase two, and we cannot quite see how the possibilities realised by communications technology are going to be related to changing patterns of motivation and desire and need.

Cherry: Technology opens up new degrees of freedom, new modes of action, to which we all have to adjust, and it involves us all in a choice, usually a moral one. Do we act, or do we not act? There are increasing numbers of actions to which we have to adjust ourselves, including the fundamental problems of all social activity, and this includes town design. Telephones were invented 100 years ago, but it is only in the last ten years that they have come into massive use in an explosive way so affecting our pattern of living. Roofed-in cities; what are these for; why does anyone want a roofed-in city? They may be possible to contrive but what are they for?

Stone: The roofed-in city, the underground city, and so on, have been suggested seriously, and technically they have certain advantages. If in our climate, we had a city that was roofed over it would be very much more comfortable to move about in.

Cherry: We have a very nice climate in this country and who does not like walking in the rain? We have been taught by the Victorians that snow was not a thing for respectable people to go out in unless you put a veil on. But now, some how or other, we have got the idea that people should spend their lives in cossseted urban environment, and that changes in the weather are unpleasant. Rainfall is so small in this country and comes throughout the year in small quantities but if you got the rain in one dollop as they do in West Africa, or snow falls as in New York that block the streets you really would know something about it. But this country has got a climate which is so mild.

Bennett: The cost of an internal environment, with mechanical resources is frightening economically, both in terms of mechanical service, first costs, and running costs. Many of the schools in California were air conditioned but this was given up in later designs which were made to face north and use cross ventilation.

In regard to the size of a community one is a little concerned that we have completed our first new towns with a population that is too small. At places like Stevenage or Harlow, all the 'A' Level types, were travelling up to London, they cannot find the right kind of job in a population of 60,000. Unless you form clusters of towns with different opportunities many people will have to opt out of them. However, over 230,000 people leave London every year and 200,000 arrive. The reason they leave is that life is no good to them in London, and many are prepared to travel 30 to 40 miles a day and to commute beyond the green belt. Recently I was on the Isle of Dogs, where we are doing a comprehensive development of the whole area and I met some dockers there. They asked me what I was doing, and when I explained one just said 'I have bought my house at Ascot!'

Stone: It is probably economically cheaper to build a cluster rather than to build in one development. Where the problem is the cost of altering the existing structure of a town in order to make it suitable to take a larger population, if you can define any method which enables you to leave the town much in its present form and allow it to develop naturally, this tends to be very much less expensive than rebuilding it.

Redfern: A comment on this question of the size of settlements and the size of clusters, is whether people who live there can have the range of facilities that are available. The question that I am asked most often in the new town I am associated with is 'why haven't we got a Marks and Spencer?' and 'when is the new cinema coming?'. The simple factor here is that economically they are never coming because the size of the population does not justify it. The nearest Marks and Spencer, is about 5 miles away, which I suppose you would consider to be a quite reasonable distance, but it is certainly not considered a reasonable distance by women who have to go to it. There is a social side of marketing that concerns the provision that can be given to people. This is a function of the size of the community and it is one that must not be ignored. The important thing is how people wish to use the place they live in.

Stone: I do not think we will solve the problem of what people want without some form of market indication. If we were to provide a building grant for those who had a financial need, rather than offering them subsidised dwellings, then they could choose what housing they liked. There has been a movement in some quarters to bring the market in and charge, for instance, for the use of public open space in the countryside, for roads and so on. Certainly, if we could extend the market this would give us more indications.

Langdon: When I was in Germany I saw a number of housing projects and never saw any cars. The reason was that the cars were all underground. At what point, with the increase in land costs and the great process on using land, does it become economically possible to use the land under the buildings in our own country?

Stone: To provide a car park underground would cost something in the region of £300 or £400 a car, as compared with £50 on the surface. In the long run, of course, we are sacrificing agricultural land but the value of agricultural produce is so low per acre, that in economic terms one is not justified in doing anything else. One could argue that this is not the way to look at it; that one should, in fact, find some other way to evaluate agricultural land. The Local Authority, however, has to take a commercial view because it has to pay the commercial price for land.

Climate and civilisation

by

SEAN MULCAHY

THE RELATIONSHIP between climate and the location of centres of early civilisation throughout the world is most striking. All were situated in areas close to the 70°F isotherm and where wide summer to winter variations were not excessive. The number of days of enervating heat or cold were few.

The Greek and Roman cities which followed were located somewhat to the north, in areas of less Summer handicap, by reason of a comparatively advanced technology of heating whereby measures could be taken against the cold.

From the thirteenth century, with the invention of the chimney fireplace and the development of coal, civilisation went further north to areas conducive to human energy in Summer, and, where Winters were made tolerable by heating and clothing.

CLIMATE AND BUILDINGS

Early buildings were simply shelters against wind, rain, radiation, intrusion and, depending on weight and restricted ventilation, they modified the diurnal variations of air temperature and radiation. Building construction varied in weight and thermal opacity depending on the characteristics of climate. These static buildings of structure and fabric could merely temper the external climate. It required the addition of energy, of heat and light to transform it.

It was not until the late nineteenth century that the technology of mechanical ventilation, refrigeration and electric lighting revolutionised the possibility of climate control in buildings. Yet the revolution seems to have occurred in spite of building designers.

The historian and critic of architecture was, and is still, concerned primarily with matters of structural style. The art, rather than the science of architecture, is still taught and practised in historical terms. The doctrinaire so-called functional designers of Europe set out to 'civilise technology' but simply adopted a new structural style, of poor performance, inadequately corrected by technology. A building was still to be judged by the impact of its exterior on a sophisticated observer. Little or no comment was made on its performance (perhaps because it could not be drawn or even now photographed— Pevsner in a wide-ranging lecture on modern architecture showed some 80 slides of buildings, all of exteriors, not one of an interior.) Reyner Banham's new book *The Architecture of the Well-tempered Environment* deals with this subject. He propounds that those designers, and notably Frank Lloyd Wright, who calmly accepted the function of technology and absorbed it within their existing skills, did so to the great advantage of their buildings. Louis Kahn, who set out to enslave technology, albeit in a temple, and is revered by present-day architects, wrote: 'I do not like ducts, I do not like pipes. I hate them really thoroughly, but because I hate them so thoroughly, I feel that they have to be given their place. If I just hated them and took no care, I think that they would invade the building and completely destroy it'—and so he structurally designed the celebrated but ineffectual Richards Memorial Building in Philadelphia.

Yet, as Banham points out, electric lighting and air-conditioning have extended man's activity in time and place far beyond any structural innovation in history.

ENERGY AND BUILDINGS

To ensure that a building performs satisfactorily as a thermal machine the relationships between the required internal climate, the variable external climate, the fabric and the energy systems should be clearly set down.

The thermal factors of external climate are those of radiation and air temperature which act on the building fabric in accordance with its transparency to radiation, largely through glass, and in accordance with its conductivity through glass, walls and roof. Because of the unsteady state the weight of the fabric is also important. Next comes the input and control of by-product or waste energy—the by-product of light, people, machines, processes. Finally the equation is closed by the input or extraction of energy by means of the service systems.

Clearly where the difference between the external and internal climates are great buildings should be opaque in shape and fabric. Where diurnal variations are great buildings can with advantage be heavy.

Waste energy should be minimised by the use of high efficiency sources and by insulation and should be directed to use when required and deflected when not. By so optimising the equation the capital and running costs of the building can be minimized. Nor is it a matter of cost. A fabric which is badly matched to the climate and the purpose can create a situation which cannot at any cost be completely corrected by energy.

AVAILABLE TECHNIQUES

What are the techniques available? As yet external climate control is beyond our means although man has had some influence on climate by large scale plantation or deforrestation. Insulating fabric is readily available. Variable screening against solar radiation is common and photo-sensitive glass is available which becomes opaque to incident radiation. Industrialized building techniques avoid weight. It seems likely that the trend to lightness will prevail as it does in all machinery and the capacity of the energy and the response to its control will be extended to deal instantly with energy variations.

The urban building suffers particularly from three sources of annoyance, namely traffic noise, dirt, and air contaminated with carbon monoxide and sulphur. A filtered, preferably washed, mechanical ventilation system is required. Windows must be sealed. Where the facility to open windows is then no longer available, overheating is less acceptable and refrigeration is necessary, even in temperate climates.

Modern ventilating systems operate at pressures and velocities far in excess of those applied twenty years ago. The reduction in distribution size is necessary to conserve space. Distribution energy costs are consequently high. As yet constant volume ventilating systems are used. This requires the constant distribution of maximum air quantities. The possibilities of considerable reduction of energy cost by varying air volume to requirements are being studied. New developments are now gaining prominence, arising from the new generation of deep buildings which rely on mechanical ventilation and high levels of artificial illumination. The interiors of such buildings are not susceptible to heat loss or gain to the exterior. The need for continuous high levels of artificial lighting produces waste energy which in Winter is directed through the ventilating plant to the exterior heat losing zones. (There is a point here to be watched. The need for high levels of illumination is partly related to the comparative level of the daylight perimeter. If this is reduced artificial levels can be reduced. Further, luminescent techniques may so improve lighting efficiency that the waste heat available will not be sufficient. Using lighting for heating, picturesquely called 'Boot-strap Heating', is a costly process.) The refrigeration plant required for Summer use is used as a heat pump in Winter. (A heat pump is a machine which raises the temperature of low grade heat to a level which is useful. The useful energy obtained is many times the energy required to operate the heat pump. This makes it economical to use the expensive fuel of electricity for heat for which normally relatively inexpensive fuel is used.) Even in a temperate climate the capital costs of such buildings can be less than those of high perimeter ratio buildings relying on natural ventilation and daylight. I believe that running costs are higher especially when one accounts for the high cost of operation, maintenance and renewal of sophisticated machinery.

We can conceive in the future solving the difficult problems of air distribution by regenerating local air by a form of electrolysis. In fact, rather as all art is said to aspire to the condition of music, all services aspire to the condition of electricity.

'Electricity plus socialism equals communism' says Marx.

APPRAISAL BY MEASUREMENT

Bridging the present and the future will, I believe, entail the widespread application of appraisal and measuring techniques only recently and rarely in use. Such appraisals have focussed attention on the need to co-ordinate fabric, activity and energy systems. It seems that users' response to buildings relate almost entirely to heat, light and sound, the basic physics of buildings and only marginally to those aspect of buildings which have engrossed the historians and critics.

Following appraisal can come rational design. To design is to predict, and one cannot accurately predict until one has measured. This is a field of many dimensions of which the linear dimension is only one. Intuition may well be the effective basis by which man can live in the city but it is no basis for confident design.

OPEN-ENDEDNESS AND ADAPTABILITY

At the same time that we err by inadequate design we also paradoxically err by over-design. We deny the users the opportunity of taking an active part in their own environment. They become paying guests in their own buildings. We make it difficult to adapt the building to change. The structure of buildings, especially tall urban buildings, is necessarily appallingly durable. Services are not so. Interior fabric need not be so. Our designs should give the users the greatest possible freedom by facilitating the re-arrangement of fabric and the re-routing and upgrading of services.

The difficulty of upgrading services relates not so much to the cost of plant distribution and outlets but to the difficulty of accommodating the distribution in the structure and fabric. Systematic routes for future services are essential in the design of adaptable buildings.

FUTURE BUILDINGS

Banham has already said that a building cannot be said to be modern which does not avail of, nor has been influenced by, energy systems. There are some indications that energy rather than structure could be the essence of shelter in the future. One thinks of inflatable buildings, motor caravans, space capsules but these are not urban shelters. The new urban culture will be an interior one and will also be a leisure one or could be if urban leisure were tolerable. The enjoyment of leisure-time I believe to be more closely related to the physical environment, even more so than the productivity of work-time and I believe that the essence of the desirable environment is to be found in the ideal out-of-doors climate.

There is still a wide gap in quality between the controlled artificial climate and the ideal natural climate. In the case of lighting it seems to relate to the distortion of the natural colour spectrum of daylight and perhaps also to its static state. Thermally it may relate to lack of radiance, in terms of temperature and of the ultra-violet component of daylight radiation (it has been demonstrated that plants and fish respond favourably to controlled ultra-violet radiation). The photo-biology of man is inadequately known. What is it that makes garden or beach so pleasant? If we could create such an atmosphere in a city dwelling our vexations would diminish.

THE WELL TEMPERED CITY

Indeed it may be that the entire city will become a well tempered garden. The technology already exists. Buckminster Fuller's domes can shelter Manhattan. Electricity can temper without contaminating. Sewage and contaminated air can be treated electrolytically. Breezes can be made to stir the leaves of trees. A radiant sun can be made to traverse the sky. The science and technology exist. It will in time be used. Whether in time man can identify what it is he requires remains to be seen.

No doubt irony will intervene, the only reliable element in any situation. By the time we perfect the control of urban climates we will no longer require to do so. We may well have adopted the nomadic culture of the caravan and the capsule.

Discussion

Bentham: A building for which the South West Electricity Board has planning permission is a building with high lighting intensity and with little glass on the outside. This reduces solar gain and thermal loss while allowing people to look out. It is a low cost building both in terms of capital and running costs. There is no heating and the air conditioning is heated from the lighting output, and there is cooling only.

Jones: Buildings which are almost completely glazed seem, nevertheless, to keep all their lights on in the daytime. If we look at the room we are in, it has vast windows and all the lights are on.

Mulcahy: In some sense the more glazing you have the more artificial light you need to balance the high levels of lighting near the windows.

Langdon: Experimental psychology has shown that in almost all the comparative judgements we make we use some kind of anchor point, to give us a reference from which to judge and develop our attitudes. We are accustomed to buildings with electric lighting or high levels of illumination compared with those to which our grandparents were accustomed. In the past the day ended for the mass of people when daylight disappeared, and the wealthy few who could afford sufficient illumination to carry on their activities after the end of the day had only got lighting levels that were quite low, so the whole anchorage point would be much lower. How do we look at a problem such as this which arises in a situation in which we can do almost anything we like. In the past there were few choices we could make and nature governed our activity to a very large extent. Now we have the possibility of having illumination at any level. Surveys will not give us the answer because anchorate points change and attitudes are formed in the context of a technology that is fluid and can produce situations at will. It is very difficult to know how you would find out or even how you would set about finding out what the right answer would be.

Odell: With electricity we have a source of energy that is inherently expensive because of the gross inefficiencies of conversion from the original source of fuel. By the time we use electricity something like two-thirds of the original input has been lost in the process of conversion and transmission.

Mulcahy: There is a great deal to be said for having a flexible fuel such as electricity is.

Bennett: Of fifteen houses in Andover we visited in the winter we found that in ten of them the average temperature provided by the tenants never exceeded 50°F. We found nobody living in a house with a temperature of 60°F. simply because they could not afford to pay the bills for heating which is provided under Parker Morris. In our new houses, except in rare circumstances, we do not provide an open fire. The lack of money to provide the right heating conditions in the home is leading to appalling situations of condensation and mildew, and the effect of it is getting into the timbers. On one estate timber replacements, because of condensation, has cost hundreds of thousands of pounds. These houses are designed to Government standards of insulation and materials. But the families who live in them cannot afford the comfort conditions that are minimal. All these families were without a car and many of them without television.

Floyd: What balance should there be between the physiological needs of the user, the technical equipment, and cost.

Mulcahy: I believe that the over-mechanised buildings are likely to be extremely troublesome, costly to run, and will be badly maintained as there is no tradition in engineering maintenance of buildings as there is in ships, but there is the need for the same standards. These buildings may be capable of giving good conditions but in fact very frequently they don't and won't. I would strive hard to design conditions and buildings which do not need these mechanical services.

Stone: On the question of different standards in different sorts of buildings, there are two factors which are relevant in commercial buildings. One is the cost of the building in relation to turnover, which makes the cost of the building look very small. The other is the tax system. While companies do have some two-thirds of their profits taken in tax, the cost of servicing is small in relation to it, whereas in the case of the house-holder there is no way in which he can offset his heating system. This comes out of what he can afford to pay and is competitive with other goods or services. So there are bound to be differences in standards.

The artificial environment and its implications

by

R. G. HOPKINSON

My purpose is to raise the question of the psychological and physiological background to our environmental standards and to stimulate some discussion about whether it is a good thing that recent advances in the techniques of artificial lighting and heating and in the scientific control of noise have made the totally artificial environment a reality, at least in the developed countries where the cost can be afforded. Changes in the relative costs of human labour on the one hand, and of building materials and maintenance on the other, coupled with changes in human living habits have led to economic arguments in favour of the total artificial environment. This artificial environment is talked about as being a good thing in itself, not merely a substitute for the natural environment, especially in closely built urban areas.

These arguments have not yet made a great deal of headway except in those areas of highly unfavourable external climate in countries like the United States, Canada, and Russia, and to a limited extent in Australia and South Africa. But although in this country these arguments for the total artificial environment cannot be so easily sustained, nevertheless we very often get advocates for semi-artificial environments, that is, a building which is enclosed acoustically and thermally but with some windows.

I am suggesting that the standards for such environments need careful study and that there is need for both a sociological and an analytical approach. At the moment there is an over reliance on sociometry and I feel it is unwise in that it gives people what they want rather than what they need. In a novel situation such as the totally man-made environment people cannot know what they need because they have never had it. I know that the idea that 'the man in Whitehall knows best' is not too popular at the moment but nevertheless I would say that an analytical study of human physiology and psychology is at least as important as are social surveys in providing information in order to determine standards and comfort limits. One of the things that most of us who were born before the last World War have noticed is that the attitude to the artificial environment has changed almost completely. Central heating is now built into every new low-cost dwelling, and every office or factory burns its fluorescent lighting as a matter of course during the daytime whether the sky is bright or not. It needs a definite effort of memory to recall that less than twenty years ago nobody switched on the artificial light during the daytime; if the light was not sufficient they would take their work over to the window. Fewer still had any heating in their homes other than an open fire and one or two low-power electric radiators, and central heating was considered an unwanted luxury appropriate only to the inhabitants of the arctic wastes of Canada and Sweden, or the hedonists of the United States.

The environmental revolution has been partly economic and partly technological. More money has become available for environmental services, though whether it is real or merely borrowed wealth now seems to be a crucial question. This money has been spent on higher standards of artificial lighting for continuous use, day and night, and on full central heating, though as yet not on a full American standard of air conditioning, but no doubt this will come. This money would not have been spent in this way if there had not been commercial pressures as well as technological advances. In the 1950's the upper limits of lighting with filament lighting had already been reached in this country, and they had been surpassed in the U.S.A. where complaints of glare and heat radiation from the lighting were already prevalent. The upper levels of illumination (30 lumens/ft^2) which were then current in the U.S.A. gave rise to direct radiant heat effects beyond the comfort limit, and the temperature rise due to convective heat load was already posing a serious problem. The fluorescent lamp, which had been gradually replacing filament lighting during the 1940's, more quickly in America than in this country, and more readily in industrial building than elsewhere, received a major spurt in acceptability with the development in this country, of the halogen–phosphate luminescent materials which made it possible to get light of a reasonable approximation to natural daylight with a bonus of added luminous efficiency. From this time the fluorescent lamp was truly launched by means of massive sales campaigns and became the accepted illuminant in offices and in all buildings other than private dwellings and hospitals.

The comparable technological advance on the thermal side was less dramatic but there were improved methods of getting the heat to the consumer, particularly warm air circulation, such that any engineer whose training in lighting and heating was completed by 1950 would find himself lost if he had failed to maintain a continuous learning activity.

At first these new technologies were applied to the lighting and heating of buildings as we then had them but it soon became apparent that, simply because it was now possible to provide an artificial environment, there was no longer any reason why buildings should not undergo a radical change. If we could light artificially, then why have windows: they are major sources of heat loss and draughts, they let in the traffic noise and if they are no longer providing the working light, then their only function is to provide a view and this is not really necessary. Once rid of the windows, buildings need no longer be limited in depth, spine corridors are no longer necessary, rooms can be shaped and sized to their operational function, rather than by the need for daylight penetration. Industrial processes need no longer be restricted to single storey buildings in order that the roof might be glazed. So the arguments ran, and to the service engineer and the property developer they were very attractive.

Curiously enough this period of technological development in the artificial environment, the 1950's was also the great period for the development of daylighting technology. It is impossible with hindsight to see any more logic in this than in the up and down movement of women's hemlines. It needs a James Laver of the environment to perceive the deep-seated psychological urges which led to buildings with excessive glazing becoming fashionable just at the time when technologists were, at last, freeing designers from the need for having any windows at all. Even those of us who were deeply involved in the environmental technology of the time are not all sure just what happened and why.

At one end, architects seemed to be determined to make the fullest use of concrete or steel framed building techniques as an excuse for, or at least a means of, putting clear glass in every external surface they possibly could. It is important to realise that the framed building can be clad as easily with opaque materials as with glass, so that although the framed building construction permitted the glass curtain wall, it did not require it.

At the other end, the daylight technologist had for the first time at his disposal methods for the quantification of glare on the one hand, and for internally reflected light on the other and as a consequence he could go farther than ever before to prescribe visual comfort, although his prescription was often poured straight down the sink by the architect (to the subsequent acute discomfort of the occupants of the buildings). Nevertheless many enlightened architects, particularly those concerned with social service buildings (like schools and hospitals), made use of this new daylight technology to make their buildings better.

Even with this attempt at a rationalisation of events, there remains an element of the inexplicable, and no doubt architects, technologists and above all property developers, were seized by the zeitgeist and carried along, some very willingly, some protesting and prophesying doom. Concurrently, and no doubt for the same unexplained reasons, architects wanted to build high. The building regulations and the by-laws in urban areas like London were concerned partly with fire risks and partly with the desire to enable every room to receive adequate daylight. Every large block therefore had to have its light well, and its upper floors had to be set back from the street. Once again the technologist saw the way to realise the architect's dreams. A return to the fundamentals of daylight technology demonstrated that high building was not incompatible with adequate daylight penetration. The old idea of ribbon building right up to the street boundaries necessarily demanded the set-back and the light well, but by designing a group of buildings to include some low-rise and some high-rise, daylight could penetrate between high buildings instead of over them.

This was the basis of the new Daylight Code, which is still in operation in London and many other large cities. Although simple in concept the Daylight Code required high technical sophistication in its detailed working out. It did a useful job, not least in that it made technically respectable the high rise building which it was every architect's ambition to build.

It is not always fully understood that environmental standards are often a compromise between cost and efficiency as well as acceptibility. This compromise operates in many different ways. As an example, I have recently been helping to design a school near an airport where a totally acoustically insulated environment is required. The consequent limitation on window size affected the levels of light, especially of artificial light, and this in turn brought in the problem of the penalty on the cost of electricity. The decision had to be made on whether it would be more costly to have natural daylighting with large double glazed windows or the higher levels of artificial light incurring the higher cost inherent in overstepping the maximum demand tariff limit. The environmental factors taken by themselves, i.e. the scientific factors alone, cannot lead to the decision. The decision is an economic and political one.

The argument for a totally artificial environment leads to the windowless building. The history of the windowless building again is obscure, but quite different from the high-rise building. Architects did not particularly want to build it. It was the technologist, primarily, who demonstrated to the developer that the windowless building was a solution to an environmental control problem. At first windowless buildings (apart from defence buildings) were confined to industrial processes where the closest control of temperature and humidity was essential, and where the penetration of the exterior climate, e.g. in the form of irregular solar radiation, is not permissible. Experience with these buildings demonstrated that they are tolerable working spaces, and it was not long before the wider possibilities of windowless buildings were being examined, especially in North America and Russia, where unfavourable climatic conditions supported a high degree of insulation against the unfriendly exterior.

Among these advantages, important particularly in North America, and unfortunately no longer to be ignored in our own, is that the absence of windows renders them relatively free from damage by vandals and hooligans; this is a factor which has weighed with designers of schools in the disturbed areas of urban America.

Once the legitimate reasons for windowless buildings are left behind, however, considerations of convenience and profit for the developer are balanced against the deprivation of man's natural right to the sight of sun and sky. Experience with windowless industrial buildings has, according to some, indicated a higher rate of sickness, or at least a higher rate of quasi-malingering sickness, both in Russia and the U.S.A., at least to the extent that long and costly research studies have been made of the causes of this unease and the means for its amelioration.

Much emotional and hysterical comment is aroused by the mention of the ills arising from deprivation of daylight. The facts are so few that the field is open wide to opinion, and so the arguments cannot be clinched. Above all, one hears the misleading phrase 'no evidence has been produced' that anyone suffers physiological harm from working for long periods in a windowless building. The phrase is meant to imply, of course, that no harm results. The truth is that no evidence has been produced and so we just do not know. Eventually evidence may be produced that windowless buildings are not harmful but for the moment we are in a state of lack of knowledge.

At the opposite pole, those concerned to advocate the cause of man's right to natural light seize on what inadequate evidence there is of psychological disturbance, particularly the evidence of the troubles which certainly are experienced by southern people who go to work in arctic latitudes for long winter periods during which they are deprived of natural light.

The problem of the windowless building has been investigated by Hollister on behalf of the Greater London Council, and his study is by far the best unemotional critique on present knowledge, but because it is uncommitted it gives only limited help to the designer who really needs advice in arriving at decisions as to how people are going to react to a building of this kind.

The high-rise building and the windowless building are therefore two new forms of environment for man which have become technically feasible, and economic, because of the rapid rise of sophisticated environmental engineering during the past two decades.

The former is generated by the desire of the architect to build it and the latter by the ingenuity of the technologist. In neither case was the occupant asked for his opinion in advance, and it is only belatedly that his opinion has been sought in retrospect.

The arguments in favour of the high-rise building so far as the developer is concerned are substantial. For example, a big industrial concern can house the whole of its enterprise in one large building. Among the arguments advanced for the occupant are that being high up he will be away from the traffic noise. When the Daylight Code was put forward, the technologists rightly offered as a bonus, over and above good natural light, the reduced amount of noise penetrating from one building to that of its neighbour as compared with street boundary ribbon development. It was also assumed that the high blocks would be relatively free of traffic noise on the higher floors, although more knowledgeable acoustic technologists knew this not to be the case and said so. As one progresses up a building like Alexander Fleming House on the Elephant and Castle traffic roundabout in south east London the noise level changes, but not for the better. What happens is that down below all the individual noises of the nearby traffic are heard, while as one goes higher the whole of the traffic noise from a large area around the site dominates. The character of the noise changes but the amount of it does not. Hence the trouble with the Daylight Code is that, by spacing tall blocks to let daylight penetrate in between, it also encourages traffic to be routed between the blocks, with a consequent noise problem which effects the whole environment. On sunny days the occupants throw open the windows to get some fresh air. The resulting noise level is intolerable and they have to close them again and then the heat is intolerable.

The effect of height above ground level on the amount of noise which is experienced in a high building has been given surprisingly little study. There has been a carefully worked out study by the Scientific Advisor's Division of the Greater London Council, which shows that as one mounts a high building in a large traffic complex, the total noise level decreases very little (e.g. from 80 to 75 dBA in thirty storeys) but the loudness pattern changes, that is, the character of the noise changes. There are very big fluctuations in noise level on the ground floor whereas on the top floor thirty storeys up the fluctuations are very small, although the average level is in both cases about the same. On the ground floor of the building one hears all the individual noises such as people going by and particular vehicles passing and people making remarks whereas on the top floor one only hears a steady loud rumble. Although generally it can perhaps be agreed that height in a big city does not give quietness nevertheless there is no simple law which enables a precise prediction to be made of what is going to happen in the case of a particular building.

These comments apply to the noise *at* a window. The effect *inside* a room will depend very much on the frequency content of the noise. Closing the window on a ground floor will in general be much more effective than closing the window on the upper floor. Closing the window on the ground floor will cut out all the irritating articulated noises of higher frequency whereas on the top floor closing a window does not have anything like the same effect on the low frequency noise which predominates at that height.

If noise is a serious problem, as it often is in the towns, the argument for full air conditioning then becomes very powerful indeed, if windows are opened the noise is intolerable, and then if they are closed then rooms become intolerably hot and stuffy on warm and sunny days.

This of course does not by itself condemn the high rise building. Freed from the requirements of the present Daylight Code, high rise buildings can be spaced more closely with traffic routed round them rather than between them and designed so that they have heavy acoustic walls facing the traffic routes, with acoustically insulated fenestration. The resultant insufficiency of daylight can be made up by a permanent supplement of artificial lighting. Even so, we are not yet sure that this solution will be acceptable.

There still remain the other objections to the high rise building, the difficulty of rapid access and dispersion in an emergency (inadequate lifts) and of course the psychological problem of fear of heights, and now the fear of progressive collapse stemming from the Ronan Point disaster.

Some but not all of these psychological difficulties both of the high rise and of the windowless building might have been avoided if some care had been taken to find out if people would be able to live and work in them. It is not easy to find out what people *need* in their environment. It is much easier to find out what they *want* and this is not necessarily the same thing. It is very easy of course to criticise the kind of methods which are available at the moment but it is much more difficult to find some means of substituting something better. Technologists and sociologists ought to get together to discuss their respective disciplines. Sociology finds out how people respond to what they have now, whereas the technologies of physiology and psycho-physics find out what are the basic functions of the body and the mind and hence what they need. These methodologies need to be welded together in order that we can predict more reliably how people are going to respond to very considerable future changes in their working environment.

One of the things we badly need to do is to determine whether standards which are appropriate to the natural or the partially natural environment are also appropriate to the artificial environment. The Russians have made real attempts to study this problem particularly as far as lighting is concerned, but much remains to be done. Standards of lighting are still presented in the form of a detailed schedule of minimum recommended lighting levels prescribed for each visual task. This is an anachronism which dates from the time when artificial lighting was expensive and required precise engineering to direct it on to the work. The schedule of minimum lighting levels is in fact a schedule of tolerable inadequacy. No task however visually easy is performed better at the minimum level than at a preferred higher level, hence the minimum level is an expression of how much less than his preference the worker is prepared to tolerate. With the advent of fluorescent lighting it is possible to afford levels of lighting which reach, or closely approach, the value which the eye would choose to have, given free choice uninfluenced by limitations imposed by cost or inexpert engineering.

These preferred levels of light are not those of outdoors. It is misleading to imply that the ideal light is that outdoors on a bright day. This may indeed be ideal for agricultural activity of playing cricket, where the ground and other objects reflect only some 10% to 20% of the incident light, but is far too great for work on white paper, which reflects 80%. Already in the over-abundant economy of the U.S.A. levels of lighting are going into 'prestige' buildings which are causing a significant proportion of people to complain of too much light. Some people are happiest with 500 lux, some prefer 2000 lux, and the level should lie somewhere within this bracket. It is the level of good daylight, near a window, on a medium bright day. This should be the design objective for the overall building lighting.

The work itself, if it is visually exacting, may require additional preferential lighting, but this must be at the choice of the worker. He should not be forced to have it if he does not want it, nor should he be deprived of it if he does. Young people will probably not want it, elderly people probably will, but there is no rigid rule.

Standards of acoustics must necessarily undergo some changes also in coming years. The world is rapidly getting noisier, and we must learn to live with this noise until we eventually devise means of sheltering ourselves from it as we have sheltered ourselves from the vagaries of the exterior thermal climate without, at the same time, shutting out the world.

The human being responds to noise in a not altogether predictable manner. The same noise, or almost the same noise, may be tolerated or even welcomed if it comes from one source, and may cause extreme irritation if it comes from another. The ticking of a clock on the kitchen wall is a pleasant background to the housewife's work, a regular noise which causes no disturbance. A dripping tap, with the same regular frequency, a very similar sort of noise, is totally unacceptable. Why is it that some noises madden us and some are completely tolerable?

Some recent work on hospital noise reveals that the traffic noise which comes in from the street outside is actually welcomed because it masks the much more irritating and distressing noises which are generated inside the ward, the noises of the nurse clattering the bedpans, the noise of the patient next door groaning in misery. Patients actually welcomed the week days, the Monday morning after the quietness of the week-end. In fact it has been suggested that it may be possible to design some form of artificial noise that one would pipe into the wards when the traffic noise was not loud enough. It is unlikely that this will work. If patients know this noise is man-generated, it will be just as maddening to them as the internal noises of the ward. The reason why the traffic noise is tolerated is because patients know that nobody can help it. It is something which is there and they accept it.

In schools there is now a move for teaching in large open areas. These large open-planned areas need very careful acoustic treatment because here again some sort of ambient background noise is needed to mask the noise of individual teaching groups. The requirement is for selective absorption to reduce the intelligibility of distant noises without affecting that of near noises. Sound absorbant and reverberation materials have to be employed to ensure an acceptable character, one that is neither dead nor which is too reverberant to be produced.

The attitude of people to aircraft noise is complex. Houses in the vicinity of London Airport can get a Government grant towards acoustic insulation against aircraft noise to the extent of half the cost. It costs about £200 to insulate a house, so the owner has to find £100. Only some 3,500 householders out of about 60,000 have as yet taken up the offer. One of the explanations is that as soon as the Government makes the grant and the acoustic insulation is installed, the Local Rating Authority adds a supplement to the rateable value of the property and so, in a few years, the grant the Government gave is taken away by the Local Authority. In spite of this, the prices of houses, which are still bought and sold freely in the area, show a surprisingly small reduction over other comparable and quieter areas, and this questions whether all the effort being made to give freedom from noise is worthwhile or whether it is of less monetary value than we believe.

While this paper was being prepared, an announcement was made of the formation of a new scientific group called the British Society for Social Responsibility in Science and this is being headed by Professor Maurice Wilkins, F.R.S. and Nobel Laureate. The purpose of this Society is to consider the ethical problems of science in a self-destructive society. Most workers in the building field have probably read this announcement as being something that concerns other people. Professor Wilkins and his friends are concerned with the problems of developments in nuclear physics, armaments research, biological warfare, unrestricted use of pesticides and this kind of thing. Many of the generation of Professor Wilkins, he himself certainly, were engaged on research on the technology of warfare at early stages of their careers, and then they transferred, as soon as they were able, to branches of research of a different kind in order to free themselves of an unwelcome responsibility. Research on the human environment might well be felt to be such a non-committed activity but if this was felt to be a successful retreat from an unwanted position I do not think it is any longer. Any feelings of smugness are quickly dissipated by a consideration of just where environmental research is leading us. It is directly because of the developing sophistication of modern environmental engineering that property developers, both private and public, are able to consider as serious economic propositions the enormous high-rise dwelling block with nowhere for the children to play, or the totally enclosed, windowless, isolated artificial environment. Perhaps this is dramatising the situation too much, but it seems that environmental researchers and designers have to ask themselves if their work is capable of being directed towards ends which are not in the long term interest of humanity as a whole and if it is, then what attitude do they take—do they halt their research programme or do they go along with it. I discussed this problem many years ago with Dr. Gunner Pleijel of Stockholm. Pleijel had just returned from a visit to the United States to study problems of solar overheating in glass-walled buildings. At that time Sweden had not any of these buildings and he was going to find out all about them. I asked him why his studies were concerned solely with the physics of the facts and the problem as it existed in the U.S.A. rather than with demonstrating, which was well within his considerable competence, that on an environmental basis such buildings were a dreadful mistake in a climate like that of Sweden. His answer was simply that 'these buildings will come—we cannot stop them—it is like the supersonic airliner, nobody wants it, but it will come, and all we can do is to prevent, if we can, the most painful consequences of man's folly' and of course he was right, the glass buildings came along and also the Concorde. It is too late perhaps to do anything about these buildings. It may not be too late to do anything about the totally enclosed windowless artificial environment. Nobody wants it, that is certain, except on economic grounds. The fact that people who already work in windowless buildings are not noticeably prone to revolt against their circumstances does not seem to me any more significant than the undoubted fact that in the early days of the 'dark satanic' Lancashire cotton mills, people flocked into them in order to earn a better living, or at least to earn more money. At some stage the questions must be asked, and answered; first, do we want the artificial environment, and second, shall we be getting it anyway whether we want it or not and if so what are we going to do about it.

The two examples of the artificial environment which are the main subject of this paper, the high-rise building and the windowless building, are two different examples because the high-rise building came because we thought we wanted it (perhaps we are not so sure now) whereas the windowless building has come not because we want it but because it is the result of the inexorable logic of our dissatisfaction with certain aspects of the normal windowed building. The chief, perhaps, of these is unwanted solar radiation, but do we really want to lose all the other advantages that a window can produce.

The lesson is surely that new building developments, or projected developments, should be thoroughly examined for their implications, so far as we can predict them, before they are allowed to progress too far. It is obviously possible that any planning machinery to conduct such a thorough examination would be yet another brake on progress, and it is also all too clearly possible that machinery might be responsible for the follies that all such bodies, from the fine arts and historic buildings commissions and the like downwards, seem predestined to commit. Nevertheless I think we should take the risk because the alternative is worse.

BIBLIOGRAPHY

Windowless environments (Dec. 1967). GLC Research Paper.
HALL, P. (1964). *London 2000*. London: Faber.
HMSO (1963). *Traffic in towns*.
HOPKINSON, R. G. & KAY, J. D. (1969). *The lighting of buildings*. London: Faber.
MUMFORD, L. (1961). *The city in history*. London: Secker & Warburg.
TETLOW, J. & GOSS, A. (1965). *Homes, towns and traffic*. London: Faber.

Discussion

Grey: My window in the City looks on to St. Paul's, but if I had to transfer to one of these windowless buildings my outlook is gone. In one of the windowless schools that was mentioned there was no form of artificial substitute for the window.

Hopkinson: A lot of thinking is going into ways of alleviating the artificial environment. Among the things that are being studied is the critical minimum size of a window which is needed to give visual release, and to allow you to feel that you are not boxed in. It seems possible to make some sort of judgement about this and to suggest guide lines. On the question of getting some relief from the artificial environment, a school I visited has top light only, and one of the teachers said that at the end of a two hour period she needs to take the children outside for 10 minutes in order to freshen up.

Jones: I want to put the thought that there are different sorts of buildings, which create different sorts of problems. That if, for instance, you are working in a factory that is 100 meters long by 100 meters wide, this may be an acceptable windowless environment but if, on the other hand, you are working in a room which is 10 meters square this is a very different problem, and the lack of windows in these circumstances could be very disagreeable. The other point is this. Diagrams have been shown relating to light penetration on which a complete architectural theory is being built. These diagrams dictate where we put our blocks and how we place our buildings. If in fact the question of the depth of penetration of light into the buildings is not very important, and I suspect that it is not, then the whole of the theory collapses. Is this a fair comment?

Hopkinson: Yes I think so. There are certainly different types of windowless environment which give rise to quite different responses even in the same room if different sorts of work is being done. For example I find that doctors and consultants are quite happy working in a windowless room because they have to deal with a constant stream of people to whom they have to give their total attention. But it is entirely different for someone working on a stack of files with nobody there to concentrate his attention.

On the question of daylight technology. If, in fact, you can demonstrate that it is acceptable either to have total artificial light, which I do not think it is, or partial artificial light, which I think is acceptable, then it does call for a revision of the Daylight Code. This we have been saying for some time but one is very reluctant to give up something which has benefit until there is something better to put in its place. We are helping the Department of Education and Science to think in terms of something other than their 2% Daylight factor for school building but we have to go carefully because we may throw away much of great value in our attempts to improve.

Redfern: The question of noise for hospital patients gives the answer to a problem that has been worrying me. Surely the hospital patient prefers to have real noise coming from the outside, rather than an artificially created noise, because then he is in contact with the work outside.

Langdon: The building research station is doing work to discover acceptable window shapes and minimum acceptable sizes. But I still ask myself whether when we have done this work, we can finally make a decision because what people want is one thing, and what they need is another. I cannot see an experiment or method which willl help us to find out what people need, and it seems to me to be an impossible requirement to try to discover what people want; in any case if we are guided by what they say they want we may find a very different situation. Recent work by the University of Tennessee has shown that undergraduates who belong to 'Pop' groups often have marked hearing loss with hearing levels equal to a 50–60 year old person. Further studies have shown that this goes back to school years, and the onset of measurable hearing loss can be said to start at 8–12 years. Now, clearly, all these people wanted this and who is to say that they are not to have it.

Loten: There is a misunderstanding which has grown up about the use of surveys; the survey is interpreted by the practitioner.

Survey answers may report that people want such and such but the premise behind this is not that what people want they ought to have. No sociologist makes this premise. A guide in interpreting surveys is what the sociologist calls Thomas' theory which goes 'if man defines a situation which is real then it is real in its consequences'.

Bennett: In County Hall we were prepared to consider giving waivers for windowless kitchens for family dwellings, we had already given waivers for kitchens in dwellings for batchelors. When a responsible local housing authority from the City of London came forward with their Barbican scheme for 2000 flats, they were all designed with internal kitchens. Many of these were family kitchens where the mother or child might be for many hours a day. Instead of giving the waiver the responsible Committee asked the architect whether his kitchen at home had a window, when he said 'yes' the Chairman replied 'well when you have bricked it up will you please come back for a waiver'.

Hopkinson: The environmental research people are trying to dig into people's requirements and even into their foibles. If people want things then, may be, they also need them. The Lighting and Building Committee when they were unable, after much study, to find out what people's sunlight requirement was, said that in their opinion the important reason for having sunlight in dwellings was people's evident desire to have it.

One further point relating to something said earlier. The social scientist may not make claims beyond the findings of his study, but it becomes a temptation to respond helpfully to the persistent demands of the administrator and the politician who badly needed answers. Consequently, it has become more common for extrapolations to be made beyond the legitimate findings.

Human interactions and communications technology: a two-way process

by

J. LANGDON

I have done my best to disrupt Professor Douglas Jones' efforts to get a nice, well organised Symposium, by saying I was too busy to write a Paper. The truth was that I do not really know what to write. This has given me a slight advantage in that I have been able to hear other Papers first before deciding what I might say myself; whereas other, courageous people, went ahead without bothering about that.

On the other hand, I will claim the right to listening to what other people have to say before opening up myself because I want to try to do something different from other speakers. We are all specialists, experts, or so-called experts, in some aspect of environment, some aspect of communications, some aspect of providing for people or finding out what they want, or what we think they want, and so on, and I am in this boat along with all the rest. But it seemed to me it might be useful to stop being an 'expert' and recall that, once upon a time, before I got involved with buildings, I was a psychologist; and I thought it might be interesting to stand back a little and ask some questions about the assumptions we are necessarily forced to make in carrying out our work.

If one is a specialist, one has to take a lot of assumptions as given, as points from which to start. Then you can begin the research process or the design process. You can feed data into a computer, or you can design studies, or experiments which can produce data to be fed into a computer, but in doing this you have to make some assumptions.

For instance, you may have to make some assumptions in carrying out an experiment on people that you are going to get, say, a normal distribution of data; or you may have to assume that a scale you want to use is of a particular shape, that it is linear or an interval scale of some kind; or it is a rank order scale. You are forced to make these assumptions. You may try to test some of them but when you do so, you only find yourself back at a further set of assumptions about the nature of probability distributions, or the nature of linear, or non-linear interval, or category, or rank order scales. Sooner or later you find yourself at a point where you are back in the fundamental theory of statistics and you realise you cannot go any further.

So you go ahead and design your experiment. It may be, of course, that some assumption which escaped you, or more likely something that you did not think was an assumption at all, but a plain and self-evident fact, went on to control your experiment for you, and help produce a set of results which somebody is going to show to be nonsense by publishing another paper in five years time. Nor do we escape the necessity of making assumptions by saying that we are going to stand back and try to look at the philosophical, or epistemological, or psychological theories on which the work rests; we do not cease to make assumptions in doing this, we simply transfer to another field and start making assumptions in the realms of philosophy or theory of knowledge, and then apply the outcomes of these assumptions to the specialised fields of technology.

We cannot claim that to get beyond assumptions; this would be futile. But at least one can use such a process to question the more detailed procedures in which we are normally engaged. This is, of course, rather like taking off your clothes in front of the audience because in this case our clothes are our expertise and experience.

It would not be difficult to start talking about the work we have done at Building Research Station on environmental and communication problems; in fact it would be easy to give an interesting lecture lasting an hour. As it is, I am voluntarily leaving these clothes behind and plunging into icy water, realising that I do not know any more about what I am going to say than you do. So, we are on an equal footing; the only difference is that I am standing on a dais and you are seated down on the floor. But that does not represent the state of knowledge; the real state is that we should all really be down on the floor and what I would like to see is not so much a discussion, more a talk-in, and I hope that it is you that will have to talk this afternoon just as much as me.

Having got away from technological expertise, I think the first point I would like to consider is that when we engage in any specialised activity, and particularly any technological exercise, such as design, or research, we are forced to go to such a level of detail, such a level of expertise, which is the outcome of many years experience in a very well defined, comparatively narrow field of human activity, that our own activity becomes more real to us than anything else. It becomes more real to us than the objectives to which it is supposed to be being applied. This is understandable because the designer becomes so interested in the design process that it becomes difficult for him to do this to a high level whilst keeping to the fore-front of his mind not the building itself, but the purposes it is supposedly serving. It is therefore quite understandable for all of us, when we indulge in our own skilled activities, to find it difficult to keep equally to the fore-front of our minds 'what is it for?'.

This is the first difficulty which the expert has to face. The second difficulty is that we have to live in a wicked world. We live in a world filled with human stupidity, short sightedness, and squalidity, and we know that we are imperfect instruments, in an imperfect world. We have so little control over our own activities and over the outcomes and products of those activities that we never can be sure that anything we do may not end up very differently from the way we conceived it.

For instance, one finds one's self in the difficult kind of situation to which Professor Hopkinson referred this morning. Somebody says 'Windowless buildings—do we *really* need windows in buildings?' and if you are a researcher, you are soon faced by someone else saying 'Well, I, personally, doubt it'. Now, I do not myself think that windowless buildings are a good thing. But this is a purely personal point of view and there are other people who think they are. If we think there is a danger that this would lead to bad conditions, to worse conditions, then it can be argued that at least we ought to do some research to find out the answers, so that we would be able to stop, or put up some resistance to a move which we knew to be against people's best interests. One is then in the same position as the man at Porton Down who says 'I find biological warfare horrifying, but if I do not do this research, what defence are we going to have against it?'. This is, I think, the position we all find ourselves in, and this is the second reason that we have to scrutinise, very carefully, the assumptions that underlie our work and its meaning; because in the example of windowless buildings, you know very well that when you have done the research you are not going to produce a clear answer in black and white; yes, no, we do not have windowless buildings because they are bad, or we do have them because they are good. You know that you are going to come out with a complicated set of answers which show that under certain circumstances this is beneficial and under other circumstances this is deleterious. Or that if the hours of, say, exposure a day are limited there is no harm in it, and so on. And then there arises the question of costs so that the whole thing gets very complicated, and in the end it is difficult to see a clear decision. But you do know one thing; and that is that you have opened up the whole field and made some addition to human knowledge, and now somebody else will make the decisions. And maybe they will not use the criteria you hoped would be used. This is often the outcome of your research. Eventually, you come to feel that the research you are going to do is something that is only in your hands while you are actually doing it. As soon as you have published the results you have lost control over it altogether.

So, this is the second reason; in addition to the fact that in order to carry out one's work as a designer or a researcher, one has got to keep in the fore-front of one's mind, not just the object, but the details, the process, the technology, the mechanism, in order to carry it out competently. But, apart from this one is forced to do this in a sense because of the realisation that if you thought too much about the objectives of the work you will end up by not wanting to do it at all.

Consequently the technologist is driven back to consider only his own specialities; only his own technical skills, and what he can do with them. He may tell himself that on the whole what he does is for human betterment; he may tell himself that on the whole his activities are benevolent ones, or at least his intentions are, but he sees also that this ethical point of view often remains ineffective.

When we try to look generally over the whole of historical political economy; that is to say, the process of historical development of civilised society, and to draw from this some generalisations, one of the things that strikes us immediately—and which many generations of thinkers have pointed out—is that when society is at a relatively primitive stage of development, obligation falls upon all. With man at a primitive level of development, it is not possible to survive without the inter-dependence of one man upon another. The price of survival is unity. In a very primitive society men can only produce as much as they consume, there is no surplus. There is no such thing as leisure, because there is little time free from labour, from food gathering, hunting and the recuperative processes of digestion and rest needed to provide the energy for the next foray. Men also are extremely weak, they are weaker than their natural enemies, and at this stage have little protection of an organised kind against the elemental forces of nature. The only thing that has ensured man's survival is his ability to learn, his ability to use tools, his ability to increase the rate of production, his ability to increase the rate of energy conservation as compared with his consumption, and thus derive some immediate possibility of further improvements to this same process. And from this come a number of things.

The first thing that comes is the specialisation of activities; instead of having to police the whole backyard himself, instead of having to be a universal handymen, he can develop specialised skills so that there comes to be something that he can do better than somebody else; to the extent that we are all doing this, we gain an immediate productive advantage.

The second thing—which he derives as a benefit from this—is leisure; that is, some part of his activity which is neither work, nor food gathering, nor recuperation, nor sleep. Moreover, this specialisation, when it goes far enough, and when the level of productivity has become high enough, is sufficient to enable the specialisation itself to be carried into the field of leisure. So that there eventually come to be specific categories of people entrusted with the responsibilities for what one might term the cultural development of the environment. Hence, it is possible to have religious administrators, poets, law givers, to develop some kind of historical record in the form of folk myth.

I think in all this we should note that communications, which we often talk about as if it were a thing in itself, is merely an aspect of the productive process. It is an aspect of specialization, an aspect of differentiation within the total biological and social life of man. And, also, like the other specialisations, it has a hierarchical order of production and non-production. That is to say, there are those aspects of communications which can be properly considered as part of the productive process itself, and there are those aspects which shape off away from the productive process and which are regarded as belonging to cultural and leisure pursuits.

The difference between the ecological processes I have been describing and those occurring at the present day is sometimes expressed when we say that it was more difficult to do anything in the past. The development of production, the development of technological means of production, technological means of communication, has made things less difficult. Although this is true I do not think it brings out the essential difference. The essential difference, it seems to me, is that in the past, things were not merely more *difficult*, but they were more *laborious*. Technology, the development of production techniques, makes things less laborious, and I think there is an important difference here between difficulty and laboriousness. It was the laboriousness of life, the fact that everything had to be done by hand, the fact that man's frailty compelled him to unite with his fellows in order to achieve any important result, generated and was the constant stimulus of inter-dependence between one man and another.

Whether it was the family, or the tribe, or clan, the sole condition of survival was the direct inter-dependence of one person upon another. It is the decline of laboriousness which, acting against this, generates independence, independence of one man from another.

What I have in effect been describing is the effect of technology on the ability to escape our social obligations. This has always been possible for a limited section of society and, in some societies, this grew to such proportions that eventually, the society collapsed or was overthrown. In a tyrannical society, or in a feudal society, it was possible for some men to escape obligations laid upon others, though, in fact, it was not possible to escape all obligations. The feudal lord escaped the obligation to labour in the field by day, but he did not escape the obligation to defend the community, he merely substituted one obligation for another.

But there have been societies where it has been possible to escape almost all social obligations. For example, the only obligation upon the aristocracy in France at the time of Louis XVth was to attend Court, because failure to carry out this would lead to loss of status, and loss of monarchical favour.

Today, we have rather a different situation, in which there are a number of minimal obligations which we are compelled to observe. For instance, we are compelled to observe a whole mass of regulations, which we call Law, in order to carry on a more or less civil community, but these are so arranged so that they are, in fact, not very tiresome to obey. Beyond this we can live a quite confortable existence, supposing that we have the where-with-all. Life is possible throught the technological developments of science, through the technological developments of the productive system, and through the storing of energy in the form of cash or inheritance it becomes possible for quite large numbers of people to exist on a minimum of obligations. And, we have been discussing in these last few days, a future in which it is possible to see this spreading in ever wider circles.

To put this on a very simple anecdotal level: I want to obtain something from a local shop, and I want to obtain what I need at a reasonable price, and obtain a selection of quality. I can obtain any old rubbish simply by asking for it at the first shop I come to. But if I want to obtain any sort of choice and quality in the commodity, it may be that I have to develop particular relations with a particular man that I have in mind. I have to know my grocer, as you say, and this depends on a certain ritual of politeness, of polite enquiries on one side or the other, as to one's health and the flourishing of one's family, and 'How is Aunt Emma' and all that sort of thing, and out of this grows some kind of human relationship, or it may be a substitute for it, and I can say I know the grocer and I can always rely on him that he will have whatever it is that I want.

This may be an attenuated form of tribal inter-relationship but, nevertheless, it is some kind of relationship. What one can look forward to is the point where even this has been done away with as a result of technological super-abundance; there is no such thing as a scarce resource in grocery. So there is really no need to develop any relationships in order to get it, as anybody can get it as long as they have the money to buy it, and in any case we shall replace the grocer by an automated super-market. Then I can simply arrange to push a button, or even have somebody else push the button for me, or push a button at home, and have the goods brought to me by pneumatic chute. When the attenuated relationship I sketched has disappeared the outcome of improvement in technology and in the communications process is to bring about the entire disruption and eventual disappearance of the elements which the communications process was brought into being to relate.

I want to pass on to a second effect; that when I go to the grocer and I want a particular kind of biscuit—say, I want Bath Olivers—when I do this I am able to discuss with him all the various pros and cons of different kinds of biscuit. It may be that he knows something about biscuits, it may be that he does not, but talking about biscuits with him is part of getting some of the kind I want and in the process of doing so the grocer comes to build up some sort of picture in his mind of the sort of person I am. If he does this for enough of his customers, he finds his shop succeeds because he knows roughly what they want, stocks it, and he knows just about how much stock to carry and so on. Now all this of course, is on the basis of communications between customers and shopkeeper and these have a particular shape or form. They take the shape of conversations, they take the shape of orders, of regretful inability to fulfil them and attempts to do so, adjustment on his side and adjustment on mine. Over a longish period we eventually come to some sort of a modus vivendi. As a result I get something to eat, and he gets the wherewithal. The effect of technology in replacing him is that instead of a comparatively rich dialogue, made up of words and phrases, pointings and tasting, there comes to be what you might call a 'specifying brief' as my grocery order, expressed either by ticking or punching holes in a piece of card or pressing buttons or whatever may be.

Of course there is probably no card yet made, and certainly no button pressing mechanism yet made which can be connected up to include all the marginal items and almost subliminal indications of quality and difference which I expect my grocer to respond to; this is beyond any machine or computer that we can yet imagine. In fact, if I use a supermarket, and if I was to give an order in this way I would not expect to receive the same level of service, for instance, as when I use a large department store. Not simply because it is not possible to stock this variety, but simply because employing such a medium it is not possible to make a choice effectively within it. I cannot discriminate or differentiate well enough. Hence the second effect of this kind of communication medium is to narrow the 'bandwidth' of the communication; it impoverishes the number of discriminations and new answers which can be expressed.

We see this in an extremely absurd and rather frightening form when we contemplate the behaviour of car drivers on the road. I am in a car, and I want to do something, but how can I let the chap behind me know what I am going to do? About all I can do is to move a little switch in the car, which causes an arrow to light up at the back and front, either one side or the other, or I may be able to open the window and make some curious kind of flapping signal.

I certainly cannot speak to him, cannot yell at him—he won't hear me if I do, I cannot even turn round and make a face at him, I will probably bump into somebody as I do so. We have no two-way radio between us, our means of communication is confined to little flashings and flappings, and perhaps eventually to allowing him to overtake me, so that I can make some gesture at him as he passes by. We know from a number of studies that a large part of driving behaviour, and large part of the accidents that happen, a large part of the general bad state of vehicle driving is simply due to the poverty of the communication link between drivers. Two drivers who are driving one another round the bend eventually come to the traffic lights, and are both stopped by the red light, and they both get out and face up to one another, and start punching each other. This is not really because they need to punch one another. They have been brought to this situation by the relative inability on either side to understand what the intentions and desires of each were, and this is because of the relatively attenuated set of communications between them. While I think that McLuhan has taken too far the idea of the medium as the message, I do think it would be reasonable to regard the message as being very largely characterised by the medium.

Therefore in considering all the technological developments of processes, whether they relate to the production of environment or to communications, we have to ask what effect is this having on the medium, and what effect on the productive relation itself. Is it having an effect such that it goes beyond the critical balance point so that the characteristics of the communications medium, the characteristics of the production relationship, or system dominate the product or the relationship?

I have a feeling that we have already reached this point. It is, to my mind one of the very great dangers, when we are tackling about rapid development in design, rapid development in building technology, rapid development in communication technology, that we can now pass beyond this critical balance point, when the environment, instead of being an outcome of what we want it to be, eventually determines the way we live. Or where the communications process, instead of being an outcome of our desire is the determinant of what we shall know.

When we try to make these general assessments, in much that we say about our problems and the ways in which we try to face up to them and solve them technologically, there is an unspoken assumption that science and technology are somehow self-generating, logical and historical processes which come about through the appearance on the scene of certain well endowed individuals around the seventeenth century. And that as a result of their brilliant discoveries we can go ahead and develop an even more complex self-generating, self-developing, self-perpetuating mechanism. So that the production of everything that we plan today, whether it be windowless buildings or expressways, or living in thirty-four-storey apartments must necessarily be the outcome of the continued activity of science and technology. And if we ever feel worried about it we can relax by saying—well there it is, we are in the grip of this, you see it's bigger than us, it's just got to go that way, if people want this, this is what they are demanding. Or else we may say— we have to have houses for people, they have to be got to work somehow or other, it's the only solution. Or we may say there are going to be 70,000,000 people in this country by the year 2000, so it is just too bad if they want an old fashioned farm-house existence, they can't have it, they will die in the process; they have just got to live this way. What we are doing when we take such a point of view is to forget that science and technology are not just self-generating processes of a purely logical kind; they are historical products of human society at a particular stage in its development.

The dominating characteristic of science is a desire for truth, a desire for empirical knowledge, a desire for efficiency. A desire for efficacy, as opposed to the desire to create myth, the desire to create poetry, or the desire to find purpose in life.

From the seventeenth century on, science has served the purpose of removing ideological obstacles to the maximum utilisation of natural and human resources on an efficient basis. In doing so it has been primarily the agent in developing a consumer orientated society. This is a society which is devoted primarily to the mass production of consumer goods. Such society operates always to maximise the scale of its operations, to maximise the growth of its profits, and the benefits derived from this. I do not really need to go over this ground, it has already been gone over by Marx and Weber, and recently by other thinkers. We all know this, and have very little excuse for regarding science and technology as if they were laboratory processes, with a peculiar sanctity of their own.

Technology simply follows the historical objectives of our society, and the one which it follows at the moment is the utilisation of skills to conserve and develop a mass market to the greatest extent. It must be a mass market because any other market is more expensive and less profitable to operate. The best way to run a business is to reduce variety; it's cheaper to produce that way, it's cheaper to sell that way. It is not difficult to re-design motor cars so that you produce two basic models instead of seventeen. It is slightly more difficult to persuade people that you have *not* done it; but that is possible as well, as you can see by certain advertising. You make two basic models, and make people think that they are offered seventeen. Thus the major problem for the entrepreneur is to persuade people that this reduced variety is either not really reduced—that they still have variety—or if that cannot be done, of creating the impression that variety production is not so much worth having as against the best. Because if you have got the best and also the cheapest, then why do you want variety? If we can produce enough housing for the population, and this involves perhaps very little variety, well it is better to do without the variety and have a roof over your head.

When we come to communications, which as I said earlier is merely one specialised aspect of the technology of production, we see again that sociological thinking about communications reflects exactly the same biases, exactly the same patterns that we find in production technology and production relations; that is, it is one formulated to serve the needs of a consumer orientated society. The way we think about the communications process is a curiously one-sided one. It is to think of it primarily in terms of a perceptual process, the receipt of information.

In all the talk of communications process you will find in every discussion, in every paper devoted to it, a concentration upon the image, a concentration upon the perceptual process, a concentration upon vision, upon hearing. Whereas in actuality, communications involves respondents, it serves a purpose, of doing something, or of being unable to do something. But this has taken the back seat in the way that we think about these problems. The way we think about these has been formalised ever since the seventeenth century by the theory of psychology in its account of the perceptual process itself. For the nineteenth century psychologists, who based their psychological theories on the philosophical outlook of the seventeenth century natural philosophers, perception was a process primarily seen as of a developmental kind, in which sensation is primary, and response secondary. An S. R. Bond in which stimulus comes first and action is a response to it. I suggest that this basic notion which has been operating in psychological theory until comparatively recently, with various elaborations and sophistications, can be shown to be nothing more than a reflection of the ideology and outlook of a society of the kind I have already described.

It is only comparatively recently that attempts have been made to re-formulate psychological theory on a different basis. For instance, in Piaget's work on the development of child thought and perception, Piaget traces the history of the perceptual process in a different manner and he begins by referring to the initially quasi-random movements of the child's tongue and mouth in its search for food, as a result of which, the primary perceptual space is generated. This Piaget locates in the mouth, the buccal space, as being the primary space of perception because this is the space actually explored by motor activity in the search for food. He then traces the progressive development of perceptual spaces on a wider and wider basis, but always in response to primarily motor activation mechanisms. More recently Taylor has formulated this idea in the form of a behavioural basis for perception, and where Piaget spoke of, for instance, schemata, meaning the sensori-motor frameworks developed to structure perceptual spaces, Taylor speaks of a vast number of links, which structure multiple simultaneous states of readiness for response, and suggests that these correspond to perception.

Now I think the question that we have to ask is, does this model make any difference to the way we think about communications as a social process? I think it does, because it means that we have to begin by looking afresh at the communications process as a relation between doing and sensing; the Gutenburg Galaxy Marshall McLuhan speaks of, the new development among young people today in participating, touching, being involved in a happening. This is very interesting really because it is a considerable elaboration to speak of participation, touching, being involved; why not simply the word 'doing'? Of course this answers the question itself, because if you do replace it by the word 'doing', you then realize this is not quite what McLuhan has in mind. Because there is not anything really for these people to do, they are there to receive and they are only being made to feel that they *do* in a vicarious way by the touching, participating, being involved, etc., and if this is a typical sort of happening, one realises that when they have wiped the paint off the floor and cleaned the mud out of the buckets, and the girls have put on their clothes again, packed up the whole show and gone home, the world is exactly as it was yesterday, and the day before. I believe that if we think about communications using the sort of model I have discussed, namely a sensori-motor network based upon primacy of action, rather than primacy of perception, and we consider this as a dynamic process in communication between seeing and doing, hearing and doing, if we do this, then we would have to develop a different sort of communications theory.

This is what it would mean to talk seriously about putting the needs of people first. We start off by claiming that we want to put their needs first, but very soon along the line we find that these needs which we put first are not their ultimate needs, but what Aristotle would have called their 'efficient' needs, the needs that have to be fulfilled in order that they can take part in the situation that we have designed for them.

I have a feeling that therefore, our original model of communications, the way we see this operating, the way we use technology in order to further our operations is based upon the outlook of a consumer society, and that we have to think further than this. I believe we have to think of how communications, how technology, can serve to bring people out of such a degraded state of affairs, where their main function in life is to act as a purchasing agent for massed produced goods and services. We have to think of how we can use technology to produce an environment where essentially human needs, essentially human characteristics which have been the origin of love and art, can be put in their true positions, and the 'efficient' needs relegated to a less important position. For if technology, if communications, can truly serve a positive purpose, it should not serve the purpose of bringing forward the mundane aspects of human life as the chief source of intense speculation and discussion, but relegate them to a relatively trivial position.

To a certain extent one can say that the dissatisfaction and frustration which young people in our own society feel with the quality of life, is that they are in effect saying; well if your technology, if your communications, if your clever tricks, are really so clever, why can't they increase the number of options that are open to us in life to do what we want, instead of merely reducing them? How we are to do this I do not immediately claim to know, but I feel that it would be wrong to hold a Symposium such as this without trying to think about what this means, and consider how we may avoid falling into a technological bottomless pit.

Discussion

Odell: The ideas Dr. Langdon has put forward on the perception of space and the need for involvement were put forward in terms of the child. Has adult perception, as a result of changing technology, changed in the way he perceives space?

Langdon: The trouble is that one is in danger of trying to deal with this at a superficial level. The idea is one of perception in structure and space resulting from primary motor needs. In the Development of the child in Society it is suggested that the doctrine that perception is of a developmental kind is wrong because it reflects the interests and require-ments of Society rather than the needs and structures of that child. In other words the doctrine puts forward the idea of perceptual reality as an affliction which serves the needs of Society in place of the needs of the child. One can elevate this idea to a form in which perception relates to the objectives of society or of its dominant social class. So, when one tries to link up a theory of this sort or a theory to class analysis or to technology, I think one has got to be very careful in distancing off these background considerations and assumptions. The study of a particular and detailed problem of every day life, may show no immediate improvement in the way any particular social process goes on. What it would do is to enable us, when thinking of any particular technological process, to put it into the framework of a developed social theory.

Dakin: McLuhan seems to link what he calls the 'sense ratio' of various generations with his concept of 'hot' media and 'cold', the difference being that in the one the actual definition of the object perceived is very sharp, therefore the imagination has little space in which to play so that the action demanded from the recipient is relatively small, whereas the other one lacks physical precision, therefore the imagination is left some space for working, therefore the participant is really able to pratitipate and is absorbed by it. The cinema, which has a very high degree of precision in the parts of the picture, is an example of the first. You may call a child half a dozen times, and he does not hear you, the child seems to be obtuse and tiresome; but the reason he does not hear is because he is absorbed in the business of actually participating.

Langdon: How, in principal, this thing could be verified is difficult to know.

It is easy to say, for instance, that you can apply this theory to Shakespearean drama, which works better without any scenery because the imagination is given maximum scope, whereas, if you put in scenery, the more realistic it gets the more limiting it will be for you to get anything out of the verse. That is perfectly true, but it is not because of scenery nor the lack of it that the imagination is not set to work, it is simply because the poetry does not affect you. In music, for instance, precision is absolutely necessary, but precision does not take away from the imaginativeness with which a score can be per-formed. It seems to me that the opposite of precision is vagueness.

Hopkinson: It is worth pointing out perhaps that we do know something about children's behaviour in respect of television. We have made lots of surveys, and one of the disturbing things for the 'McLuhanites' is that children are very responsive to contact, and they like some things and they don't like others; but when you are arguing this with 'McLuhanites', they tell you this characteristic of Freudism.

Brandt: Is it not true that McLuhan's methodology is suspect? He never gives chapter and verse, he writes in epigrams rather than in measured statements, and the technique he uses is the technique of advertising, that is to say coining plausible and ringing statements by way of explanation instead of really looking at the phenomena under observation.

Bennett: Dr. Langdon mentioned the grocer and the supermarket. Personal choice, must, to an extent, be lost if we have a system of supermarkets: and although the choice may be bigger in some ways it will be less in others. If we relate this to architecture, would Dr. Langdon like to forecast what type of losses are likely when we fully codify everything in building?

Langdon: My grocer came out of his house one morning, got run into by another car, and was in hospital for several weeks. I had, from time to time, accounts of how he was getting on, and finally he made a complete recovery. My interest in this man just happens to be part of the texture of my life, and perhaps my concern for him, and the concern of his other customers, was part of the texture of his life. The point I am making is not simply that I do not have a wider choice of goods, but that I do not have this slice of my life at all. This is, I think, the important point.

   As for the question of the design in buildings, you know better than I do, that what we are heading for is reduction in variety.

Bennett: One of the aims of System Building is to give an almost infinite variety of combinations. But this does not seem to be coming through.

Cherry: Do I understand you to mean that, as time goes on, the variety available becomes less and less, so that certain types of goods, certain manufacturers, disappear totally? I find young people have no conception of certain things which used to be available, and so there is no longer a demand, and therefore there is no production. The American attitude is that if goods are wanted they will be produced, but this, I feel, is a false argument.

Langdon: Market sales depend upon market demand. You only create a demand for things which it is convenient for you to manufacture. But if a manufacturer wants to 'muscle in' in a field which is already occupied by a competitor, and if he cannot beat him on his own ground, then he has to beat him by producing a variant and creating a demand for it. Thus manufacturers are forced to make concessions. Without that, you would get down to a very basic list of goods, simply because the demand for others is ironed out.

Odell: I would like to ask for evidence for this thesis. Certainly one can think of products that have disappeared but, on the other hand, one can think of products that are now on the market which were never demanded in the old days.

Mulcahy: In Dublin our eighteenth century buildings are much revered, because they are uniform, whereas the real problem of modern building is that it is so varied.

Parsons: At the moment there is a vast number of people who lack food. Is there no point in reducing variety if we can thereby give everyone enough food.

Langdon: The reduction of variety is not intended, nor does it effectively contribute to the alleviation of the misery of those who are dying from lack of food. We are not turning out quantities of corn flakes and packaged biscuits in order to alleviate the miseries of India. I am not against supermarkets because, for the majority of people, they represent an advance in standard; but I am querying whether they represent the best performance or technological aids that we have today. We are not saying that life is getting worse in this country, it is getting better, but it does not adequately reflect the technological means at our disposal. On the contrary, it may represent a degradation in terms of what is available.

Medhurst: Coming back to the problem of communications, my grocer has not broken his leg but recently, in a supermarket, I was approached by the manager because I left my change there a few weeks before. Surely communication takes place wherever there are people. However, one of my main grumbles has been against sociologists and psychologists who will analyse what has gone before, but will not give an indication of what to do in the future. The Architect who has to have a building on the ground in six months' time, or the Planner who has to have a new town there in 15 years, what are they to do? We are designing whole environments now, and in towns and cities we are building buildings. These are going to be criticised in the same way that we are to criticise what has taken place in the past. How, in fact, do you correct the faults of the past in the developments of the future?

Hopkinson: The reason for the apparent ineffectiveness of the social scientist in relation to planning, is that very often the questions which you ask are not necessarily amenable to solution. If you say, why is such and such going to happen, or what is going to happen to such and such, then my reply is that the structure of society is such and such, and in the past 10 years its history has dictated so and so. This is no answer because it does not dictate action. All you can expect from the social scientist, at this point in time, is information.

Burberry: At present there is a rigid division for the responsibility for the design of buildings on the one hand, and for the processes that go on in and around buildings on the other. There seems to be a possibility that the design of buildings could include both the hardware and the function.

Communication between people: the available technology

by

J. C. IRELAND

'TELECOMMUNICATIONS', ON WHICH I am going to talk, cover the whole art of communications apart from face to face contact.

I say 'The art of Communications' because it is essentially an art, which takes the fruits of scientific development and by manipulating them meets the practical needs of the everyday world and in meeting those needs moves forward. Communications has to move forward in step with a world that is moving forward, not lag behind it nor run too far ahead. As an instrument of progress it must match the job.

What is the present form of this instrument and how is it shaping for the future? But first a brief look back.

From the earliest days the runner has been a communication agent. In Egypt the message was inscribed on clay tablets, and the invention of papyrus may have been stimulated by a competitive agency who found that they could thereby make their runners go faster and further.

The Persians posted slaves at intervals who shouted from one to the other, but the error rate of a system of this sort is very great.

Aeneas invented the floating message board—which is, perhaps, the first example of a coded system. On receiving the cryptic message, say six, the operator would draw off six pints of fluid in the top and the floating board which would then ascent to the appropriate line and the message could be read off at the rim.

Polybius introduced the first real telegraph code. The alphabet was written in five columns and each letter had a co-ordinate position, which was signalled by lighting multiple torches.

The Romans introduced the first vehicle-borne mail service—a method which was continued unchanged in principle until it reached its apotheosis in the mail coaches of the nineteenth century.

In the twelfth century, Ghengis Khan launched the first air mail service by using pigeons, and tradition has it that the Rothschilds made successful commercial use of the pigeon post after the Battle of Waterloo.

The semaphore was first introduced in 1767 for signalling racing results direct from the course. Napoleon set up semaphore chains from Paris to Marseilles and it is surprising how fast they were. It took time to 'fill the pipe' (for the first signal put in at Paris to reach Marseilles) but thereafter, signals poured out at a rate of about seven words a minute—on a clear day.

With all these means of communications which depended on sight or sound or on carried messages, civilised man had not really advanced very much beyond jungle methods until in 1831 the properties of electromagnetic fields were discovered and formulated by Michael Faraday. For the first time man had a reliable means of communication which could 'go further than voices and faster than horses'.

By 1851, with the laying of the first submarine cable between England and France, the linking of England and America became a possibility and in 1866 the Transatlantic Cable was laid by the Great Eastern, the only ship in the world large enough to carry all the cable needed to link England to America.

In 1876 Bell invented the electromagnetic telephone and then Edison produced the carbon transmitter. This was the audio break through, which allowed not just the long distance transfer of intelligence that the telegraph had given, but the transmission of recognisable personality in the voice.

Each of these voice prints is a picture of the same syllable spoken by different people and each is completely different from the other. The picture is built up by electrically-plotting frequency against time, with amplitude (or loudness) shown by seven steps—like the contours on a map. The evidence points towards the voiceprint being as personal a characteristic as the fingerprint—though not enough have been taken to establish this statistically. This confirms the basis of the peculiar intimacy of contact which the telephone gives, and also opens up fascinating possibilities in the future for identification and verification.

The personal and immediate contact which the telephone offered led swiftly to the distribution of the service to the office and the home, and so the telephone exchange was born.

Now we accept our telephone system as commonplace and we are quite used to dialling trunk calls all over the country. The key to this has been the economic provision of long distance circuits by carrier telephony. With this technique many circuits are carried on a single transmission path, each individual circuit is separated out at the ends by tuning—basically in the same way as one 'tunes in' a radio broadcast station. Present day transmission paths, formed by co-axial cables and microwave radio links, can be used to give no fewer than 2700 separate trunk telephone circuits on a single transmission path.

Submarine cables with submerged amplifiers at regular intervals, fed with power along the cable itself, have extended these techniques into the international and intercontinental connections. These under-ocean cables and the communication satellites now make conversations with many parts of the globe as simple as ordinary local calls. There is, of course, the time difference to consider—remembering that your correspondent may be in bed.

All this takes its place in business life today. What is not so well known is that telegraphy, taking a leaf out of telephony's book with switched distribution into private premises, offers in the telex service, direct connection between business offices on a similar world wide basis.

Now, you will see, that the actual teleprinter message as it comes in will be displayed on the closed circuit television monitors that are around the room. The message will be sent out when we have called the appropriate number and it will be transmitted by sending a punched tape through the machine and then we shall get the reply message back from our distant correspondent.

'Voiceprints', or, more correctly, Contour Spectograms, of a single syllable spoken.

Copyright 1962, Bell Telephone Laboratories, Inc., Murray Hill, New Jersey, U.S.A. Reprinted by permission of the Editor, Bell Laboratories *Record*.

Quick as the telex service is, the speed of transmission is comparatively slow. The advent of the high speed computer, which has been made possible by the development of electronic storage and manipulative circuits able to work at a very high speed, has brought about the transmission of large amounts of data at very much higher speeds. This can be done over the ordinary switched telephone connections by applying data transmission equipment.

The data is prepared on punched tape, but is sent at more than ten times the speed of conventional teleprinters, and is reproduced on punched tape or fed directly into a computer at the far end. It is vital for accuracy that no errors creep in during transmission, and since even the best switched telephone circuits are liable to occasional 'clicks and bangs' which cause errors, an error detecting code is used which includes electronic circuits that reject faulty characters and cause them to be re-sent and received correctly before passing through to the final output. So, although there may be trouble on the connection, this is detected; the receiver demands further re-transmission and the final message is not put in to the computer until it is correct.

A typical application of this technique has been made in this country by a large group of Insurance Companies who have linked their branch offices to a central computer. It will be apparent that there are many other cases, for instance, Banks and Business Houses, which have a wide geographical spread of their offices, that can make use of this type of facility.

The combination of high speed data manipulation at a central point fed from a multiplicity of outside collecting points is finding wider and wider application and will form an integral part of the communications of the future. The availability of a single central memory or inventory, that is being continuously and immediately updated as each transaction takes place, has obvious advantages in the industrial field, in stock control, and in the general field of seat reservation.

An airline seat reservation system is quite small and compact and can be located in every office where seat booking can be effected, at airports, air terminals, travel agents, hotels, and so on. Each set is linked back to a central electronic inventory that works so fast that, although it may have connected to it quite a large number of these out-stations, it can deal with them one at a time. Thus the bogey in seat reservation, which is double booking, is completely eliminated. The whole core of this type of business communication aid—as indeed of any computer—is the central 'memory', or information store and electronics has given us the technique for making stores of all sizes and for all speeds of operation suited to the task in hand.

A different application of storage is the Repertory Dialler. In this the storage of information is not centralised, as in the case of the computer, but is dispersed to the users telephone. This device, which incorporates a magnetic memory is connected to a loud 'speaking' telephone.

Subscriber dialling is being developed to cover the National Network first, then the International and soon the Intercontinental network, and the number of digits that has to be dialled will up and may reach fourteen or even more. The Repertory Dialler memorises several hundred numbers and dials them correctly at the touch of a button. This device is now under trial.

With more and more long distance automatic working, the time taken to set up a call becomes significant, both economically and as a matter of convenience to the caller, so telephone exchange switching must become faster in operation. To do this information must be fed in from the Subscribers Telephone faster than the ordinary telephone dial can do it.

The Push Button Telephone gives something like a five to one speed up over the traditional telephone dial. The advantages of push button signalling cannot really be used until all the associated switching equipment is also fast enough; the latest types of telephone exchange now being installed can do this, but it is quite practicable, as an interim stage, to store the faster incoming signals from the push buttons at the exchange and then allow the switching to take place at the present normal speeds. This means that the subscriber will have to wait for an interval after pushing the last button before anything happens—but evidence so far indicates that this is not as frustrating as was feared. The advantage in being able to clear a long number out of your head quickly shows up in fewer mistakes and obviates the misgivings that sometimes arise half-way through dialling a long number. A trial of this push button working has been carried out on a group of subscribers on the Langham Exchange in London and has proved all these points. The users have been enthusiastic. The first full scale application of the push button telephone in this country has been in private automatic exchanges, and in private branch exchanges for both internal communication and connection to the public network.

There are many refinements which include the loudspeaking telephone; the immediate calling of selected people by push-buttons, or by key operation; the ability to transfer calls coming in from the public network from one extension to another; the priority 'butting-in' on to calls by senior management; the setting up of conference calls between a number of extensions; and the association of the ordinary desk telephone with centralised dictation recording. These pieces of equipment are so designed that they are worthy of front hall display rather than of relegation, as in the past, to somewhere in the basement. The installation at the Shell Building in London offers a good example of the sort which business communications have reached today and from which the future will spring.

Communication development must pass through the sieve of economic viability and, with certain esoteric exceptions in the political and military field, has got to pay its way and keep in step with the users acceptance. This is a hard taskmaster for the development engineer who often has to abandon, at any rate for the time being, fascinating but uneconomic lines of approach. One such new facility which is now passing through the economic sieve is the addition of sight to sound. The original invention of the telephone was the audio breakthrough and the work of the 1920's and 1930's gave the video breakthrough. But the great frequency band-widths which are needed for instantaneous picture transmission, limited its commercial applications to the mass media such as television broadcasting, or to limited closed circuit application. By advances of technique and by the acceptance of an adequate standard, as opposed to a perfect standard of definition, the video telephone looks as though it is approaching the realms of practicability as a distributed and switched service like the public telephone.

In a wider field, one of the most exciting arrivals has been that of world wide communication via satellites. Here the communication engineer is presented with an opportunity to use radio propagation under ideal conditions without the previous frustration forced upon him by the curvature of the earth. In principle it is very simple. A radio repeater station is put in space at a height where, in radio terms it is visible from a very substantial part of the earth's surface; signals are shot up to it and are then sent down to areas which could not be reached by the traditional methods. In practice there are problems—and I would like to consider some of them.

An attractive initial approach was to put satellites at a height at which they would orbit at the same angular speed as the rotation of the earth and would therefore appear to be stationary. Such a synchronous satellite has to be at a height of about 22,000 miles, and with three suitably placed each would be radio-visible from one-third of the earth's surface. At the 'overlap' points two of them would be radio visible, so it should be possible, with two 'hops' up and down, to establish radio communication between any two points on the earth's surface. But, there is one fundamental difficulty—propagation time. Radio waves travel at the speed of light (186,000 miles per second). For a single 'hop' connection, a signal would have to travel 44,000 miles to the satellite and back which takes just under $\frac{1}{4}$ second and for a two 'hop' connection 88,000 miles or nearly $\frac{1}{2}$ second. This means that on a two 'hop' connection the message is not received until $\frac{1}{2}$ second after it is sent and the reply takes $\frac{1}{2}$ second to get back. So the reply is heard 1 second after the sender stops speaking. By this time the sender has come to conclusion that the recipient did not hear him so he starts to speak again, and in no time there is confusion. For a single hop connection the $\frac{1}{4}$ second delay is tolerable, and many public telephone circuits are now working on this basis via the sychronous satellites that have already been placed in orbit.

Another aspect of this same problem is echo. Unless very special preventative steps are taken some of the speech energy is electrically reflected back on the return path. The sender of the message hears this as a delayed echo of what he has said, and this makes his speech incoherent.

An alternative to the three synchronous satellite is a series of nine satellites at a height of no more than 8,000 miles to give an effective coverage between any two points on the earth's surface by three up and down 'hops' of 16,000 miles. This would impose an overall time delay of about $\frac{1}{4}$ second which would give acceptable conversation conditions. As the satellites would move in relation to the earth, the ground stations would need steerable aerials and computer controlled tracking equipment to follow the appearance of each satellite from horizon to horizon. Although this is a fairly complex operation it is proved and practical, as has already been shown by the trials made with the satellites Telstar and Relay.

The equipment for receiving, amplifying and re-transmitting the radio signals is contained in the body of the satellite, and the power to operate it is derived from an array of solar cells which give a direct conversion of energy from the Ultra Violet light energy into electrical energy.

A commercial application of a world communication system, using the nine satellites, is quite practical. The equipment in the satellite is rather more complex than in the case of the synchronous satellite because its task will vary according to which part of the world's surface it is moving over. When it is over the Atlantic it may be required to provide amplification for a large block of circuits between Europe and America, but over the Indian Ocean it will be required to amplify a number of small blocks of circuits between different countries. To offer this multi-access will give a satellite system a flexibility which has greater commercial value, but it can be seen that if it is to work satisfactorily it will call for political co-operation between the earth users of a high order. If this was achieved it would be a major step forward in international relations which could pave the way for co-operation in wider fields.

Satellite communication circuits will be integrated with those that are provided by land and submarine cables and by microwave radio links.

The electro-magnetic wave-guide offers a breakthrough in that, unlike any other transmission means, the attenuation or loss of power in the transmission through the wave-guide gets less as the frequency that is transmitted gets higher. This is completely contrary to all other forms of transmission and such guides are already practical propositions. The transmission path that can be given by a wave-guide of a 2-inch type would carry no fewer than 200,000 telephone circuits or 100 television channels. This now awaits its commercial and economic justification. This is beginning to show in the United States and in this country, where a requirement for circuit provision of this magnitude is seen to be needed in the not too distant future.

Another field, now opening up for the transmission of a large number of circuits on a wide band width, is the use of light as a transmission medium. Fundamental work has produced the laser—the initials of LASER stand for Light Amplification by Stimulated Emission of Radiation—which offers the opportunity for producing a very high frequency energy narrow light beam which can be guided and regenerated at intervals. The modulation of such a light beam to carry communications is quite practicable.

The direct use of beams through the atmosphere does not seem likely because of the loss by dispersion through fog, smoke or rain, but the possibility of the transmission of light by an optical guide—such as a tube or a fibre—may give an interference free transmission.

Technology which is now available will lead, in the next ten to twenty years, to an increasing influence on communication so that more and more people will be brought closer and closer together. Direct contact between them will be faster and sight will, in many cases, reinforce sound. Routine work will be handled more by electronic data processing and computer will talk directly to computer.

It is clear that telecommunications will be a vital tool in the hands of the overall planner.

The extent to which it is used, and the imagination with which it is applied to changing conditions and to differing demands lies only partly in the hands of professional men. Much will depend on the investment agreed by the Government and on changes in the social attitudes of business firms and individuals. Our contribution is to provide the technological signposts, and to achieve the economic production of the systems that are needed.

A leader of the Bell Laboratories when talking about a universal communicator back in the 1930's, made the comment that 'When a child is born he will be issued with a small device—the size of a wristwatch—engraved with a number which will be his World Identity Number for all purposes. Through this device, and using this number, you will be able to communicate with him at any time wherever he may be. When one day you try and there is no reply, you will know that he is dead'.

Plessey with the help of the G.P.O. provided equipment for use as a background to this paper. Among this equipment were the following:—
Teleprinter used during the paper to communicate with New York and Zurich; Repertory Dialler; Video Telephone; Electro Magnetic Wave Guide.

BIBLIOGRAPHY

ATKINSON, J. (1968). *Telephony* (2 vol.) Pitman.
MARTIN, J. (1969). *Telecommunication and the computer*. Prentice-Hall.
RENTON, R. N. (1965). *Telecommunications principles*. Pitman.
SYSKI, R. (1960). *Introduction to congestion theory in telephone systems*. Oliver & Boyd.

Discussion

Findlay: Why could not the delay brought about by messages going from satellite to earth and back to the satellite be reduced by sending messages from satellite to satellite?

Ireland: This would mean that messages would have to travel nearly as far. But, the main trouble is to get the satellite to differentiate between sending one signal back to earth and another one off to the next satellite. This is not really a very restricting situation, because such a large proportion of the telephone calls one wants to set up are within the range of a single hop.

Moxley: Concerning the abbreviated dialling. I remember seeing this at least five years ago and we were impressed and delighted with it. Why has it taken such a long time to become accepted?

Whyte: There are two less costly competitors. One of them offers a smaller number of numbers which can be stored, but it is still costly. The other, which is the cheaper, uses plastic punched cards, which are dropped into a slot in the instrument. Each of these cards has been pre-punched with holes to indicate the number you are calling. This has the attraction that the number of numbers that you can store is completely unlimited, you just have a card for each number but it is rather more cumbersome to operate. There is, at present, the matter of capital priorities and the demands on capital. If you did not have a telephone at all and were being told that you had to wait still longer for your telephone, you might feel that our limited resources might be better applied to putting that situation right than to providing additional facilities to the lucky people with a telephone. This is a passing situation and shortly they will be offered to the public.

Nealon: In my village, when one rang up on one of the 45 lines we had on the exchange, and the person was out you were told by the operator that 'he will not be back till 12 o'clock'. Will our automated systems ever be able to give us this sort of personal service?

Cherry: The same thing happens in other fields, does it not? My bank accounts, for example, are totally incomprehensible and do not give the information you need. We cannot have the advantages of both worlds.

Langdon: Is it inevitable? Why cannot we, for instance, develop more computers that will do just what that local operator did? My bank uses computers and sends out accounts which are comprehensible. It is not sufficient to replace one mode of doing something with another mode that does not do the same thing but does something else.

Ireland: This is true, and technically this can be achieved but at a price.

Bayliss: I understand that a service is commercially available in the United States whereby one can leave a trail. If you are going out this can be recorded centrally and calls are automatically re-routed to your next telephone destination.

Ireland: This 'follow me' facility is available on certain telephone exchanges over here on a limited scale, but its use is almost exclusively confined to Doctors. This facility is going in at a rate of about ten a month in the Electronic Exchanges.

Clarke: Are there any centralised interconnected computer systems in this country?

Ireland: There are a number of these systems operating with industrial companies, which include one of the big Insurance Groups, and two of the Banks. The facility of linking all the branches into a central computer point exists. There is no technical difficulty, it is a question of whether the customer is prepared to pay the price.

Clarke: On the planning side this is important because it means that the location of certain offices, particularly central offices, are independent of the old forms of communication.

Telecommunications in the next thirty years

by

J. S. WHYTE

THE POST OFFICE and the telecommunications industry are standing on the threshold of a new era in telecommunications in which a wide range of new services is becoming technically possible. Some of these are of such importance to the community at large that any studies of the long-term future trends of the various activities of the community either commercial, industrial, governmental, or social, cannot meaningfully be made without consideration of the implications of these new developments. Telecommunications can no longer be considered separately from other aspects of organisation but are now so intricately interwoven with organisational concepts that they must be considered as an integral part of the total planning activity.

Telecommunications provide means of linking places which are remote from each other and the technological and social developments that we have seen under way, for many years, are all leading to a growing radius of communication requirements. Thus whilst the original telephone systems were provided within a single town only and there was no means of inter-connecting the systems of different towns, these quickly developed so that trunk circuits, inter-linking the different systems, could be provided. This growth of inter-city telecommunications complemented the growth of transport facilities and, later, the growth of international telecommunications complemented the growth of international trade and travel. While new developments in telecommunications in the future are important in their impact on the town itself, we must keep these local benefits in proper perspective and not let them dominate our view of the future.

The very capabilities that telecommunications will offer in the future will affect not only the design of dwellings and their layout, but may lead us to question existing ideas about the need for cities as we understand them, and their location. Will there be need for travel for business purposes, or will there be relevance for contemporary type shopping centres, and so on.

Whilst the telephone service will remain, for many years, the cornerstone of Post Office business, nevertheless their function covers telecommunications in all its various facets, national and international, voice, vision, and data. They must provide, on a sound economic basis, comprehensive telecommunication services meeting the communication needs between person and person, machine and machine, and person and machine.

In looking towards the future and postulating what the telecommunications services may look like in thirty years time, three features may stand out:

1. Major growth in existing types of service.
2. Introduction of many new types of service.
3. Growth in machine to machine communications.

We must bear in mind the needs of both domestic users and commercial, industrial and business users, because development will not be equally applicable.

The very substantial growth of existing services such as the telephone, both in terms of the numbers of customers served and the volume of traffic they generate, may appear to be self evident. Nevertheless the scale of the growth has extremely important consequences for the system designer. It is a statutory obligation of the Post Office that the operation is conducted on a profitable basis. To be fully responsive to the national needs, the system must be flexible in its design so as to admit change and growth, and it must be open-ended and able to absorb new customers whether they be in existing established communities or in areas not already served. These requirements must not result in diminished profitability as the system grows because, if it were otherwise, the long-term economic viability would be endangered.

The number of telephone stations in the U.K. (Fig. 1) at the end of the war was under 4 million. This has grown to 12 million despite the many years of capital investment restraint that were a feature of this period. We would expect, by the end of the century, to see at least the equivalent of a telephone in every household in the country. This observation has implications for the planning of new housing.

A full-scale experiment is being undertaken in Washington New Town, by the Post Office in collaboration with the local authorities, in which a comprehensive communication system is being provided to all households at the time of construction. This will involve two telephone pairs and a wideband coaxial cable to provide VHF, sound and television programs. The two cable networks will be separate electrically, and the main economic benefits of this first experiment will accrue from the sharing of common plant such as ducts, trenches, jointing boxes, and to some extent, from the common planning for the simultaneous provision of the conventional and coaxial cable networks. The distribution will be wholly underground and the lead-in to each dwelling will use special ducts provided by the development corporation engineers. Householders will connect their own commercial-type television receivers to the system and will be able to tune them to any of the channels in the television Band 1 and 3 as well as to BBC Radio 1, 2, 3 and 4 and the Durham radio local program in Band 2. Spare capacity in the line frequency spectrum is available for future exploitation for other wideband services such as educational or closed circuit television. The first 300 dwellings in this scheme are due for occupation early this year.

This is the first step. Schemes that are technically more advanced than this are under study in the research laboratories.

One possibility, for example, would be to have a single coaxial cable running around the district like a ring main and carrying streams of extremely narrow high frequency pulses with feeders off into each household. Apparatus would be provided for gating out selected pulses carrying information relating to individual households. As a variant on this, local distribution to households might be provided by means of millimetric radio beams from tiny transmitters installed on the tops of lamp-posts.

MILLIONS

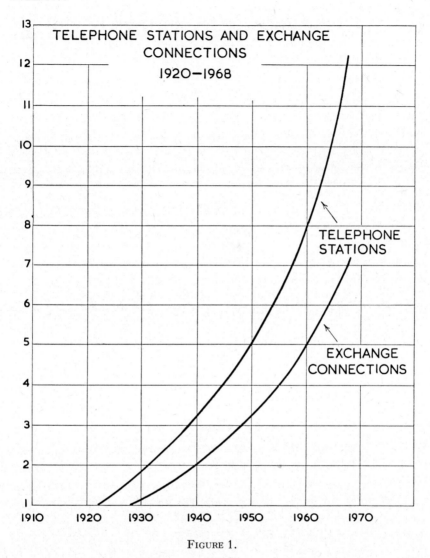

FIGURE 1.

Another alternative, under study in the research laboratories, is the use of specially produced glass fibres which have the thickness of a human hair, but which would offer the possibility of transmitting on very large numbers of channels. Although such exotic forms of transmission medium are unlikely to enter service on a commercial scale for many years, one or other could provide not only the entertainment and telephone channels of the Washington scheme but, in addition, make available viewphone and high speed facsimile services for every household.

In person to person business telecommunications, there is one development that has recently been demonstrated by the Post Office which could have the most important consequences for its users; I refer to confravision. In this system a specially equipped television studio is provided, looking rather like a company boardroom, which will accommodate up to five participants who can hold a business meeting with a similar number who are miles distant. There are two large television monitor screens. One of these shows the participants at the distant location, and the other can show either one's own colleagues or material that is being presented. Associated with these facilities is a high quality loudspeaking audio system which experience has shown permits a relaxed and free-flowing discussion. If it was decided to initiate a national service it would be possible to provide studio facilities in major centres of population so that they could be booked for use by any interested organisation. Alternatively, very large organisations might wish to equip their own studios to connect to the network. A demonstration system between the G.P.O. Telecommunications Headquarters in Gresham Street and their Research Station at Dollis Hill in North West London has been installed.

One of the developments that may appear in the late part of this century, is that of 'non-voice' telecommunication services. The nature of some of these can already be predicted but it is likely that others will emerge. During the past decade there has been a rapidly growing appreciation of the interdependence of scientific disciplines and the beneficial results that flow from technological cross-fertilisation, and there can be few fields where there is more scope than that of telecommunications and computers.

Both computers and telecommunications are concerned with the collection, storage, processing, and dissemination of information. Figure 2 shows how they are interlinked and their important relationship to the whole field of control. The first steps are being taken, in factories, towards the completely automatic control of processes. Some industries, notably the petroleum and chemical industries, are considerably in advance of others in the introduction of these techniques which seem destined to spread to most areas of manufacturing. Increasingly, after the establishment of automation on the local scale, control will be exerted remotely from computers operating over data transmission facilities and acting on the basis of information received from other locations. These developments will lead to the direct exchange of information between computers, and between computers and other types of equipment and plant. Management will rely increasingly on the computer to pre-process the vast amount of data relevant to its decisions. The inter-relationship of data is becoming so complex, and the volume of data so great that managerial decisions, to be adequate to sustain the profitability and efficiency of the business operation, will not be possible on a personal, intuitive basis. The decisions remain the manager's responsibility, but the machines must help him.

The fourth inter-locking area that Figure 2 shows is that of publishing. Its link with the information processing and dissemination capabilities of computers and communications is obvious. However, we face a new problem in this area because of an information explosion which threatens to engulf us; nowhere is this more so than in the realm of scientific publishing. The scale and urgency of this problem is illustrated by the number of scientific journals subscribed to by the National Library at Boston Spa which was 20,000 in 1965 and which rose to 26,000 in 1967. This figure does not include trade journals except those that have a significant scientific element. It has been estimated that there are nearly 10,000,000 scientific papers in existence. A quarter of a million chemical abstracts were added to the collection in 1967 and nearly a third of a million will be added during 1970. This enormous volume of material which pours out every

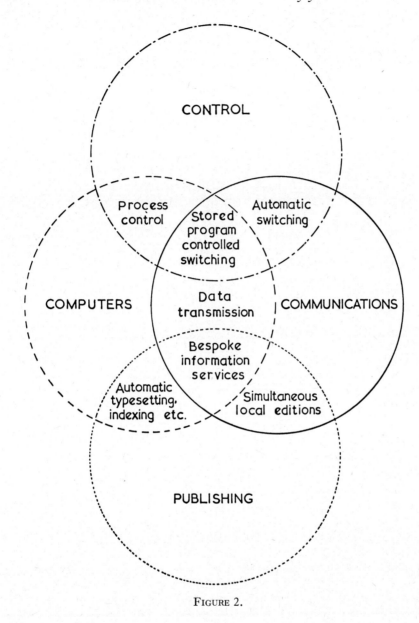

FIGURE 2.

year cannot possibly be appraised and assimilated by working scientists. If we are to avoid being overwhelmed, and of committing resources to the duplication of already known results, means must be found of bringing machines to our aid. It seems likely that the computer can help in the automatic classification of material, its storage, and its selective retrieval under interrogation from remote locations. This would enable the contents of national libraries to be accessed from the laboratory, office or home and hard or soft copy produced.

In the everyday world of publishing similar possibilities are opening up with the application of computer type setting which, aided by telecommunications, can be operated remotely. There are possibilities for simultaneous type setting in a number of different places and using material originating from a single source. The blending of national and local news and advertising is thus possible. Since the delivery of newspapers involves high labour costs and the inefficient use of labour, there is an obvious incentive to eliminate physical distribution to the home. We may see, one day, the printing process carried out in the home with the information coming in over data links. It would seem to be a feasible proposition once this stage has been reached, for the customer to have a considerable element of choice in the type of material that is printed for him so that the balance of the resulting document would vary considerably from one customer to another.

What else would be possible in the home? Before answering this question in the context of thirty years to come, it would be interesting to stand back to 1939 to look at some of the commonplace items in our homes today that were not widely available then. Polythene, nylon, and PVC were unknown as were many types of synthetic material for carpets, curtains, and clothes; the work tops in kitchens; the tiles on the floor; the insulant in the roof space; together with fluorescent lighting, television, washing machines and electric blankets.

It is indisputable that the technical possibilities which we can now foresee greatly surpass those that were foreseeable 30 years ago.

We may expect the 'viewphone' to be available for those who can afford it.

The dial on the telephone instrument will almost certainly have given place to a series of push buttons. This apparently trivial innovation may have far-reaching consequences because, with its aid, a telephone call will be set up and used for the remote control of a variety of apparatus. These could include the interrogation of computer-based data banks with program-controlled voice responses from the computer; the obtaining of access to a wide variety of information services; the interrogation of one's telephone answering machine when away from home; the remote control of the cooker or the overriding of preset instructions; the control of central heating; or the shutting of greenhouse windows from the restaurant where you are dining.

A cordless telephone is possible which can be moved from room to room without attached wires, by making use of either induction loop or infra-red broadcasting techniques.

Nation-wide or continent-wide radio paging schemes, to enable an individual to be located and called to a telephone no matter where he may be, are already under study. Small schemes are operating in Belgium, Holland and Switzerland. One may feel of this development, as with some other telecommunication developments, that we are raising questions of the invasion of privacy, and the community will have to make decisions about this. But all manner of surveillance services for the very young, and for the very old and the infirm, and other forms of alarm are natural extensions of the communications system. Home video shopping could be achieved with goods displayed to the housewife on a viewing screen, her orders would be given by using a simple keyboard, or even by pointing at the screen, automatic packaging and invoicing taking place simultaneously at the warehouse, and automatic debiting of her bank account. The only step that cannot be eliminated is the physical delivery of the chosen goods.

All this seems technically possible but when it would become economically viable is much more difficult to suggest, and it is pertinent to consider whether the housewife will ever really want this. Perhaps, in part, shopping is a social exercise offering a certain pleasure and satisfaction which would be lost if the family shopping expedition was replaced in this way.

A more promising very long term aim is the virtual elimination of the physical transmission of letters. This will be achieved when inexpensive, simple to operate, full colour facsimile machines become available. When such devices become available there would be a problem about their introduction because the value of this service would depend on the number of people who would wish to use it. There would, therefore, be a difficult interregnum during which both delivered and wired mail would have to co-exist. This would make the economic viability of both systems more difficult. The telegram service, whose economic viability has been disastrously undermined by the telephone, is still maintained to meet a social need and is an example of this sort of problem.

Some of these potential developments would involve pre-wiring all buildings for communication services at the time of construction, and might also include laying the necessary loops of cable to produce induction fields for use in connection with the cordless telephones. The laying of the services to each house might well become a combined operation with those of the other public services.

This prompts me to ask whether a much more fundamental issue is involved than the pre-wiring of buildings. New services that have been discussed, particularly confravision, viewphone, video shopping, together with the possibility of wholly automated remotely-accessed library facilities, make it possible that travel to the extent we practice it today, may become unnecessary. If one pursues this line of thought ad absurdum, one can imagine a fully-automated situation in which the individual need rarely leave his home but merely manipulate the knobs and dials and screens around him in order to obtain his education, conduct his business, do his shopping and get his entertainment. Such a prospect would certainly be unacceptable to many people and there may be strong psychological reasons for suggesting that this form of insularity would be socially unacceptable. In the case of confravision, we do not know enough about what makes people travel or the nature of business activities, so it is not at all clear whether a service of this sort would be accepted by business men as a substitute for personal visits. There is a body of opinion that suggests that business men like to travel and enjoy the experience. Nevertheless, we see the beginnings of an era in which major advances in communication facilities will, by annihilating distance, remove many of the restraints which have hitherto been associated with the location of industry, business, and houses, and the interrelationship of these with shopping centres. Planners of the future may have a greater degree of freedom in the choice of sites for new enterprises than formerly. Certainly the growth of communication facilities, both physical and telecommunication, has reduced the dependence of some areas on a single industry which were a feature of industrialisation in the late eighteenth and early nineteenth century. The 'single industry' town led to some appalling social conditions in times of depression, and it is a matter of some satisfaction that the development of the technologies will give new freedoms.

While recognising that telecommunications are often in direct competition with physical communications, they are often complementary. Examples of this can be seen in the extensive data transmission facilities that have been provided in West London and Glasgow to permit the area control of traffic by central computer. Such schemes will be expanded in the immediate future. Looking further ahead it is possible to see data transmission facilities being used in connection with real time, on-line working of computer systems in association with passenger control on suburban railways. Already the new Victoria line in London makes use of automatic turnstiles and magnetic recording on passenger tickets, and it is not a very great step to extend the facilities to link the turnstiles with a central computer for a variety of other purposes. Such a scheme is already under study for the Bay area rapid transit system to be introduced in California.

Yet another possibility for the future is that of arranging for 'personalised' bus services. It has been suggested that a prospective passenger could go to a bus stop and press a button which would send signals to a central computer which would automatically direct the nearest bus to that pickup point. A number of variants of this scheme have been put forward to deal with the problem of low densities of traffic and with the less busy hours of the day. This is another example of the partnership between telecommunications and 'physical' transport.

We shall need to question whether these developments in communication will have a major influence on the siting of towns or on the type of facilities that are provided in them, shopping, dwelling areas, and business and industry. Are we moving, perhaps, towards the concept of the universal village and away from the concentrated town?

The consequences of some of these telecommunications possibilities may appear to offer society negative opportunities but this need not be the consequence if we are selective about the options we take up and are careful of how we use them. There are many ways in which a lot of menial work can be removed with the aid of computers and electrical communications, so freeing people to do more valuable things. We should be aiming to use the new opportunities to build a better society and not a sterile mechanistic one.

The application of these possibilities cost money, and it seems likely that their introduction will be determined more by economic viability than by technical possibility. Certainly, at the domestic level, affluence will be a major factor, and services like viewphone will initially be in competition with other ways of spending any surplus family funds. Even at the end of the century the average income in the U.K., for the head of household, is likely to be less than that enjoyed today by each of us in this room.

We have then a picture of massive growth, of many new technological possibilities annihilating distance and reducing the need for travel, and certainly many more possibilities than there will be the resources to develop. The environment in which we live is held by us in trust for our successors and when we pass it on to them it is our duty to ensure that we have not spoiled it by neglect or impoverished it by pollution.

REFERENCES

KAHN, HERMANN & WEINER, ANTHONY. *The year 2000*. Macmillan.
LORD, T. K. & JONES, R. G. *Confravision—the new aid for business communication*. P.O. Telecommunications Journal. **19** (4) 20.
MARSHALL MCLUHAN. (1967). *Understanding media*. Sphere Books.
Towards the year 2000. Daedalus. **96**, (Summer 1967). No. 3 Proceedings American Academy of Arts & Sciences.

Discussion

Hutchinson: The evidence that has been collected in studies of transportation show that 'trip making' increases with increased affluence. The substitution of business travel by telecommunications is unlikely.

Cherry: Certainly telecommunications has developed and the amount of travel has increased, because in those areas where this is happening the world is getting richer, but we can argue that travel for certain purposes can be reduced.

Brown: You mentioned that developments in telecommunications should not pollute the urban atmosphere, but this is one of the problems that has not been tackled. Our cities have to contain enormous buildings for the apparatus that makes telecommunications work. Is there a possibility of miniaturising this apparatus?

Whyte: At intervals along main roads are little brick buildings which are the repeater stations of the coaxial cable transmission system. These stations handle traffic of 2,700 channels per coaxial tube, and this will grow to 10,800 channels per tube. But those buildings will become redundant for new work because the apparatus they contain has been shrunk so that they can be buried along with the cable. The development of schemes for larger numbers of channels by coaxial cable requires, for unavoidable technical reasons, that the repeater stations are closer together as the number of channels to be accommodated rises. The fact that we have been able to miniaturise the repeaters and bury them in manholes has spared us the embarassment of finding surface sites. In the city centre buildings are needed to accommodate the switching plant which is additional to the transmission plant that I have just been speaking of. Here the progress is not so fast and, indeed, the switching plant has not changed in size significantly over the last 30 years. We are, however, just starting a new era in which electronic exchanges are being installed and these are smaller in volume than the electro-mechanical exchanges that they replace. The stage reached so far gives a modest reduction in size but the phase after this, which is in the research laboratory, uses micro-electronic circuits on a very large scale, and will increase capacity without a great increase in overall volume. Traffic growth figures are enormous. Growth in telephone stations since the end of the war has multiplied threefold with nothing like that increase in the total building volume, and the growth that is still to come will be accommodated in an even smaller increment of building.

Jones: Two points. First: the Post Office has an enormous capacity to do great visual damage and this is something that is causing concern to many people. The second point relates to confravision. Interaction between people in the studio is partly conditioned by their relative positions, and the nature of the discussion is therefore conditioned by the design of the studio.

Whyte: But visual improvements so often cost money. Is the community prepared to pay? On the design of confravision studios, certainly it is more convenient to look ahead rather than to turn sideways, but it is also more convenient for the people at the other location if all face the screen. The G.P.O. have a human factors research group in their Research Station and are working in association with the Medical Research Council and with one of the Universities on facets of human behaviour.

Langdon: Systems of communications of the kind discussed will need a great deal of servicing, with a large number of skilled men to keep them running. Thought is being given to the development of electrical networks on the lines of nervous networks in which the circuits are self repairing.

Human factors and the interdisciplinary approach to the problems of public transport

by

P. A. B. RAFFLE

PUBLIC URBAN TRANSPORT, while planning for the distant future, is dealing with the problems of the present and of the immediate future. I have taken as my brief what can be done and what is being done at the moment. I have resolutely resisted the temptation to look ahead too far mainly because the decisions that have to be taken are usually out of the hands of the transport organisation which is running the services.

Public urban transport has three main problems. There is a shortage of staff prepared to do the irregular shift work hours and weekend working which are needed to provide the service the public requires. Public transport is a labour intensive industry. Commonly, wages are three-quarters of the expense of the undertaking and it is difficult to pay wages which adequately compensate for the irregular hours without charging fares which would price public transport off the market. A view that service is equated with servitude has gradually developed over the years and many service industries are finding difficulty in getting enough staff of the right type. Perhaps, too, the lack of tangible evidence to the efforts of the day—nothing has been created—makes the service industries less attractive than the manufacturing industries. On the other hand, shift work attracts those with interests and hobbies which are best followed when others are working and, for certain people, the contact with passengers and the lack of direct supervision have attractions which outweigh the advantages of working in a factory.

The second main problem of public urban transport is the vicious circle of traffic congestion which causes delays and irregular bus services; this, in turn, leads to public protest and boycott, so that more cars are used to commute into cities, causing more traffic congestion. In 1967 between 7 and 10 o'clock on weekday mornings, 70,000 private cars brought into central London some 98,000 people whilst 4,400 buses (equivalent in road space to about 13,000 private cars) brought in 172,000 people.

The third problem is that there are quite substantial financial losses, due mainly to fraudulent travel and partly to vandalism. It is quite astonishing how many people believe that not paying the correct fare is perfectly acceptable social behaviour, whereas it is only making the other passengers pay more than they should.

I should like to consider some of the possible short term solutions to these problems, illustrating them by the work which is being done in London Transport at the moment, in particular the reactions of passengers and staff to changes in traditional methods of running bus and underground services and collecting fares.

Other cities and other countries are trying different methods but the published reports give few details of the human factors involved.

The general aim is to provide equipment and services which reduce staff, which circumvent traffic congestion, and which reduce fraud, which are readily acceptable to public and staff, at an acceptable capital cost. The solution needs collaboration between the operators who run the services, and between the systems analysts, civil, mechanical and electronic engineers, architects, ergonomists and operational research and market research workers.

People seem to expect public transport to provide a service in this order of importance: regularity, speed, cost and comfort. I shall deal with developments in bus operation and design first because the majority of cities depend on the bus for mass transport.

About 40 of the larger cities in the world have abandoned trying to move everyone who wish to use public transport in two dimensions and gone in for, mainly, underground railways. Those few cities with overground railways, and this includes trams that run in reserved lanes, have been abandoning them because of their effect on the amenities of the city and because of the cost of upkeep. Trams which mingle with traffic simply obstruct the flow of other vehicles.

It is clear that the longer a bus route is through built up areas, the more likely it is that traffic congestion will increasingly delay the service causing the irregularity and bunching of buses which the public finds so irritating. The bus operator can mitigate this by shortening bus routes to reduce the spreading effect of traffic delays from one section of a bus route to another. (These routes mainly radiate from central traffic objectives like shopping areas and railway stations.) As the majority of bus passengers travel short distances they, at any rate, are not inconvenienced by the shortening of the routes and so should have a more regular and faster service. The longer distance passengers are inconvenienced by having to change buses. This inconvenience can be reduced if interchanges are arranged at bus stations, where, because of the more regular services, the second bus is likely to be waiting.

When the buses are delayed in one direction, the delay will eventually affect the other direction unless some of the buses are reversed short of their normal destination. This is difficult for a controller to organise logically unless he knows the position of all the buses on the route at a particular time. BESI, which stands for 'bus electronic scanning indicator', is one method of providing this information. Buses are fitted with coded reflector plates and at interrogation points a light beam is reflected back to road side apparatus indicating the route and bus number. This information is transmitted to a central teleprinter where the time of passage of each bus is recorded and compared with its scheduled time. The traffic Controller can then decide which bus to reverse, and where and when to do it. Instructions are given by telephone to a roadside inspector, which is a somewhat inflexible method, or by speaking by radio to an inspector in a patrolling car. The most successful method yet used but in limited trials only is by radio to individual bus drivers.

The popularity of the Red Arrow bus services in central London indicates that the public rates regularity and speed higher than cost and comfort, and this has been confirmed by a market research report. These single deck vehicles travel on short routes with limited stops with a fare slightly higher than those on the conventional double deck vehicles. They carry nearly as many passengers as the new double deck buses, but the ratio of standing passengers to seated passengers is nearly 2 : 1.

This reshaping of bus services will limit the effects of traffic congestion but will not eliminate them. All the efforts of transport operators will be frustrated unless town planning, traffic management and, perhaps, police control ease the passage of the bus through the main streets of cities.

Fare scales and methods of fare collection can be simpler on shorter bus routes, but it is seldom feasible in large cities to have a single fare for all journeys unless the service is subsidised from some other source. If it is not subsidised, the flat fare is so large that it discourages bus travel. Simplification of fare collection brings immediate dividends because 'one-man-operation' is feasible, the fare being collected either mechanically, or by the driver on less busy routes. The 'one-man-operation' driver can be paid a higher wage, sharing the increased productivity with the employer. Collection of a fare by the driver, or by a machine, also reduces fraud because the fares are collected on boarding the vehicle.

The development of these new vehicles enabled us to design the driver's cab and the controls to accommodate, with ease, more than 90% of the range of sizes of men. This cab is much more popular with the drivers than those of other commercially available vehicles.

Considerable attention has been given to the design of different types of fare collection equipment. On the high intensity Red Arrow service the height of the coin entry area, the height of the tripod gate, the width of the gangways, the amount of padding on the arms, and the amount of damping in the mechanism were all human factors which had to be taken into account. Originally, a coin change dispenser was fitted on these vehicles but it had to be abandoned because of mechanical difficulties due to vibration and because of operational difficulties in keeping the machine loaded: change is now provided by the driver. Approximately 15% of the passengers require change on these buses compared with nearly 50% who ask for change from a conductor on a double deck bus.

On less intensive services and where children's fares are mandatory, a different type of fare collection equipment is provided. In this the adult passenger puts a 6d. in a machine which operates a tripod gate but when a child, paying half fare, wants to pass through the child presses a button on the machine which gives the driver an audible warning so that he can check that it is a child. Further ergonomic problems arose because the equipment had to be suitable for younger children travelling alone. A children's tea party was organised in which part of the game was to use mock up equipment. This showed that the first theoretical solution to the problem was acceptable.

On less intensive and longer routes mechanical methods can be replaced by the driver himself collecting fares. Higher fares for longer journeys can be charged without providing complicated mechanical equipment, and in this type of service passengers leave through the front entrance so that the driver has some check on those who travel a greater distance than they have paid for.

One matter of concern in these developments is the time taken for passengers to get on the vehicle and pay their fares. On the conventional two man vehicle, the average time taken at a bus stop, per boarding passenger, is one second. With one man operation, using the driver as the collector of fares, the average time of boarding is 5·1 seconds per passenger so this method cannot be used on a busy route. On the Red Arrow service, the average time is about 2 seconds per boarding passenger, but using two gates. Automatic fare collection, where the passenger has the correct money, is much quicker than manual collection; but passengers must be able to change money and change machines are unreliable on moving vehicles. Where there is a variable fare which they may not know about they have to be able to ask the driver, and he can do both these tasks on a route which is not busy without being overloaded. The next stage is the development of a split entrance vehicle, one side of which provides automatic fare collection, the other side of the entrance leads to the driver who can issue a ticket, and give change as necessary. In mock-up trials of this dual method of fare collection, the average boarding time was $2\frac{1}{2}$ seconds for all passengers. Following laboratory trials of coin insertions which were filmed and timed and then analysed, it was decided to concentrate on one coin slot accepting several values of coins rather than using different sized slots for different coins. The speed of use of the single slot, with mechanical sorting of the coins, was significantly quicker than when passengers had to put the coins into appropriate slots. As change giving is the slowest part of fare collection, as much help as possible is given to the driver by providing simple coin dispensing equipment, but the drivers prefer to collect the change into trays and into pockets which suggests that there is something wrong with the mechanical device.

The dual type of fare collection also has the advantage that some older people are frightened of mechanical things and may also be confused by the multiplicity of fare collection methods.

No manufacturer has yet designed a bus chassis which would conform to Ministry of Transport requirements and which is sufficiently low on the ground to eliminate the two steps into the vehicle so helping the partially disabled and the aged. On the other hand all these vehicles have doors operated by the driver so that boarding and alighting accidents are considerably reduced.

What are the reactions to these changes?

There is always resistance to change, of course, but the majority of regular commuters readily accept the new pattern of bus services and the new methods of fare collection. Their main complaint, as before, is of irregularity of services, but this is very often outside the control of the transport organisation. The off peak traveller and the housewife with children or with shopping manage the fare collection side without trouble. They do complain about the reduction in seating capacity on some of the vehicles especially as some seating at the rear is reached by another step. The Red Arrow commuter, on the other hand, is prepared to lose a comfortable seat on a less frequent service for standing room on a frequent and regular service. However, we must beware lest the development on busy routes, fare collection methods and types of vehicles should produce a small underprivileged section of the community which cannot use public transport because of these changes and who therefore become isolated.

The staff reaction to these changes has been encouraging. Transfer to one man operation has been voluntary, and the men with longer service get the first opportunity to transfer. These drivers, who for years had been incarcerated in their cab in the front of the vehicle with no contact with passengers, have found that they enjoy this new human contact. Most of them have blossomed forth into good public relations experts and give considerably more help to passengers than might have been expected. In addition the enhanced wages have helped to increase their status.

In underground railway operation there is more scope for automation and mechanisation than there is on buses. The trains, which run on reserved and fixed tracks, can be driven automatically and routed automatically. There are fewer fare collection points and these are static so that the fare collection equipment can be more elaborate. Because the journeys are longer, reduction in fraudulent travel is even more important.

Many of the recent developments in underground railway operation have been incorporated in the new Victoria Line which was opened in March (1969). The aims of the methods used in fare collection are that a passenger should be able to serve himself with a ticket and get his change more quickly than he can obtain one from a booking office; this reduces the need for booking office clerks. A mechanical check must be made that he has a ticket before he enters the railway system and that he has paid the appropriate fare before he leaves, so making ticket collectors unnecessary. A passenger takes 7 seconds to get a ticket from a booking office window compared with just under 5 seconds from a single value slot machine including taking change. This difference is very important at a busy station in the evening peak hours. The new single value ticket machine will accept a variety of coins and give the appropriate ticket and change. It is developed from earlier machines but accepts a greater variety of coins and recharges its change hopper from the coins put in. The key to this fare collection system is the ticket which is cardboard but coated on the back with plastic containing iron oxide just like magnetic recording tape. The time and date of issue, the station of origin and the fare paid, are encoded electronically on this coating. The passenger then inserts the ticket into a gate and if the ticket is valid doors open allowing the passenger in, the photo-electric cells open a second pair of doors and close the first pair behind him. This method of operation ensures that only one passenger can pass through at a time and that he has a valid ticket for that day and station. There is always some inconvenience with baggage though passengers do not complain. At the other end of the journey the passenger puts the ticket into a similar gate and if it is valid the gates open, and if he is using a season ticket, similarly encoded, the ticket is returned to him as he goes through, until the last day of validity when it is retained. If the passenger has changed his mind about his destination during the journey, he can go to an excess fare window and be issued with a new ticket.

Tripod gates are also being used on the underground as they have been in New York for many years. Their dimensions are virtually the same as the ones being used on the buses. The low door gates were designed after considerable consideration of the ergonomics of human movement.

There will be considerable reduction in the number of booking office clerks, and even more of ticket collectors, as this method of fare collection is extended. Consideration of human factors in the early stages of the design of the equipment has ensured that few alterations will be necessary in future marks of the equipment to improve them. The only outstanding ergonomic problems at the moment are the ticket entry area of the gates which could be improved, and the design of the coin entry area on the new ticket machines, which is already being modified.

Closed circuit television equipment is now sufficiently cheap and reliable for use in the control of crowds in stations, again saving staff. The station supervisor can watch the ticket hall through 'one way' glass and the platforms and so forth on television monitors. He can speak to passengers over the intercommunication system, and he can answer questions in response to an enquiry button.

An additional valuable facility is that the Line Controller, who supervises the whole line, can monitor what is happening on the station platforms throughout the line simply by cutting in to the station circuits.

The Victoria Line trains are designed for automatic operation, and the train 'operator' combines the function of driver and guard which saves staff and increases his status and wages. The 'operator' only opens and closes the doors for the passengers, and supervises. Out of his window he can see down the train and on a television monitor, sited on the platform, he has a picture of his train viewed from the back so he has no difficulty in supervising passengers boarding and alighting. Through two telephones the train operator can communicate at any time with the Line Controller, and he can also talk to the passengers.

He starts the train by pressing two buttons (two for safety) and the train moves off if the signals are in its favour. It accelerates and obeys coded signals, which are transmitted through the rails, all the way to the next station where it stops automatically. Technically, the doors could have been designed to open and close automatically, but on applied psychological grounds, it was thought that the train 'operator' would not be alert and efficient if he had nothing at all to do. Yet one underground system is being constructed in which the 'operator' has absolutely nothing to do with the operation of the train. It will be interesting to see whether the right type of man can be recruited or retrained to remain efficient enough to diagnose defects in the electronic equipment and to get the train underway. The Victoria Line 'operators' are all experienced underground train drivers, chosen by seniority or by volunteering. They have reacted very well to the change of task without the resistance one commonly expects when manual skills are replaced by automation.

Automatic control of the train ensures that electricity is not wasted in excessive acceleration or insufficient coasting with power off, and provides a more regular service than does manual operation. Every train driver has his own pattern of manual operation; some are extravagant in the use of current while others get ahead or behind the schedule because of their driving methods.

Much thought has been given to the passenger accommodation in these new trains, including the ergonomic design of the seats. Because many upholstered seats get slashed on some of the London Underground lines, plastic seats were considered. Though these are hard, they are more comfortable than one would imagine from looking at them. Market research on passenger reaction to these experimental seats showed that in spite of the hardness and coldness there was no strong reaction against them even from mini-skirted girls. Many praised them, especially for their cleanliness and durability. A number of underground railways in other countries use plastic seats on their rolling stock. They are, presumably, acceptable because of the relative lack of coarse vibration, compared with road vehicles, and the comparatively short journeys travelled.

The nerve centre of train operation is the signal cabin. The traditional signal cabin and signalman are being replaced by automated signalling. This reduces the number of signalmen to a quarter or a fifth of those previously needed. The whole of the Victoria Line is supervised by one man! Automated signalling not only reduces man power but improves regularity of the service by eliminating delays due to human error. While the service is operating normally, the Traffic Regulator does not have to interfere with the automatic control of the service in any way—he might just as well not be there. If, however, he does have to take over, he can alter the routing of trains, alter the signals, put in extra trains, take out trains and so forth. The Traffic Regulator gets his information from two diagrams. One shows the position of each train by a red strip of light, together with the signals. The other diagram indicates each train's destination which is picked up from trackside equipment. Coloured lights indicate the mode in which the automatic equipment is working.

When the service is upset the Traffic Regulator may have to take complete control of the whole system. This is a heavy mental workload and goes from the extreme of doing nothing to being at maximum pressure. This could be stressful but, so far, there is no evidence that there is a problem. Yet, when one is in the regulating rooms during periods of disruption of service, one has the feeling that these men are being stressed. Because of this we are giving facilities to Prof. Sayers of Imperial College to undertake some measurements for us and the Traffic Regulators are collaborating very well. They are wearing equipment that records their hear beats which are then analysed by computer to see whether the change in heart rate will show some measure of mental stress. This information is needed not only for this problem but for others such as the Air Traffic Controllers and airline pilots whose jobs swing from doing very little to doing a great deal in a short time.

The public reaction to this 'new-look' underground is favourable. They are impressed with the thought which has gone into the design of ticket halls, platforms and passages which has reduced the impedance to passenger flow to a minimum.

This is in part due to the contribution of architects and civil engineers who have made a close study of queue movements.

The passengers will, however, judge the success of these developments not by what is going on behind the scenes but by the regularity of the service and the reliability of the automatic fare collection equipment.

The success of any development in urban transport depends on the provision of a service which the public wants where and when it requires it, with equipment which is easily understood and is quickly and safely used.

REFERENCES

MURRELL, K. F. H., *Ergonomics*. Chapman & Allen.
Article on the Victoria Line. Supplement in the *Financial Times*. 5 March, 1969. Supplement in *The Times*. 7 March, 1969.
SELL, R. G. & RAFFLE, P. A. B. (1960 & 1970). *Applied Ergonomics*. Vol. 1, 4 & 113.

Discussion

Cresswell: If the floor at the front of the vehicle is kept low there is a huge differential between the level inside the vehicle and the wheel arches at the back so one ends up with a sloping floor or with a higher floor, and this means steps. The problem may be one of tyre size, and if the tyre manufacturers could come up with small tyres, about car size, either filled with gas or with compressed air then it might be possible to get the low floor. Alternatively, as the doors open, part of the floor might also be designed to drop to the ground so that mothers with pushchairs could get in.

Medhurst: The methods of fare collection which have been described seem to be so complicated that they might be self-defeating. In Montreal you buy a dollar's worth of 10 cent tickets, and you can buy them from the tobacconist, the drug store, or from the bus driver himself, and you hand one in as you get into the bus. This has been working extremely efficiently.

In a new town near Washington there are proposals to use mini buses, carrying a dozen or so passengers, and operated by women, who are working part time. There will be a flexible system of routing which in a small town seems to have opportunities that might be applied to this country.

Raffle: A number of cities have adopted the system of pre-purchasing tickets and have given it up. This is because they have to be sold, as you said, by the driver, which holds up the procedure, or by agents, tobacconists or newsagents or people like that, who want 20% 'rake off'. I think Copenhagen is the latest city to give up this method.

Odell: Is this not a question of whether the agent's commission offsets the additional cost of installing complicated machines plus the additional cost of the driver's time? Some cities are introducing a differential to discourage people from buying tickets from the driver.

Raffle: The interest on the cost of the equipment is less than losing 20% on the value of the tickets.

Stone: One problem on the underground is that of congestion and getting in and out of the tube trains, and this is made more difficult by the fact that there is not accommodation for heavy luggage. As more of these services connect main line stations this becomes more important.

The other problem is that of ventilation, the tubes are about the hottest and most unpleasant places to be.

Wolfinden: British Railways are now going in for a policy of streamlining toilet accommodation at main line stations. There is now one toilet at Temple Meads station for eight platforms and that is underground; think of this in terms of old people, we are an ageing population, women with children, baggage, and handicapped people!

Boyne: There has been some emphasis on economics and that one cannot afford to give a better service, or one cannot afford to pay the men more. In fact there is no other way to get to work except by public transport. The private car is being priced out because one cannot park in the streets and most cannot afford to park in a garage, so Public Transport can charge what they like.

Cherry: Why cannot you have machines on the street for the sale of tokens? There is no need for agents surely, and why does this country not have flat rate fares? We are financing our transport as if it were a producer industry when of course it is a service industry. When I go through a gate to enter the Victoria Line I feel I am a prisoner. If we had fixed rate fares there would be no need for gates.

Lastly, a man driving in a cab with nothing whatever to do, will, from the experiments I have done, face a mental collapse in time. He will be a prisoner and he will be searching for his guilt.

Langdon: A lot of the points just made are ones I would like to be associated with. In Stockholm they use both flat rate and variable ticket systems and they employ advanced methods of probability sampling to check the ticket returns. To get on the Stockholm system you buy the flat rate ticket that controls your entry to the platform. If you travel only where your flat rate applies you come out and that is the end of the matter, so there is no control. Alternatively you can buy a variable price ticket at the booking office, but if you cheat you may get caught in the process of random sampling. It seems to work so they have the best of both worlds.

It is possible to have a system of door entry without steps if one thinks of the kind of transport now in use at airports which have articulated driving units separate from the body, so that the question of wheel arches does not arise.

In terms of the tube system, the Victoria Line is in no doubt our most advanced, but one gets the impression that it is only a Mark 4 and that there is little new thinking that has gone on. The control system may be advanced but the trains and the stations remain unchanged. Platforms are narrow and without seats along the whole length, whereas the Paris Metro has a seat the length of the station. The trains still have this wretched board flooring, which collects cigarette butts between the slots, instead of having a smooth composition floor which can be washed out every day. The steps in the stations are not made with water runways so that they can be washed down and cleaned hygienically. The old watering can system is still used with a broom.

There is still insufficient insulation of noise between the motor system and the coaches; and we do not seem to have thought at all in terms of gas liquid suspension or pneumatic car suspension.

Human communication:
technology and urban planning

by

COLIN CHERRY

ON THE evening of 9 November, 1965, at the height of the rush hour, the City of New York was plunged into total darkness in the twinkling of an eye, together with the whole of North-Eastern United States and the border area of Canada. Why? Because of the breaking of an electric power line in upstate New York. Subway trains instantly stopped. Traffic was soon in chaos, because traffic lights were obliterated. Thousands of people were trapped in sky-scraper elevators (and many of them held there incommunicado). Shops were looted in Harlem. In a very short while mass rioting broke out in Boston and in other cities. All New York airports were blacked out, together with most radio stations. International cable and teleprinter services collapsed. Emergency police and Civil Defence workers were immobilised by the traffic jam. A substantial part of the human race was paralysed and demoralised—by the melting of a wire. 'At his ranch near Johnson City, Texas, President Johnson *kept in close touch with all developments*',* though how he performed that remarkable feat was never revealed. In New York shops the price of hand-torches rose abruptly from $1 to $5.†

New York hangs like a monstrous spider at the end of a long copper thread, whose breaking plunged that city of lights, Lethe-wards into the abyss.

A modern city is a technological artefact that is only just tenable, held together by the skin of its teeth. It is only just possible to transport the million commuters by train, in and out of London daily, because we all know the disastrous effects of a slight fog or a broken rail. Less than 10% of that number of people get in and out by car, by murderous struggle, where they camp out on our streets, poison our air and stun us with noise. In the Los Angeles business district the total area of 'parking lots' is half as big again as the whole area of the streets. A major city can only just feed itself, water itself, clear away its rubbish and its sewage. Law and order are only just maintainable—until apparently a piece of copper melts! It is becoming easier and quicker to fly between countries than to travel between some cities. It is becoming well-nigh impossible to dig a hole in a London street without cutting some pipe or cable; indeed nobody knows where some of them go to, until they are cut and the users squeal. (Sometimes nobody squeals). It only takes a strike, of railwaymen or postmen, or oil delivery-men, to bring it home to people how frail is the structure of our 'technological society', especially in the concentrated artefacts that we call 'big cities'.[1,2,3]

* Italics are mine.
† *Guardian*, 10 Nov., 1965.

This near-untenability of cities is due to more than physical causes, however. For example, they are nearly ungovernable too; computers may come to help them, but how can our Councillors be expected to grasp the immense complexities of inter-related systems?[2] Or, again, at emotional level, many cities are, for many of us, horrible places of ugliness, dirt, stench and noise. Or, again, at moral level; in Bethnal Green, I am told for example, one child in three appears before a magistrate before he is twenty-one years old. But what else can we expect? There is nothing for boys in cities to do that is danger-ous, and at the same time, is legal. Cities are packed with constraints, forbiddings, frustrations, taboos, for the young.

Now, all this may seem no more than diatribe to many of you, but I have hoped this week to hear serious discussion of these sorts of topics and oddly enough, I would like to ask now, in my own language, whether it is relevant to ask this question: is the large city necessary today, or is it becoming an outmoded artefact? In particular, I would like to examine briefly the implications, to this question, of my own field of technology—communications.

Now first, I think it worth noting that the resident population of London has been steadily decreasing for the past 30 years. (See Fig. 1). Commuter traffic too, from south of the Thames, had ceased to grow by 1967. Some forty trainloads a day have been persuaded out of London by the Location of Offices Bureau. Increasing rents of office space in the City have also had some effect. Various social forces have been reducing London's working population, especially clerical and office classes; some 90,000 people per year have been migrating from Greater London, nearly halved by the increased birth-rate.

Now it might seem a piece of fanciful speculation to think that the trends of the Indus-trial Revolution may be reversing—though only at the moment so slowly. But are the *causes* there now, if latent, for this reversal? England is the most urbanised country in the world, with 80% of its people living in urban areas. The so-called Industrial Revolution brought whole populations into the new cities, because shafts and belts machinery forced social collectivisation, and these grew fast in the early Victorian period. As always, the tech-nology of the period was a major determinant of the social structure and today we have the technologies of things like telephones, Telex, data-transmission, computer links, closed circuit television, picture-telegraphy, and a host of electronic systems and heaven knows what in the future, in principle and in principle only, to remove certain constraints which have long existed upon the ways in which we have been free to organise our econo-mic life. Apart from those forms of work which require heavy objects to be moved or large numbers of people to work together on one object in the manufacturing industries, we have an increasing variety of forms of work today which handle that abstract material *information*—messages, documents, data, accounts, filing records, in a host of what I shall refer to now as *clerical operations*; this vague term is roughly to be equivalent to 'office work'.

There seems, to me, to be an urgent field of research to be explored, for I can find little evidence that this is yet being done. This can be described as centring around the general questions: In what ways and to what extents will existing and future information technology affect urban planning? How is this technology likely to replace the movement of people's bodies by movements of their minds? Will this technology lead to major decentralisation of our present urban communities?

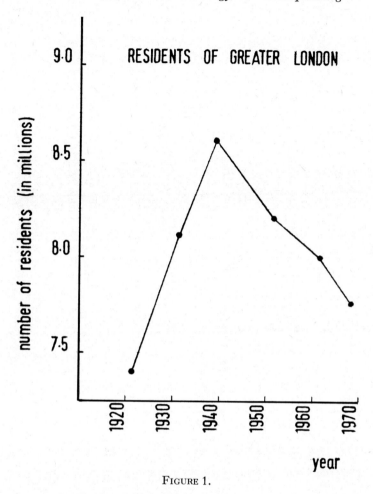

FIGURE 1.

There seems, to me, to be here two forms of study:

(a) Analysis of what has happened already, in our cities, through the adoption of existing techniques (telephone, Telex, closed-circuit television, data-links, and so on).

(b) Theoretical study, or prediction, of what might possibly happen in the future, when existing techniques come into massive use and new ones become introduced that can be physically possible. What are the implications of future possible techniques for *present-day* planning and building?

With regard to this latter, the theoretical study, I should like to ask this audience, in my innocence, whether anything yet is already being done? But, concerning the former (studies of present-day trends), I can find only very few isolated examples. One of these is a study which has been made by the Location of Offices Bureau, of the City of Leeds, which contains some very interesting information.[4] Their Report deals with offices, the sizes of their staffs, and how they had moved their locations over the past 20 years, or expected to move during the next 5 years, with the reasons why, and so on. Now their definition of 'an office' was rather restricted, to cover only 'an establishment in which no-one was engaged in non-office work and physically separated from other forms of establishment', which, of course, is only a small fraction of total office work. Even so, it appears that office staffs have increased by 8% over the past 5 years only.

This Report also points out that modern information technology, including that of computers, is as yet very little used by these white collar classes but, where it is used to some extent, the office staffs number forty or fifty or more only; that is, in larger offices only. This is not surprising, but such staffs total only $5\frac{1}{2}$% of the whole office population of Leeds. If, by some miracle, all the other $94\frac{1}{2}$% of small office staff could be electronically collectivised, how would that situation change? Is there a lesson here, in fact, for future urban planning?

As I have said, there are some slight signs that offices are moving away from London, but many if not most of these are moving out *en bloc*—a whole Head office, or a whole Insurance Office, when they remain there as large collectives, to which their staffs commute. The kind of decentralisation which I envisage now as a theoretical possibility, goes further than this and leaves each individual in his local town, or village, or suburb, or whatever it is, or other local cummunity. Rather than travel to and from his firm's office, he might one day travel to a local centre used, near his town or district, by very many people of other firms and institutions; housed in the local centre would be telephones, Telex desks, facsimile screens, computers and various forms of *terminal equipment* we cannot envisage at the moment, whose usage might be covered by, say, forms of rental. In other words, are we now approaching a time when it is becoming more socially desirable to substitute message-transmission in place of the transport of persons, in a major sector of working life? I fully admit that I cannot now give you the relative economics of this change, but some enquiry that I have made suggests to me that nobody else has done such exercises. If anyone at the Symposium can help me here I shall be most interested, for I feel it to be a matter of urgent co-operative research. This is a far less fanciful suggestion than floating cities, or blocks of flats a mile high, or towns under the sea, or real-estate on the moon.

There are certainly some conclusions to be found in the L.O.B. Report to which I have referred, which support this vision of the future.[4] First, office staffs in Leeds were found to be extremely small, for some 70% of offices employed between only one and ten persons and 93% less than forty persons. It is only above that size of staff that offices begin to use modern data processing and computers and, even then, surprisingly, those offices whose business has a nation-wide sphere of interest use information technology *less* than those with local interests! No doubt all these offices, of all sizes, use that antique instrument, the telephone, with due respect to the Post Office but, as the Report notes, 'the main direct impact of data processing equipment or computers on offices is . . . yet to come'.[4]

Second, it was noted in the Report that offices tend to cluster together in districts according to function (such as Finance, Insurance, Legal, and so on), presumably determined by long traditions and by the need for easy and rapid communication and contact between them. This is supported by the finding that the vast majority of offices still value face-to-face meetings above all the forms of communication, even though the larger proportion of those meetings takes place *out* of the offices, necessitating travel. As I see it, this is reverting to the eighteenth century Coffee House traditions. How might these preferences change as the technologies of communication and information of the next ten years come to be introduced—and as motor traffic congests our streets yet more? It is indeed interesting to note in the Report that the main reason, by far, given for moving offices out of the centre of Leeds into the suburbs is the better car-parking available there (it is not the reduced rents, nor the attraction of staff)!

These and several other points made in the Report support the opinion which I have offered, that, should decentralisation of cities proceed in the future and if advantage be taken of out exploding technology of communication and information, the new patterns might grow, not around office centres serving the various traditional businesses, but around specialised Centres, concerning many industries, where the technology exists, in all its variety even yet to come.

The likelihood of such change coming about will depend upon many developments, technical and social, including the physical constraints of such things as car-parking limitation, increasing rigour of commuting, blocking of streets and others, which would otherwise occur and of course, upon economics. But how does one make such an economic comparison between moving people about and moving their minds? I must admit having little idea, but feel that it should be more deeply explored. But I do not believe it to be wholly an economic matter.

It is, of course, no use basing such an economic estimation upon the existing costs of telecommunication traffic, for it is a fact that, in relation to the value of money, the costs of all modes of telecommunication have continually and steadily reduced, including the postage. The reason for this is that the amount of traffic has steadily increased. As the demands on a given route rise the costs per individual demand reduce. And such developments as I have suggested would require a great increase in our already fast-expanding inland communication network and traffic, and so we must expect greatly reduced costs.

There are, of course, many practical difficulties to these proposals. There are social ones too, because great changes in people's habits would be needed, in the traditions of office life, in uses made of face-to-face meetings and interviews, and so on. One dominant factor may be that cities are, in peace-time, remarkably durable and long-lasting physical things, whereas the various electronic media, whose effects we are considering, have come upon us in changing forms so rapidly as to justify that name: 'a communication explosion'. Furthermore, electronics seems an unlimited source of *new* ideas and methods; they are always putting themselves partly out-of-date. If you wait a little longer, some new method will appear which is better, faster, or more reliable, or cheaper. This has happened now for 25 years.

Some communication techniques are quite old as *ideas* (the telephone, and the telegraph, for instance), but in their case what has exploded is the traffic and their social availability to more and wider classes of people. Although the telephone was invented over a century ago, it has come into massive and wide-spread use only since the end of the Second World War—especially in international use as we have seen this week. The diagrams here shown, illustrate this 'communication explosion' (Figs. 2 and 3). The Telex has spread perhaps faster than any, although in idea it is an adaptation of the old-fashioned telegraph.

By contrast, traditional building has been remarkably steady and permanent. Buildings are long-lasting things. It is true, tall building techniques have undergone a radical

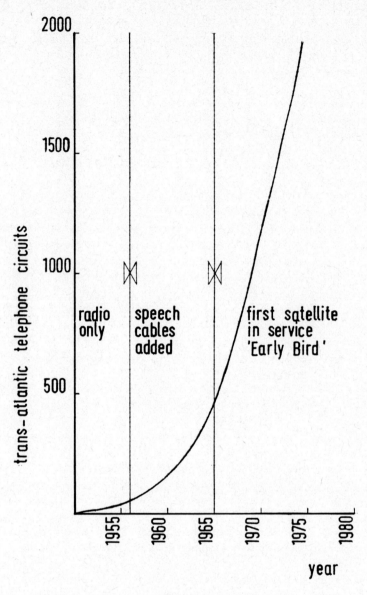

FIGURE 2.

change since the War but, with due respect, I do not think that these changes of technique approach the revolutionary changes and innovations in electronics. Just consider for a moment: radio broadcasting sprang upon the world in 1922, it was an utterly new concept; then it was only 15 years later that the world's first television service started. Then, after the War, we inherited such things as radar, microwave beams and other new concepts for international telephony. Computers appeared in the 1940's: cybernetics, automatic control, satellites, data-transmission, and many others, all within some 15

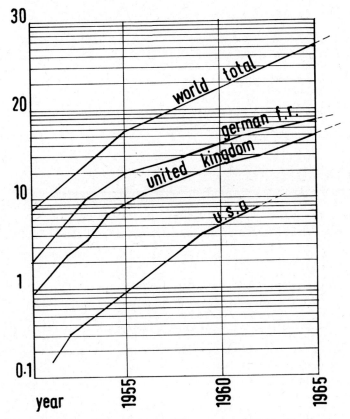

FIGURE 3. The Rapid Post-War Growth of International Telex Traffic (incoming and outgoing). With acknowledgements to the British Post Office.

years and whole new industries have been born in this time. What is going to happen in the next 15 years I cannot predict.

Dr. Edmund Leach Provost of King's College, Cambridge, recently remarked upon the long-lasting nature of towns and cities in a speech before the Town Planning Institute, in London, when he said:* 'Our trouble is that so many of the main features of our man-made environment are so infernally long-lasting. They survive long after the institutional arrangements which called them into being have ceased to exist, and what can a planner do then?' He pointed out the moral: that 'Whatever the planner may do, one thing is quite certain: he is designing the slums and the architectural white elephants of the future'.

There seems to me here to be no criticism of architects and builders as people, or as a profession, but a comment rather upon the permanence of materials and perhaps upon the natural human adherence to those monumental aspects of our visual environment which establish people's identities and feelings, especially for those of social stability.

This sheer solidity and permanence of urban environments in the past must have been one of the major constraints upon many of our social institutions; we have had to conduct

* 20 Nov., 1968. With kind permission. See Ref. (5).

our affairs in such and such a way because we have had buildings, streets, or factories, prisons, railways, schools and many other long-lasting artefacts. I think it is a sad comment upon our civilisation that our understanding of the physical world, and our progress in technology, has far out-stripped our understanding of our social institutions —and yet it is the products of the first, science and technology, that produce our physical environment, which itself is the impediment to evolutionary changes in our social institutions. We may desperately want to modify our environments, often drastically, or urgently, yet it seems easier to fly round the moon—nor can we necessarily predict the social and institutional consequences of such environmental changes.

To me, as a layman, one of the hopeful signs today is the steadily growing element of *flexibility* in architecture and town-planning and building techniques, because designers and planners are taking increased notes of many new technologies, especially that of new materials. Continual adaptation and modification to existing buildings is now more possible and cheaper. I feel this idea of evolution is coming in more readily. To make my house warmer, I didn't need to burn it down and start again. I had a heating system fitted. Walls can be moved, ceilings lowered and raised, ventilation can be changed, elevators installed, kitchens refitted and so on. In the streets too, closed circuit television can now permit traffic light schedules to change according to the road traffic demands;* pedestrians can stop the traffic and cross the road (with a delay of about 15 seconds); we may soon see travellators, adjustable traffic lanes, and other techniques for permitting flexible changes in our urban environment according to the changing needs, sometimes even hour to hour. In such ways we may slowly break some of the constraints imposed by our environment upon our social institutions and habits. Yet far more than mere flexibility of this kind will be needed to permit us to change many of our major social institutions. Nevertheless, this 'technology of flexibility' does remove some of the more serious constraints upon our living that the solidity and long-lasting nature of traditional architecture has forced in the past. We may socially adapt today in change a little more readily without destroying *all* symbolic values of traditional building.

The rigidity and permanence of traditional environments may not only restrict what people are able to do and how they can arrange their affairs, but also, and more important, restrict what they may *think* of wanting to do. I have sometimes heard it argued by architects and town planners that our citizens should not be given what they want, but what they *need*. The moral justification for this apparently dictatorial attitude has, in the past, been that 'the public' is never the originator of new ideas, but that all creativity, and all invention, arises from the insight of specific individuals. With that view I would agree. Certainly in my own sphere of technology, the new inventions have not been the result of public demand. The demand has grown, often explosively, sometimes after a delay, only after innovation. Thus railways, telephones, radio, public libraries and all other modes of communication were the fruits of the labour of specific individuals. All progress comes from the departure of certain individuals from the norms of his society; and I think it was Johnson who said 'all great truths begin as heresies'. All innovation is an act of courage.

Nevertheless, as time passes and as educational standards rise so rapidly, what we call 'the public' will become increasingly *critical*. That is the point. I am not suggesting that everyone will become an inventor or innovator, but become a more severe critic.

* For example, at some London street junctions, or in the Mersey Tunnel.

A man living in a pre-technological society, with no division of labour, his whole life spent upon the struggle of keeping alive, having no choices or controls over his own fate, may have no knowledge of his own separate existence, anymore than does a codfish. If you cannot have a thought of an individual kind, you cannot have the thought of acting upon it. With division of labour and the development of technology, his freedom of action being increased, his powers of *choice* are more available. Such things as *decisions* must be made, and *awareness* of constraints become more clear; people then demand their '*rights*'; they can *refuse, protest, criticise, object*, and adopt many other social values.

This in principle only; I am certainly not saying that the specific forms of our own technological society today are good or bad, or that the constraints which its technology has removed today, and the freedoms introduced, are good or bad, or better or worse. I am saying only that, in an existential sense, it is in the nature of Technology that it controls certain constraints upon the ways we can *act*, can *think* and can *feel*.

Let me take this point of view further, for I believe it to be very important. The existentialist thinker, Heidegger, saw technology for what it really is—it is 'mediator between man and raw nature'. It is essentially a *mediator*. Basically, it is the means whereby I come to form my own view of the physical world, of my relations to it and to other people. Who I feel myself to be, what I am like, what are my powers, what is my freedom of thought and action, my social relationships, my morals, all depend upon the various technologies, freedoms of action, which I possess.

I have used the word 'Technology' a good deal, but I am using it here in its broadest sense.

Academically speaking, the fields which we name 'Architecture', 'Art', and 'Technology', have developed to a large extent independently and in Britain we have many Schools of each. This historical separation, however, I think is due not to any inherent distinction between the fields as human activity, but is more due to the social history and traditions. All deal with men's created artefacts. It is my view that this schism is becoming more meaningless every day. Architecture and all the arts have a certain common feature in their natures; in the proper sense of the word all are modes of 'Technology'—that is, the creation of artefacts—and the creation of artefacts of unlimited forms and variety is an essential component of human nature. Man is the artefact maker and user *par excellence*. All 'Technology', in this correct sense of the word is both *useful* and *expressive* and the relation between these two is what we call 'design'.

It is in this sense, then, that I use the word 'Technology' here, as an all-embracing term to cover the useful Arts, Architecture, Town Planning, Landscaping and all the other subjects which have been discussed this week. Note that, according to this definition which I have adopted, Technology also embraces *Law*!

I would then hope to see the values of my own Technology (Communication) brought to the service of architecture and environmental planning by providing increasing flexibility, adaptability and choice and to this end far more research should be done, with collaboration between Architects and Town Planners and Communication Engineers, in order to seek out the ways in which our exploding technology of communication of all kinds that we have talked about this week—telephones, data-transmission, closed circuit television, computers . . . (what next?) may remove constraints upon our traditional modes of building, living and working, and so of thinking and of feeling. We need collaborative research.

The rigid long-lasting aspects of our urban environments may perhaps become things of the past, but it may well be that some forward thinkers are envisaging something other than flexibility, adaptability and personal choice—that is some people may be thinking of 'throw-away' cities. I must admit that sudden and total destruction and replacement of whole large-scale environments frightens me very much, for it could well mean a destruction of part of myself.

This is not to say that certain elements or even whole artefacts should not be destroyed —if economic constraints permit. Thus 'throw-away' technology has rapidly entered the field of electronics, because the cost of highly-skilled service men is too high; motor cars too reach a limit of repair. But I feel very anxious, myself, about the 'throw-away' city, or other *gross* environments. 'Throw-away' buildings? Yes, some of them; it does seem necessary, if certain social changes are to be made. With due respect, most Town Halls would well be blown up; most prisons too, if the pattern of punishment and treatment has to be changed. Many old school buildings constrain the modes of education; many old hospitals handicap introduction of new medical techniques, and the like.

The one class of social institution which seems to me to be most constrained by the rigidity of traditional environments is that which might be termed 'our pattern of work' —our daily routine, in industrial countries, that we come to accept, of commuting, of starting and leaving hours, day and night shifts, regular meal-times, division of life into 'Work' and 'Leisure', the chaos of rush-hour, the weekend ritual, the summer holiday habit; something that has come to seem part of Nature's intentions to those people living in urban areas. To end my talk I should like to speculate upon the implications of Telecommunication technology for the future of this routine work-life pattern of civilised countries in urban areas and upon our own environments.

We are no longer ruled by the rise and set of the sun, nor by the seasons coming and going, nor by sowing and lambing, nor by the harvest. We are ruled, in so-called 'advanced', countries, by two major obsessions: these are the clock and the news, and my own technology has been partly responsible for both obsessions. However, I would like to leave the second here—that is the over-pressure of news, and consider only that tyrant, the clock.

Figure 4 shows, in a very naïve way, what I will call the 'vicious circle of modern life', this regular pattern so characteristic of urban life. Let us break in at one point—say, that called: 'the Division of Labour'. The arrows indicate the verb 'requires'. Thus the division of labour in industrial life 'requires' related human activities, which 'requires' predictions as to when one's colleagues will be available, or materials there, shops open, trains available, etc., but that 'requires' prepared time tables and schedules (i.e. a clock enters) and that 'requires' programmed transport for people and goods, which 'requires' people to be collected into factories or offices, which 'requires' our traditional pattern of working life, which then 'requires' . . . the division of labour . . . and round we go in circles. We seem to be caught in this vicious circle.

Can our modern communication technology help break this vicious circle, not totally but helping to lead to decentralisation, more flexible living patterns, and increased choice? At present perhaps, very little—but then any attempt to revolutionise routines of work would lead to the strike of the century. But I feel that there are two broad qualities of the technology which we are discussing which will soon loosen the vicious circle and lead to radically changed urban traditions.

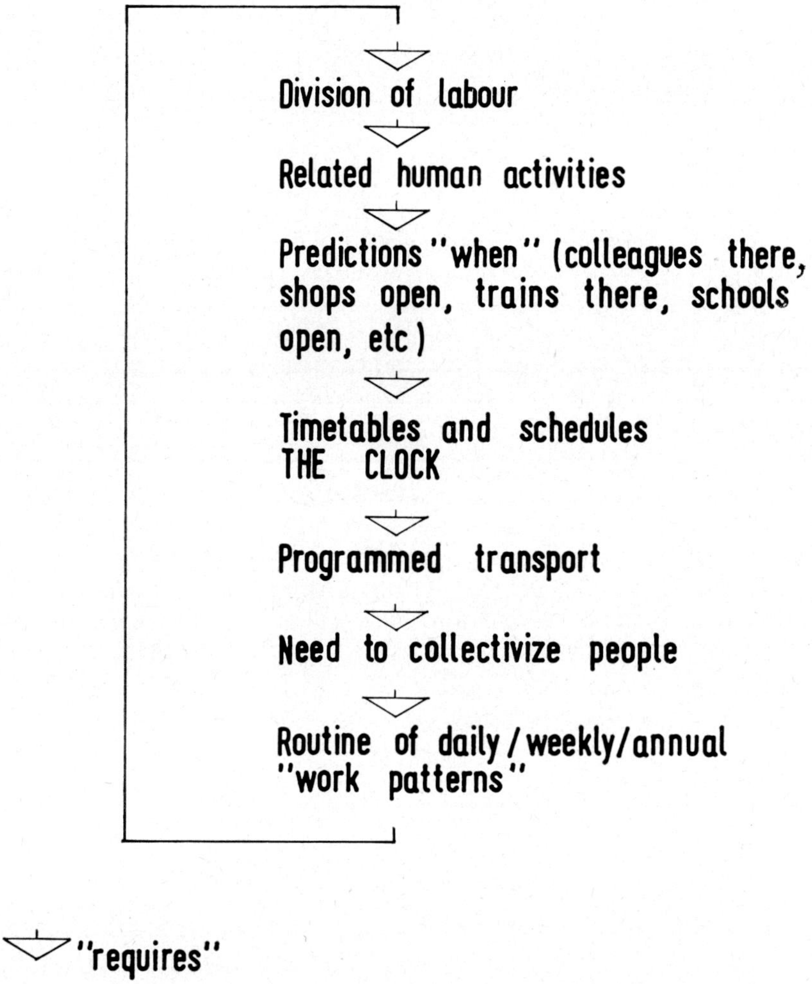

Division of labour

Related human activities

Predictions "when" (colleagues there, shops open, trains there, schools open, etc)

Timetables and schedules
THE CLOCK

Programmed transport

Need to collectivize people

Routine of daily / weekly/annual "work patterns"

▽ "requires"

FIGURE 4. The Vicious Circle of Modern Life.

There is first the obvious fact that persons and institutions at different places, but who are connected together by communication are, in certain respects, literally 'mapped together'. But they are together only so far as the particular type of communication permits. Thus, the telephone brings people together in voice only and, of course, the primary value of the telephone has enabled people to move, to travel, yet remain 'at home'—but the new 'video conference telephone' may bring people together in sight and sound. Data-links, closed circuit television and other techniques relate distant persons into common co-ordinated action, or in other different ways. This kind of telecommunication has been evolving for a hundred years—changing the shape and size of the world; it has permitted people, as I say, to travel with security and yet remain, in mind, at home. It has to a great extent separated bodies and minds. It will continue to develop, bringing us more complete and better images, sight and sound, and make human dispersal more possible and more endurable.

Nevertheless, as was remarked upon before, it is still face-to-face meeting which seems by far the most popular method of communication at the present day, within the industrial class of people whom we call 'office workers'. But this may change as future telecommunication research steadily improves and extends means of inter-person communication, and cheapens it. What I would plead for here is more research into future possibilities, to examine the principles and likely consequences of this movement of *minds*, by conceivable physical practical modes of telecommunication, to replace the present movements of bodies. The movement of bodies continues to expand and I am thinking not only of the daily commuting traffic, in and out of cities, but of possible reduction of motor car transport of persons between offices and other institutions.

The Location of Offices Bureau has commented in their report upon this present-day tendency, pointing out that, in their study of office location in Leeds, there was already evidence that face-to-face contacts were easier and more popular in the suburbs, where less traffic congestion and better car parking facilities exist.[4] The Report adds: 'Tele-communications have become increasingly important in the field of office communications, and allow a greater degree of dispersal than would otherwise be possible. Indeed, much of the functional clustering may well, to some extent, be a relic of Victorian times rather than a present day necessity, although no-one would dispute the convenience of close proximity for face-to-face contact.' The Report notes that large-scale decentralisation is *at present* not practical, though the values of modern communication have hardly yet been felt; it adds 'the implications of automatic data processing in this context (are) immense'.

It is the welter of implications offered by present-day and future telecommunication media that is important for radical changes in our patterns of living and, presumably, future planning. It is not so much study of existing cities and the changes therein, actual field work, that I am pleading for, but rather long-term academic, theoretical, studies of *what* present-day constraints may be removed and how we could conceivably adapt to them, and in what ways systematic flexibility could be introduced into design. In other words I would ask this audience of mixed disciplines: is it of value now for town planning research to have far closer association with long-range communication research? I cannot speak for the former field, but can say that the latter field has already gone very far.

So much for the first quality offered by telecommunication—the freeing of distance and mobility constraints.

Secondly, a new quality has become introduced by the fact that we have recently developed many techniques of message *storage*—storage of the human voice, of the face, of pictures, diagrams, of data, numbers . . . in increasing ways, storages which can be done in greater quantities and more cheaply every year. The broad effect of such message storage is that time can be 'suspended' and, in specific ways, we are now just that much released from the tyranny of the clock. We have, too, ever-increasing ways of duplicating and recording, which spread in scale from those used in the home to those of high-capacity centralised computers. But our ways of living, our institutions have yet far to go to adapt to these new liberties. I will just mention one, familiar to everyone—the Telex. The great value of the Telex service today is that it types received messages, without an attendant, so that the sender may be at work when the receiver at the other end is still in bed—and can read it the next morning. The world's largest airways and news services are reliant upon such services, being the most globally dispersed industries in history.

Certain excellent media of information storage we have had with us for five-hundred years—which we call printed *books*—and their numbers and circulations increase fast every year, including library loaning. The fundamental liberty introduced by that technology was of course that facts, beliefs, ideas, decisions, created at one moment in time could have their consequences felt at a later moment, which is 'time suspension'. We now have other techniques, the punched tape, magnetic computer matrix, television tape recorders and Heaven knows what in the future. In principle, these storage techniques should assist our powers of organising various aspects of economic life, because the correlated activities of people engaged upon a common enterprise does not require their being together either in time or space.

I would not, of course, for one moment, minimise the immense human problems involved in trying to break away from this dictatorial rule of the clock. Nor am I trying here to tell anybody anything. Rather, am I asking questions. What has been done to examine such social implications of data and message storage? At present we have such elementary, though useful, techniques as the recording telephone which can take down or read out a message when one party is in bed or away. But how far can this principle be taken?

Returning to Fig. 4, the point in this 'vicious circle' at which this technology of time-suspension may break in to loosen it is that which has been called: *'predictions when'*. I am thinking now, not merely of 'office work', but of schools and colleges and everything else, with their increasing use of tape-recordings, recorded T.V. lessons and lectures, and various audio-visual aids and use made by broadcasting; in shops too, and other economic institutions. If the 'vicious circle' can be loosened at that point, not broken but *loosened*, then the consequence could bear upon the next steps in the circle, leading to more flexibility in time tables and schedules, less peaked transport and some further decentralisation of our cities.

I have referred to the two specific powers offered us by communication and information technology, which will rapidly grow during the next decade. First, increased flexibility of spacial location of people's related activities; second, increased freedom from constraints of the clock. We must expect this technology increasingly to develop and improve both of these liberties, and so to free us increasingly from the constraints of both *geography* and *time*. How our social habits and institutions will adapt, in practice, remains to be seen, but, of course, adapt they will. As these liberties are found to exist they will be demanded by the public as their rights. Exactly what effects they will have upon our future cities can only be speculated upon, but it seems clear to me that they will encourage not the building up, but the breakdown of major cities and redistribute the social classes. The first class to be affected is likely to be those termed in the present day 'white collar workers'—though certainly not all of them. Another class of people who are already feeling some impact of this are those concerned with education. Certainly schools, colleges and training institutions require people to collectivise, but their organisations may become more flexible, and we are already beginning to see this in T.V. education. At present we use radio and T.V. to some extent, but the full values for education have hardly begun.

We are regularly being urged, by Authority today, to 'stagger our hours of work' and so reduce the worst excesses of urban existence—including, of course, the ritual of meal-times and the rush-hours. Unfortunately, life is such an intermingled complex of habits and institutions that this is far from easy. But as possibilities come to be seen, so they will be wanted and demanded. But there is one over-riding constraint upon their realisation—I think that is the existence of night and day. We wish to sleep at night and live by day.

A major part of that day is spent by many people inside factories and offices, where they live like troglodytes, where it might as well *be* night time and dark outside. Windows or skylights? Yes; but, for example, who likes to be forced indoors and tempted out by windows? To me, looking through a window is tantalising and I am frustrated being indoors. If I look outside I want to *be* outside, if it is beautiful there, in any weather, wet or fine. But in my own London office, eleven floors up, what do I see if I gaze outside? The beauties of Earls Court, a great slug of a building, surrounded by all the grey mess of West London. What do I do? I draw the blinds and put the light on.

So long as I live I shall never forget my first schoolroom with its large windows, just above eye level, which offered tantalising glimpses of nature outside, the wide sky, and the tops of a few trees and nought else—built with the false idea that this increased boys' attention to their slates. Many windows frustrate us, though not all.

Windowless buildings we have discussed. But if we do away with windows in many types of buildings, then there is nothing to look at anyway. So why not blow a great hole in the ground, and drop our buildings there? Are we approaching a time when a substantial part of buildings can be buried underground? Not the whole living spaces, but those in many offices, factories, car parks and other work-places, together with things like bedrooms, in which daylight is of minimal value, thereby leaving more surface of the earth for Nature's purposes? We are scarcely free to excavate great holes below the streets of London and many other cities, I must admit, but could we not consider doing so, if we are forced to build other such concentrated collectives on virgin soil—say the 'new towns'?

To conclude, I hope this paper will not be taken as impudence by Architects and Town Planners. As I said earlier, my aim has not been to tell anybody anything; rather I have tried to pose a number of questions, the answers to which have direct bearing upon my own Technology. In summary, Architects and Town Planners have increasingly overlapped their work with Civil Engineering and Mechanical Engineering; but to what extent are they considering the implications in the future of that most prolific and versatile technology of all time—namely—Electronic Engineering?

REFERENCES

1. WILLMOTT, PETER. (1966). *Adolescent boys of East London*, Routledge & Kegan Paul, London.
2. MAY, JOHN. *Living in cities*, Penguin Books.
3. H.M.S.O. The Buchanan Report, *Traffic in Towns*, (abbreviated edition).
4. FACEY, M. V. & SMITH, G. B. (Jan. 1968). Offices in a Regional Centre (a Study of Office Location in Leeds), Location of Offices Bureau, Res. Rep. No. 2.
5. LEACH, EDMUND. (Jan. 1965). Planning and evolution, *Journal Town Planning Inst.*, **55**, No. 1.

Discussion

Burberry: How does one make economic comparison of moving people about and moving minds about? A cheap day return from Bristol to London costs £2 0s. 0d. and the peak rate telephone is somewhere between 8 seconds and 12 seconds for 6d., so £2 0s. 0d. gives us 10 minutes on the telephone. Compare what British Railways do for this; they provide lighting and heating and comfortable seats, for a period of several hours, whereas we can only enjoy the benefits of the telephone line for a matter of a few minutes.

Cherry: When you are sitting in the train, you can certainly work but you are not in communication, and you might as well be at home or in your office. I am a little unhappy that we compare existing costs because the cost of message traffic may rapidly reduce.

Whyte: The economic comparison which has been made only allows you to go to London for a day. If you conduct your business by telecommunication, you can spend time in London, New York, and Sydney, all in one working day.

Nealon: Moving offices out from the centre of things has been mentioned. Young people want to be in the hub of things to meet other young people in the course of their work. Young married women want to be in a place where they can do their household shopping in the lunch time. There are many reasons for being together and if offices are moved out there will be difficulty in getting people to work in them.

Cherry: The conceptual idea is to create centres in local communities, where the apparatus of communication is available for people who are each involved in different industries and businesses and in different types of work. New types of social relationship will build up.

Floyd: About this business of flexibility. Because buildings have been around for several hundred years, they are regarded as being more inflexible than the lines of communication. But they are more not less flexible. They are built in smaller units, and they are more easily knocked down, or altered, than are the lines of communication, which tend to look upon as flexible but which are, in fact, most inflexible.

Redfern: Services generally are more expensive to move and re-route because of the property problems which they raise. Indeed port installations, airports, docks, and so on and so forth, are much more difficult things to move than are buildings themselves.

We have not touched on the question of new materials and new techniques in building which have to do with the method of financing buildings which is quite different from the method of financing telecommunications. You can only find finance to buy a house if it is built of brick and has a traditional roof and all because of the method of financing that exists. So, we have a situation where the only really forward thinking which is happening in the building industry is in the public sector. Even there we have to borrow money over 60 years, so these methods of financing are now having a terrific effect on the development of new techniques.

Cherry: I do not understand what you mean about communication being inflexible; you do not take it up and move it somewhere else. The communication system has been in the form of trunk routes carrying telephone traffic only, but it now carries everything. The future system will be by beams which will carry everything.

Burberry: Roads could quite easily be moved, but the thing which prevents it are the buildings which are all around it. While one of these can be knocked down quite easily, it would take many years to knock them all down in order to put our roads in new positions. This is why road patterns still follow the Roman arrangements. They have been most superbly flexible devices and have enabled us to put sewers and cables into them and buses along them, but the various technologies are out of step. Communication technology is moving quite fast, but building technology is fairly static and the time scale of operation is different. The motor car congests the streets, which were built before the motor car was thought of, and one day the motor car will have been forgotten. The problems in this field cannot be solved until these technologies are in better alignment.

Loten: Another constraint is the legal constraint. As soon as you start dispersing property you are up against the Law of Property, which is probably the most inflexible and the most conservative element in our society.

Hutchinson: A great deal of information has been developed in association with transportation studies on the behaviour of cities. The University of Michigan has developed a method of plugging in various assumptions about technology, assumptions about sociology, and so on, into an urban model to see what sort of urban form would come out.

Medhurst: Throw away cities; we have had railway closures and other sorts of closure and the logical next step is town closures because, some towns are in the wrong place. But we have no method of 'unplanning'. This is a completely new discipline that we have yet to learn of 'planned obsolescence'; 'unplanned obsolescence' gives us slums. What we need now is to develop a discipline of planned obsolescence.

Moxley: Human beings are going to be the same for the next thousand years. They are going to want identity, they are going to want stimulation, they are going to want security, and so on. I imagine that our new formed development is going to take account of this in some way.

The human aspects of urban transport

A. COBLENTZ

(Translated by R. Bolster)

MOST LARGE modern cities have serious traffic difficulties: the existing means of public transport are overloaded and the streets can no longer satisfactorily absorb the movement and the parking of private cars. It is easy to see that these difficulties will increase in the coming decades, due to population growth, to the development of individual mobility, to the increase in leisure time and especially to the rapid urbanisation which can be observed in all developed countries. If urgent steps are not taken, transport services will decline, whole economies will suffer, and living conditions in cities will become more and more unpleasant.

Whereas most problems raised by human transport in cities can be solved by appropriate technical progress, it is nevertheless true that in the final analysis what must be satisfied is *the wants and demands of people*, not those of some material entity with no subjective reactions. Other speakers, present here, are more qualified than I to treat the technological aspects of the problem. I shall therefore limit myself to the psycho-sociological aspects of human transport in towns, and in particular *human needs and demands in the field of public transport.*

It is, however, clear that, given the limits of this paper, I shall only be able to scratch the surface of this vast problem. I shall dwell particularly on the gaps in our knowledge and on the points where a new approach is necessary.

Present day transport difficulties in urban zones prevent town dwellers from fully enjoying the economic and social advantages offered them. For the inhabitants of our modern cities can no longer use their leisure time, easily see their friends, follow cultural and educational activities in the way they would wish to, choose freely from a wide selection of jobs and homes. The excessive distance covered by the commuter causes loss of time and tiredness such that he has no longer the possibility or even the desire to devote himself to recreational activities, even if these could be indulged in near his home. Moreover, the lack of comfort in existing public transport often causes a transfer of demand towards the private car which, in turn, increases traffic difficulties (including those experienced by buses, taxis, etc.) This is the beginning of a process which it is difficult to stop and which on the one hand results in a move away from public transport —and consequently prevents any improvement in its comfort due to the economic loss caused—and on the other hand increases journey times because of growing traffic density.

With this in mind, two elements—which are partly contradictory—must be studied without delay by public authorities if it is wished,
  first:
to avoid an aggravation of the problem;
  second:
to find a solution to it.
These two elements are:
1. Determination of human wants and demands in the field of urban transport;
2. Improvement of public transport so as to attract to it as much as possible of the travelling public.

Although a certain number of motivation studies have already been undertaken in numerous countries and although they have used increasingly sophisticated methods—such as the 'Delphi' questionnaire given to qualified experts whose views should enable one to base reasoned theories—the fact is that the needs of city-dwellers are not yet clearly enough known to serve as a foundation for long term plans. Whereas it is relatively easy to foresee total demand for a medium or a long term, it is however extremely difficult to foresee the demand of each individual method of transport. This demand will depend on external factors:—existing means of transport, speed and comfort of the different methods of transport, etc., and on internal factors: the attitude and behaviour of the user, . . . demands of a subjective nature. Assessment of these personal factors is the most difficult. It is therefore in this field that research should be encouraged. Up to now the traditional methods of interview or questionnaire have not shown themselves to be either efficient or satisfactory. Some qualitative elements have been defined, and that is all. And the limits of these qualitative elements must be stressed: my own experience enables me to say that it is very difficult—if not impossible—for a man or a woman to imagine himself or herself in a situation which he or she has not previously experienced.

In this respect, two years ago in France I directed an enquiry into the advantages of providing homes with a second living-space, that is, a children's play-room which could, if necessary, become a multi-purpose room, a rest-room, etc., in short, a room whose function was not definitely fixed and which could be varied by adapting itself to the evolution of the family. Half of the inquiries were carried out in homes which already had a second living-space, and the other half in homes of traditional type. It was quite easy to get those already having a second living-space to comment on this arrangement, but very difficult to get comments, opinions and criticisms from those living in traditional-type homes. The latter group—even when they belonged to a high social and professional category—could not be precise about the possible use they would make of a room they had never possessed.

To return to our main problem, I should like to say something about the studies which would be needed in order to assess the wishes and the needs of transport users.

As for individual needs, these appear through likings, preferences and desires expressed as well as through a judgement made on the existing situation and expressing the degree of satisfaction with this situation. But there is an element which does not always appear explicitly: that of the financial sacrifice which would be accepted to satisfy the need. So one must try to determine not only the needs, but also the acuteness of these needs. For this, the best information will be collected by providing those supplying answers with *clearly stated alternatives* and by using the results of the inquiries with the help of attitude scales (Guttman's scales for instance), which make it possible to establish a hierarchy of needs and consequently an order of priority.

In this respect it must be pointed out that we do not know to what extent the satisfaction of needs leads to the appearance of new needs, and *a priori*, we do not know the means of discerning these latent needs, as yet unknown, even to those who will later feel them. As for the needs of a community—which can differ greatly from individual wishes—they can be determined in space and time. In space, taking into account the number of persons to be satisfied, their dispersion in the town, etc; in time, taking into account the foreseeable evolution of the community, from the point of view of its mobility, of its structure, of the social and economic advantages which can be gained. These factors are relatively easy to measure in function of overall forecasts and long term political orientations. On the other hand, no existing method can be considered satisfactory for the measuring of the evolution of attitudes and for the foreseeing of the sudden changes which sometimes happen in the life of a society.

I do not claim to be able to provide the key which would make possible the definition of a new method of approach. On this question it is desirable to initiate discussions participated in by specialists in different fields, specialists aware of the limits of existing investigation methods.

These specialists—town planners, architects, transport authorities, etc.—are those who shape cities, and for this reason they can play an educational role and orientate certain needs, for human psychology is, to a great extent, ready for innovations. But the danger is great: planners are permanently exposed to the temptation to modify the desires and the concepts of others by obliging them to adopt their own. The personal wishes of these planners should not replace those of the community for which they are planning.

In spite of these contradictions, it is indispensable to orientate real and latent needs of urban transport towards *public transport*. Why? Because, for a given number of people to transport, a public transport vehicle occupies infinitely less space than the private cars which would be necessary to transport the same number of people. In fact, it is a case of giving priority to the *transport of people* instead of giving it to the transport of vehicles. As concerns community needs—which, in this case, are opposed to individual needs—there is no choice left. The giving of priority to public transport in existing towns—and especially in central zones—is a necessity, if general asphyxia is to be avoided. So it is starting from a well-defined general orientation—the giving of priority to public transport—that one must try to determine needs.

I cannot, within the framework of this paper, dwell on the deep psychological reasons which have made the majority of inhabitants of developed countries use private cars extensively. Many works have been written on this subject. So I shall abstain from comment on urban transport needs as far as private cars are concerned.

On the basis of the fundamental and necessary decision to give maximum support to public transport in its struggle against individual transport, so as to ensure satisfactory urban living conditions, two solutions are open to public authorities: either to impose such restrictions on the movement of private cars that the use of public transport would become obligatory, or to improve public transport to the point where city-dwellers would use it spontaneously for most of their travelling. It is probable that reality will place itself half-way between these two solutions. However, one can briefly examine the needs which would have to be satisfied in order that the demand should turn essentially to public transport.

The need for transport is not an end in itself, but rather a means of satisfying other needs (mobility, convenience, security, speed, and so on). Consequently, journeys must be easy, fast, considerably less costly than transport in private vehicles, which are dependable, comfortable, and so on.

The transport networks must be dense so as to avoid walking-distances of more than about 400–500 metres; the service must be dependable, that is to say it must have a constant frequency and duration time so that users can travel at the required time and knowing in advance the time their journey will take.

It is difficult to determine the order of priority of the factors, for this order may have slight differences and variations. Different studies have been made and have led to differing conclusions. In fact it seems that the problem to be solved is a total problem. The solution of one of its factors will not be enough.

However, going by the results of the inquiries undertaken in various countries to define the factors influencing choice of transport method, one observes that the two essential elements to be considered are speed and convenience. As for the cost, its importance tends to diminish as the standard of living rises: to quote a precise case a study carried out in the Paris region has shown that if public transport were free this fact would have little influence on the choice of a large part of the population.

If one examines the problem of journey duration closely, one must stress the fact that the important factor is not the time spent in the vehicles but the total duration of the journey, from starting point to point of arrival. This duration includes the time spent:

First—going to the station or the bus-stop.

Second—movement inside stations, getting into the vehicle, going from one vehicle to another.

Third—awaiting the vehicle's arrival.

Fourth—travelling in the vehicle.

Fifth—leaving the arrival station and going—generally on foot—to the point of arrival.

I think it unnecessary to remind you of the conditions in which these different operations are now carried out: the long distances between home and stations or bus-stops, waits which can be long—especially in the suburbs—between one train or bus and the next, the long duration of the journey itself because of very frequent stopping, the slowness of movement when leaving crowded stations, and so on.

But the conditions in which are carried out the different operations I have just mentioned are above all due to the fact that the population is progressively less willing to accept inconvenience and discomfort, being given that there is an improvement in other aspects of life such as comfort in the home, in motor-cars, in work places, in places of recreation, etc., and being given that information develops feelings of frustration in those using public transport.

More often than not the traveller has to put up with bad weather on his way to the station or bus-stop; when waiting at the station or the bus-stop he can still be exposed to the weather, also to crowding and discomfort; the journey inside the vehicle often obliges him to remain standing, with little room to move, and feeling the unpleasant effects of acceleration and deceleration. All this has harmful consequences not only of physiology, but also of psychological strain. The irregularity, slowness and inconvenience of urban transport cause the commuter to feel fatigue, anxiety and irritability which directly influence his work performance, his health and his social behaviour in general.

Technically it is possible to increase effectively the quality of services, provided a great effort is made in the field of research and development. The rail bus 'vehicle guide bi-modal'[1] can, for example, combine the comfort and flexibility of the private car with the frequency and the regularity of the underground. In coming years other means of transport will be experimented with in laboratories and then demonstrated practically. But one must not lose sight of the fact that short or medium term improvements in the comfort—in the widest sense—of urban transport will come essentially from a more efficient application of already available techniques. In this way it should, for example, be possible to improve bus transport by means of reserved lanes, by giving priority at intersections, by regulation in 'real time', etc.

Let us imagine we can have an urban public transport network with all the required qualities: dependability, comfort, speed. If this were to be the case, who would not say that he would stop using his personal car for journeys within the city? In any case, it is certain that a great number of users would cease to make certain journeys in their private car. That is both the solution of the problem and the problem itself. It is the *solution* of the problem in the sense that it is not so much a case of studying the open or hidden wishes of the public, its attitudes or its motivation, things which for a long time yet we will only be able to approach quite theoretically, as of studying economic, cultural, family, professional and even physiological needs which things are quite measurable. It is a *problem* in the sense that the only thing left to be solved is the principal one, namely: the creation of a public transport system possessing all the required qualities.

For, I believe, that there is no doubt about the desirable criteria for a good urban transport network. It is no good getting lost in subjective considerations—so varied and complex that decades of research are still needed before one can even approach them scientifically—when the problem to be solved is extremely urgent. It is better to orientate immediate research towards the evident, common sense needs of modern city-dwellers. This is a real step towards the solution of the problem, instead of theorising about the deep reasons behind the creation of needs, their variability, etc.

In this respect, and to show you the complexity of any fundamental study of the subjective aspects of human behaviour as concerns transport, I am going to give you a brief description of need, as currently defined: 'Need is the state of being relative to what is necessary to him or to that which seems desirable to him'. One sees already that this definition excludes new needs which might arise from future technological innovations.

To continue:

Needs are aroused—by the state or an organism
                —by man's thinking about his condition
                —by the pressures of the natural and social environment which both imposes norms and proposes objects for consumption, for needs can be manipulated by publicists as well as by planning experts. As long as a basic minimum is concerned— although it must be stressed how relative this term is due to the differences between one country and another, or even one region and another—needs are identical from one individual to another. Beyond a certain point, these needs vary according to:

—the personality of individuals
—their age
—their socio-professional category
—their cultural milieu
—the immediate environment
—geographical factors
—weather.

They can be classed in different categories (gregarious needs, the need 'to be recognised', etc.). The need may be financially reasonable or not, legitimate or harmful. It can also be felt as a state of lack, of dissatisfaction or anxiety without the thing desired being consciously perceived. This thing may be close at hand or far away. In the latter case the need can be even stronger because of its imprecision. Finally, the same object can have both a utilitarian and a symbolic value (the motor-car for example). Awareness of a need arises either from the influence of other needs, or from conditioning.

As far as the community is concerned, it can be seen that the proportion of people within a group who want a modification of the situation in which they find themselves —that is to say, they feel a precise need—contributes to a characterisation of the group. When this proportion is high, one can estimate that individually felt need is that of the whole group.

The size of the modifications to be made to the situation of the group to achieve the expressed needs depends on the dimension and the structure of the community.

Using this very shortened definition of individual need and collective need, it is easy to see the difficulties which still must be overcome before even a part of the problem can be grasped, for whereas there are different ways of satisfying needs, there are also different solutions tending not to satisfy them:

—by ignoring them, this being the simplest solution for authorities, but one which could lead to social disturbances.
—by transferring them to other needs, especially to easily satisfied ones (mass amusement, etc.).
—by adopting replacement solutions or temporary solutions.

No doubt, you will be somewhat disappointed to see that, at the end of this short paper, I am not able to propose precise research themes on the subjective aspects of urban transport. I would just like to repeat that the approach methods used up to now do not seem very effective to me, and that, in any case, they have not provided sure and usable quantitative data for decision makers.

As I am also very sceptical about the extrapolation of human attitudes and needs, even when it is carefully reasoned, I think that the most urgent research to be undertaken should be conceived in a more complete manner: what must be studied is 'man needing to travel and travelling'. In the long term view of urban transport, I think one must study *public transport* and the qualities it must acquire to provide a completely satisfactory service, it being understood that public transport can include systems other than the existing ones, for example 'DART' (Demand Actuated Road Transit System), the 'DRIAL-MODE BUS', etc.

That is why I believe that studies of applied physiology, of applied anthropology, of 'human engineering' would be the best to provide rapidly the information we need in order to foresee demand (including potential demand) and to make decisions on investments, decisions which are progressively becoming long-term ones.

BIBLIOGRAPHY

1. Compte rendus des réunions des Groupes de recherche du Centre de Recherche d'Urbanisme (C.R.U.) sur la détermination des aspirations et des besoins dans les ensembles d'habitation—1962 et 1963, Paris. (Documents ronéotés, non diffusés.)
2. 'La Recherche fondamentale en matière d'urbanisme' par Camille Bonnome, Président du C.R.U. § 1963 Paris. (Document ronéoté, 20 pp.)
3. 'Improvements and innovations in urban bus systems', a Technology Assessment Review—1969. Paris—OECD (252 pp.).
4. OWEN, WILFRED. (1966). *The Metropolitan Transportation System*. Washington, D.C.: The Brookings Institution (266 pp.).
5. 'Enquête sur l'opportunité d'un deuxième espace de séjour'. Association d'Anthropologie Appliquée, Paris, 1966 (100 pp.).

Discussion

FOLLOWING PAPER BY A. COBLENTZ

Langdon: It is very difficult, if not impossible, for anyone to imagine himself in a situation which he has not experienced, and I would tend to agree that when you look at the replies from people who have not got this extra space, the answers may not correlate with the answers from people who have. However, some four years ago, I carried out a similar study to the one Dr. Coblentz referred to, for a manufacturer, and in the course of it we found that it was possible to construct an index of what one might call 'propensity to purchase' based on the economic and psychological characteristics of that section of the population which had already gone ahead and bought this manufacturer's goods. We used the computer to work out the economic circumstances, the opportunity to purchase, the existence of social or material needs, and the psychological characteristics of that section of the population which had bought this manufacturer's goods. We then compared this section of the population, using the same index, with that section of the population who had not bought. We applied this to a National Survey, and from this it was possible to develop a state of 'propensity to purchase' not only of one brand but of different brands, including the brand of the particular manufacturer that we helped. This, in fact, has been very successful in determining this manufacturer's potential market.

Applying this to the problems of public transport, why cannot one develop such scales to measure what different sections of the public are doing, and then apply this to other sections of the public to obtain some kind of a profile of 'propensity to use' for public transport?

Coblentz: It would be necessary to have a large number of people to get a comparison of this kind. In France we have only one-third of the population who have a second living space and this is not enough to give satisfactory results.

Hutchinson: There is a great deal of information on behaviour relevant to urban transport, and a great deal of effort has been put into the design of prediction models. Embodied in these is a realistic set of hypotheses about travel behaviour and the choice of travel mode which are now finding support in empirical tests in demonstration studies that are now being conducted. The combination of semi-empirical studies with behavioural hypotheses may lead to a more realistic understanding of human travel behaviour.

Coblentz: If you want to employ new people in your office in Los Angeles, and there is not a parking place for his or her car, it is impossible to find a new employee. I really think that what is needed is common sense and not a very complicated or sophisticated approach to methods of transport.

Odell: One of the surprising things in the Paper is the statement 'that if public transport was free it would have little influence on choice'. Is there no evidence that those sections of the population that do not have to pay for transport such as employees of transport companies and servicemen travelling on public warrants do, in fact, use public transport more because of it?

Coblentz: There was an inquiry on this subject of urban transport and the results are: first, when urban transport is more expensive less people use it; if urban transport becomes cheaper, no more people use it; and, thirdly, if it is free, the number of people using it would be the same.

Clarke: The same finding has been put forward by the Consultants to the Oxford Transportation Plan, that a greatly reduced cost of travel would not change what they have chosen to call the modal split in Oxford.

Bolster: The average Frenchman who is much more attached to his car is less willing to use public transport. For example, to a Member of the Senate the idea that he should go by Metro to the Assembly, would be unacceptable, the motor car is more of a prestige symbol than it is in a place like London.

Whyte: If the degree of discomfort, the degree of overcrowding, and so on, is the same people may not want to use it. But if substantial improvements are made in the degree of comfort, and so on, would the public still respond in the same way?

   Dr. Coblentz has postulated a transport network with all the required comforts, but he only lists three. As far as I am concerned, these are certainly not all the required advantages. If you are trying to attract me away from my motor car you will have to start at my front door, at the time I want, and take me to the place where I want to go.

Coblentz: I do not think that people want urban transport to start exactly from their door. What they do not want is to walk too far, wait for a long time, and not know exactly when the bus will start and how long a time the journey will take. And urban transport must be dependable if people are to use it.

Whyte: Should we, perhaps, distinguish between public transport that is used for regular purposes, like taking people to and from their place of work, and public transport that is used outside peak hours?

Dakin: The Metropolitan Toronto Study of traffic prediction also indicated that if the fare were eliminated, and if trains ran at one minute intervals on a very extensive subway system, it still would not change the modal split very significantly.

   We have not considered the 'dial a taxi' system nor the 'dial a bus' system. If taxis or small buses were linked by radio-telephone to a computer system which you dial the computer would work out the quickest route for the driver to take. He would pick up a limited number of people, and drop them at their different destinations. While the customer would have to wait a few minutes for the car or bus to arrive, he, nevertheless gets the benefit of relatively high speed movement and great personal convenience.

Stone: Part of the recent research done by the Ministry of Transport, when trying to find out how people value time on journeys, indicated that people were not prepared to spend very much money, but were prepared to spend large amounts of time. This suggests that if the price were lowered there would be quite a large increase in the use of transport.

What the engineer can provide

(The movement of people and goods)

by

W. M. THRING

(Read in his absence by J. A. Bones)

PROFESSOR THRING starts by asking the question what do we want? And goes on to say that during the first Industrial Revolution, the primary task of the engineer was to provide the machines, particularly prime movers and powered tools, which would enable every man and woman in a fully developed country to have an adequate standard of living without excessively long working hours. This has been largely achieved in Britain and America, but there are many aspects of human life which are still unsatisfactory and Professor Thring believes that it is the job of the engineer to try to produce the next generation of machines for the second industrial revolution which will put human life on a more satisfactory footing. However, the difficult problem which has to be faced is to find out exactly what human beings want.

The engineer is not fitted to give the complete answer to this but it is hoped that this and other conferences will produce answers. For the present purpose, for the purpose of this paper, however, Professor Thring makes the following assumptions:

1. People may not wish to travel for more than half an hour or at the most three quarters of an hour from door to door on their daily journey to work.
2. They do not wish to spend long periods standing up in overcrowded vehicles, queuing for transport or sitting in stationary cars in traffic jams.
3. That more than 50% of people wish to live in two or at the most three storey houses with a small garden.
4. A labour saving system for the distribution of all goods and mail and for refuse collection is needed.

In this paper Professor Thring attempts to discuss how far we could provide such a convenient system for a heavily populated country like Britain with the development of the various machines that are being considered at the moment, and which are certainly feasible engineering devices if people are prepared to pay for them.

PROFESSOR THRING CONSIDERS PUBLIC TRANSPORT WITHIN THE RANGE OF 1–10 MILES

The requirements suggested in the previous section lead to the assumption that there would be conurbations with people spread out over fairly large areas with, perhaps,

143

central factory and office accommodation and shops round the perimeter. There would also have to be social centres of a size that would give people a feeling of integration. Experience in America and elsewhere seems to show that this development requires a good (i.e. comfortable and convenient) public transport system since the number of cars, if each person goes to work by himself in a car, would cause impossible congestion In any case, there comes a point where driving one's own car is more tiring and less satisfactory than using a good public transport system. We therefore conclude that the provision of a public transport system capable of conveying people 10 miles in half an hour, including waiting time, in comfort and with convenience, is an essential not only for the biggest cities in the country but for every working aggregate. It can also be concluded that this public transport system must not share a road system with lorries distributing goods and with private cars. Engineers have given a great deal of thought to this problem and a number of important solutions have been proposed. Gabriel Bouladon of the Battelle Institution in Switzerland, has written two important papers (in April and October 1967 in *Science Journal*) describing among other things the Battelle scheme that he calls a continuous integrated transport system. This consists essentially of a continuous belt moving along an underground or overhead track. It could for example go in the existing underground system of London. If the belt runs at twenty miles an hour, it would take people more rapidly to their journey's end than a train which reaches a peak of thirty miles an hour but spends nearly half its time stationary at stations, in deceleration and acceleration, and on stops between stations. The interesting thing about the Battelle system is that it uses considerably less power than a train system but by far the most important factor about it is that it can carry many times the number of passengers that a discontinuous train system can carry because the whole length of the belt can be full of people whereas trains can occupy only a small part of the track at a given moment. Bouladon calculates that the dead weight of the moving belt is less than 100 lb per passenger whereas in conventional underground trains the weight is 300 lb per passenger and for ordinary trains it is even greater. All the motors and brakes are stationary and the biggest problem in such a system is getting the passengers onto the moving belt and off again. This the Battelle people propose to do by a series of novel belts in parallel.

Passengers step on to these moving belts, and as they travel up or down to the main belt, they become boxed in on both sides and at the back. As the box moves forward it accelerates sideways, that is parallel to the belt, so that by the time it reaches the main belt it is moving at the same speed and the passenger then only has to step across. As this main belt, the transporter belt, leaves the station, which consists of the whole length of the region where the boxes are moving alongside it, the first belt is peeled off and goes underneath the moving floor belts and returns in the opposite direction. Any person who would be fit to travel on an ordinary moving staircase could travel on one of these transporters although people on wheeled chairs might have some difficulty. Professor Thring believes that this system is so desirable that he greatly regrets it was not installed in the new Victoria Line in London and he hopes that some city in the not too distant future will install such a system. A ten foot diameter tube could carry 75,000 passengers per hour and a double system twice that number.

The overhead system is neat with a simple single column carrying the two moving belts in rectangular tubes on each side of it. It would also be comparatively silent as it

FIGURE 1. Continuous integrated transport system. Designed by the Battelle Institute.

is smooth running, and if one wishes the belt can run on air bearings (a film of air) instead of on rollers.

Figure 1, which is also taken from one of Bouladon's papers, is a different idea and shows Bouladon's proposal for a pneumatic 'logic' tube train. The train is the dark shape and it is supported on a thin film of air and propelled by a differential air pressure. The air is blown in and later sucked out by a stationary blower. The air supply is controlled by a series of what he calls 'logic' elements which are valves operated by some external control means. There are many proposals for improving conventional railways to make them fully atuomatic by eliminating drivers or by making them noiseless so that they could run overhead without the wheel rumble which is the normal penalty of overhead railways. The best way of achieving reduction of noise is to use linear air bearing produced by high pressure compressed air so that the vehicle floats on an air layer of the order of 1 mm thick. This would have to be combined with a linear motor for driving and here Professor Thring is thinking of electrical power since normal propulsion through the wheels is no longer possible. This is, undoubtedly, a very straight forward system. All these systems, the continuous belt, the pneumatic 'logic train', and the overhead railway, could now be laid out with a central computer controlling them and without drivers.

The Transit Express Way has already been developed and built by Westinghouse in America. This uses lightweight air conditioned coaches running along their own tracks on rubber tyres. The vehicles are steered by pneumatic tyred wheels which lock into an I shaped centre rail. Modern knowledge of vibrations and control have made it possible to produce a much smoother ride than has been obtained with all previous rail systems. The system is operated by electric wires which are placed underneath and at a point where they cannot be touched by an ordinary person walking on them or when snow and ice build up. The collectors are on the coaches being on the underneath on the lower side of the conductor.

What Professor Thring does not say, and I am sure was in his mind, is the fact that these coaches are driverless and are controlled from a central computer.

Professor Thring then goes on to consider Private Transport.

A case has often been made, in the laying out of new cities, for the pedestrian and Professor Thring is sure that to walk a mile or two every day is necessary for the health of a normal person. However, the idea of introducing a new type of man-propelled road vehicle for the city of the future is a good one for distances of two or three miles. Here I think he is saying that this is a good way of getting people about in a city as well as providing the exercise he feels is so necessary. This vehicle could be a tricycle with a new type of drive and gearing and with a very light plastic umbrella covering the whole of it. Professor Thring has worked out one such means of drive based on the original method of driving a lathe. This was done by wrapping a length of woven nylon rope, hung from a springy horizontal pole, wrapped round the work and pulling it down intermittently with a stirrup. His method uses two ratchet mechanisms on the driving shaft with the two ends of the rope connected to the ratchets and taken to two pedals which hang on pendula. As I understand it the idea is that you push the pendula to and fro and the strings drive the shaft intermittently through the ratchet. It gives a very cheap and simple bicycle drive mechanism on which the effect of an infinitely variable gear can be obtained by sliding the connection points of the strings up and down the pendula.

Professor Thring believes that the city of the future should be laid out with pedestrian walkways, cycle tracks and roads developed so that those using them do not get in each other's way.

Turning to the problem of the motor car the obvious first step, which is being considered all over the world, is the miniature electric town car. Figure 2 which is taken from one of Bouladon's papers, shows the evolution of the motor car and as you can see a split into conventional cars on the one hand and the town car on the other is discernible.

A miniature electric town car which seats two or four passengers, and is of approximately square shape with the steering wheels (i.e. the wheels in direct contact with the ground) capable of being turned through a right angle to give the vehicle a *minute* circle. These steering wheels are driven from the electric motors. At present this would have to be a storage battery driven car and the weight would limit it to a maximum range to about 10 to 20 miles. However, some important developments are going on in the improvement of storage batteries and Professor Thring believes that within 10 years we shall have an adequate fuel cell with the direct conversion of chemical into electrical energy, the fuel may be in the form of a slurry which when pumped into the cell would give a 100 miles range. This would then be replaced, in another garage, in a way that is not so very different from having a tank filled with petrol.

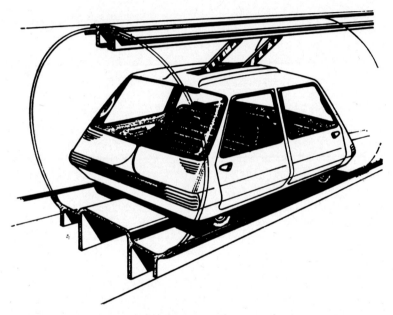

FIGURE 2. Miniature electric town car.

This 'town car' would have a moulded plastic top and sides, all in one piece, which would hinge as the existing bubble cars do. It might use the drive motors as the brakes in a regenerative form so that they could feed back power into the battery. There are, however, some more radical possibilities available for development. The first of these is the automatic self routing taxi which is being worked upon by the NRDC and Brush Electrical Engineering Company. These cars are to be automatic and self routing and are designed to carry four passengers at a speed of 35 miles per hour. This system would require 'stations' at half mile intervals in town centres to which passengers would need to go. At these stations he would 'inform' the vehicle of his destination and he would then be linked on to the main line to be branched off at the place where he wished to stop. As all the taxis on the main line would be running at exactly the same speed, there would be no danger of crashes and no effort of steering, and there would not be hold ups at traffic lights.

An alternative development is one in which people could have their own city cars in their own garages, and drive them to a pick up point where they would be integrated into a continuously moving system. This system could either provide power for their own electric motor or could hook them onto an overhead moving cable which would carry them along running on their own wheels. The cable would provide the power. This is an overhead version of the San Francisco tram! If they run on their own motors, then of course, there is a danger of somebody's motor failing and the ones behind crashing into it. Electric motors can be made extremely reliable however.

Professor Thring then goes on to consider Goods Transport.

Engineers do not seem to have given quite so much thought to the problems of goods transport, perhaps because they do not themselves drive lorries.

On the principle of freeing humans from laborious routine tasks, it would seem desirable to have an improved rail system for conveying goods from city to city in terms of automatic routing from origin to destination without any hold ups on sidings, and not simply in terms of speed. This is a matter of applying known engineering principles of control and computers to a conventional problem. However, the more important and the more intractable problem is the distribution of goods within the town from the centre up to a distance of 10 miles, and often in quite small loads. In London, the G.P.O. has had an automatic tunnel system for conveying mail from one place to another for many years, and it would seem likely that some kind of automatic system for goods transport would be brought into the city of the future. Whether this would be a tube with pneumatic transport or a continuously moving belt is not known, but it would appear to be necessary at least to have a main distribution system from the central rail station to all the major shops and shopping areas. The final distribution, from the shop or Post Office to the home of newspapers, groceries, and so forth is a more difficult problem because of the large amount of network required. Engineers could readily design a ring main tube, of perhaps 15 inches diameter, along which cannisters could be propelled by air flow on a circular route of perhaps 2 miles. Each canister would be coded with its destination so that when it arrived at the right point it would be off loaded onto a side chute which could be opened by the householder with a key. Thus he would receive his own milk or whatever else was in the system.

REFUSE DISPOSAL

The goods distributing system which has just been described could also be used for the collection of refuse, if the householder had suitable sealed canisters. He would first put the refuse into a plastic bag and then put this inside a standard canister and feed it into the system where it would be coded to be dropped off at the central collection depot.

Another important development in this field, which would reduce transport needs is the provision of smokeless incinerators in every house so that all combustible refuse could be readily disposed of: these incinerators might be combined with the central heating system of the house so reducing the amount of fuel burnt. (Household refuse has an overall calorific value equal to that of wood.)

It could be a simple matter for the householder to dump incombustible material, glass, metal and so forth into one container, and food refuse into a second which could be composted, and paper and cardboard could go into the incinerator. It goes without saying that openings for these three purposes would be built into the house in a convenient spot. Finally the incombustible refuse which had been dumped into the container would be automatically sealed up and fed into the public distribution system.

CONCLUSION

Professor Thring has not discussed in any detail the possibility that communication engineering could be developed to the point where newspapers could be printed automatically from the domestic television set, and office work could be done in a room within a mile of the office worker's home. This could be achieved if communication by video telephone was developed so that any person could consult a file, or see the face of any other person, in any inter-linked office throughout the world, ... and just by dialling the appropriate number.

This could mean the end of large office blocks and the concentration of office staff. A great increase in the number of communication channels would be needed but this could readily be provided by the use of laser beams directly connecting the offices together with a fully electronically controlled filing system. This would give access to any document out of millions by a simple number system.

Professor Thring does not envisage this being carried to an extreme in which people would do their office work in their homes; a walk between home and work, as well as a change of scene, are desirable. So he is, in fact, thinking of very much the same sort of thing as Professor Colin Cherry was talking about, a short journey to a communications centre from which you carry out your office work.

The same technology, and the same thinking, can apply to factories. The large central factory can be operated, almost entirely, by robots with a skeleton maintenance crew. This crew could live locally or, if the work load is substantially reduced, they could live in a hostel and spend the rest of the year on their leisure activities in their own remote homes.

Professor Thring has not discussed, in detail, problems of inter-city transport although here again the engineer can provide almost anything that is wanted. Particularly important is a 200 mile an hour driverless rail system, completely independent of all weather conditions, to take people distances from 100 to 1000 miles. This can be done in many ways, but an overhead monorail carrying the weight of the vehicle and using linear air bearings may be the most suitable. The thin air bearing film, the linear motors, and the electrical power, would be suitable for use over land. Support every 50 yards or so, in the form of graceful prestressed concrete arches, would be needed. Although the monorail would be supported from above, there would be a guide rail underneath to prevent sideways swaying and to give the lateral force necessary for stability.

For crossing the channel, it is quite possible to develop a kind of combined railway cum aeroplane with wings capable of taking its full weight once it had reached its running speed of 200 or 300 miles an hour. Elevating rampways in the form of overhead monorails five miles long would be needed to bring it up to speed and lift it to 500 or 1000 feet. Once it was airborn, with the wings taking the weight, it is only necessary for the rail to carry the current supply to the vehicle and to guide it so that it does not require a pilot. Thus this rail can be very light, and suspended from a catenary rope which is in turn carried on columns five miles apart.

Professor Thring hopes that this description of engineering possibilities is sufficient to show that if only people can decide what they want, and are prepared to pay the price in terms of new buildings, structures and machines, the engineer can give them a public and private system without noise, air pollution, accidents or frustration.

A film of work done at Queen Mary College under Professor Thring's direction was shown.

BIBLIOGRAPHY

1. p. 2. Bouladon, G. *The Transport Gaps Science Journal*. p. 41. April 1967.
2. p. 2. Bouladon, G. *Transport Science Journal*. p. 93. October 1967.
3. Westinghouse, Pittsburgh, U.S.A., *Private Communication*.
4. p. 5. Cooper, A. F. *N.R.D.C. & Transport*. N.R.D.C. Report 1969 p. 5.

Discussion

FOLLOWING PAPER BY W. M. THRING

Nealon: There is the problem of error and human fallibility on these belts and tubes for automatic delivery and disposal. Professor Cherry referred, yesterday, to a disaster in New York when one cable failed and the whole of New York was plunged in darkness. In these inventions we must look carefully into the possibility of human error, and even into human maliciousness.

Whyte: We had a reference yesterday, and now this one, to the New York State blackout. This seems to have attracted quite a lot of attention suggesting that, as we go further and further into advanced technologies, we run a greater risk of chaotic failures. I think it is quite important therefore that we should understand that failures of this sort are not inevitable. The failure in New York State arose from bad systems design brought about by the political structure of the industry and the number of authorities that are involved in the power distribution system in the U.S.A. It is quite clear that you can design systems which will be immune from this sort of wide spread failure. So we should not assume that because we can have complicated systems they cannot be designed to prevent wide spread catastrophe.

Floyd: If a line is blocked or broken or cut then, surely, the whole line is out of action. If this has to be got round by the provision of a duplicate line, the capital cost is enormous.

Whyte: A modern communications system is based on a mesh with many nodes linked by many lines in many different physical locations, so that the failure of individual links in it merely alters the loading on other links in the system.

Odell: I think that this statement is an extremely difficult one to take at its face value because what is being said is that perfection is achieved when there are many nodes, and many cross links. A degree of probability of failure is so small that it may only occur once in 1000 years. That, of course, may be tomorrow. If we refer back to the New York failure, the whole city was not blacked out; there were beacons of light in the darkness resulting from the decision of certain entrepreneurs not to rely on a centralised system for their lighting. With the increasing complexity of electrical and other systems which are provided over large regions, the possibility of failure is increased and I wonder whether people will not look for systems which are under their own specific control. This is done in the case of batteries or small scale motors for the provision of electricity. Because people are dissatisfied with public transport systems, they move to private ownership of vehicles in order to secure reliability and speed. One wonders if they might not adopt similar attitudes to other forms of energy provision.

151

Burberry: Perhaps wrongly I got the impression that some people feel that the distribution systems which we have been talking about are somewhat avant garde, and they have doubts about their reliability and about having a mesh system where flows can be re-routed. It may balance things a little if we remember that water mains have existed since the nineteenth century and have incorporated both of these features. Distribution is by trunk mains which are cross linked, and when one link goes out of action then the water just goes another way round. We get an astonishingly reliable service by this means. So we are living by these principles already. We would be in a very difficult situation if the sanitation in our towns came to grief, far worse, in fact, than if the electricity supply was interrupted for a while.

Ireland: First of all I would like to bear out what has just been said. You design against catastrophic failure by accepting that failure will introduce a degrading service temporarily. Guarding against catastrophic failure is largely a matter of a good systems design. The other point that I would like to make concerns the flying monorail over the channel. What happens if there is a power failure and therefore the thing stops in midflight and is then dependent on its light supporting rail to hold it up over the water? This is a clear example of failure in systems design.

Brown: I am worried by many of the subjects raised in this paper because of the effect they would have on the environment. Many of the proposals set out in this paper are large physical things that carry goods and people and while these may be easily assimilated into new cities, once you put these large units into existing cities they will cause a tremendous amount of visual damage.

Transport in towns

by

C. A. O'FLAHERTY

SOME HISTORICAL DATA

IT IS KNOWN that many of the earliest settlements were founded on the banks of rivers and lakes because of their facility for the movement of people and goods over what were then regarded as long distances. With time man's desire for communication increased and so, inevitably, other villages grew up alongside what were recognised as good and convenient trackways. In turn, these villages became towns and stabilised the trackways into travelways.

Notwithstanding village and town development there were, as far as is known, no formal roads in Britain prior to the second Roman invasion in A.D. 43. As a result, the Roman road system formed the basic framework for future road developments—indeed, it has been said that there has been no real development, no essentially new departure between the planning of the Roman scheme and the coming of the railway.[1]

It does not appear that following the departure of the legions, a single new road was deliberately planned and constructed in this country until the advent of the seventeenth century. Inevitably, the Roman roads decayed and disintegrated and, when a section of an existing road became untraversable, it was simply abandoned and a new trackway created about it. This practice may largely account for the winding, tortuous character of many present day roads and lanes in this country.

At the same time as the roads were deteriorating, opportunities for travel were increasing. About the middle of the sixteenth century the first wheeled coach appeared in Britain; prior to then most travellers, even the Courts in royal progress, travelled on horseback or on foot. Even then, travel within towns continued to be on horse or on foot with the result that, until about the eighteenth century, towns were, on the whole, restricted in size to a radius of about three-quarters of an hour travel time from their centres.

INTRODUCTION OF 'MECHANICAL' TRAVEL

In the latter part of the eighteenth century the Industrial Revolution arrived—and the steam engine—and this transformed civic life and town form as a great wave of migration from the country was initiated. The result was that villages became towns and towns became cities—this at a time when a national population explosion (see Figure 1) was also being initiated.

As urban populations increased so did distances and consequent times involved in daily travel into and within urban areas, and so the need for urban public transport facilities began to be recognised:

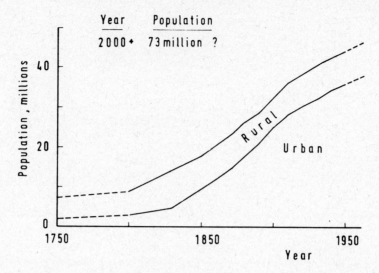

FIGURE 1. Urban and rural populations of England and Wales. (Based on data in
Reference 2.)

—1829 saw the introduction into London of the first horse-bus service.
—1860 saw the beginning of the end of the horse-bus with the initiation of a horse-tram
service in Birkenhead—it was able to carry more people more quickly over a given
distance.
—1863 saw the first section of the underground steam railway line in London.
—1885 saw the first regular electric tram service in Britain. This was at Blackpool
where the electric conductor rail was laid in conduit in the road surface.
—1891 saw the first electric tramway to use an overhead wire conductor. This was at
Leeds.
—1903 saw the introduction into England (by Eastbourne Corporation) of the first
regular motor bus service. A major feature of the motor bus is that it brought the
suburbs within easy reach of the town centre.
—1911 saw the inevitable compromise between the bus and the tram. This was illustrated by the inauguration in Leeds and Bradford on 20 June of the first public
services in Britain using trolley-buses.

While the early horse-bus, horse-tram, motor bus, electric tram and trolley-bus and
(in metropolitan areas) the railway were all competing for the opportunity to move
passengers in built-up areas, the railway was undoubtedly the prime mover of travellers
over medium and long distances. In the year 1850, the railways carried 67 million
passengers, in 1890 the number was almost 800 million, and nearly 1300 million in 1910.[3]
These figures compare well with the 1522 million passengers carried on all the railways
(surface and underground) in this country in 1967.[4]
Although the first vehicle to be powered by an internal combustion engine which
used petrol as a fuel was produced in 1865, the influence of the motor car was not felt for

many years after that. At first the motor car was greeted with much opposition. In Britain, for example, anybody owning a road 'locomotive' was limited to travelling at speeds below 4 mile/h in open country and 2 mile/h in a populous neighbourhood, and each vehicle had to be preceded by a man carrying a red flag. The passing of the Locomotive on Highways Act of 1896 marked the enfranchisement of the motor car in this country; this Act—it was celebrated in November, 1896 by an organised motor run to Brighton from the Thames Embankment in London—gave the motor car the right to travel upon the highway at a speed not exceeding 14 mile/h.

The major 'breakthrough' in motor car technology was made by Henry Ford when, between 1907 and 1909, he conceived the idea of a standard car. The result was the Model 'T' motor car, the first popularly priced motor car which, by 1914, was in mass production in the United States. The motor car era—the era of 'personalised' transport had begun.

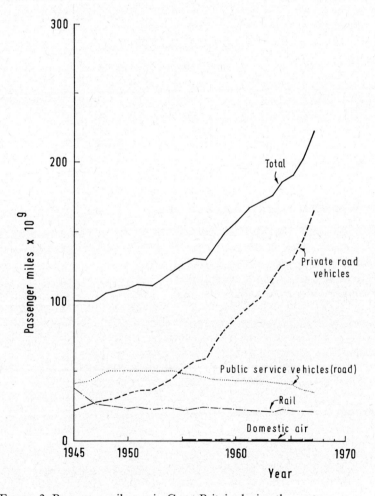

FIGURE 2. Passenger-mileages in Great Britain during the post-war years.

One major by-product of the development of the motor car—and this cannot be over-emphasised—is that it freed the suburbanite from his reliance on public transport. The motor car allowed him to live in a house which was not only geographically further away from the town centre, but also away from the main road and rail routes. The result was that the suburbanite became heavily dependent upon the motor car—and so it became the self-inflicted necessity which it is today.

PRESENT TRANSPORT PATTERNS

Figure 2 shows the post-war patterns of travel by the various modes of transport. The most significant trend exhibited by this graph is the very rapid growth in the private car motor passenger mileage, while the values for the public transport facilities (road and rail) declined.

Are these trends likely to continue? I believe that, on the whole, they are. Consider, for example, the data in Figure 3 which reflects bus transport developments[5] in 78

Municipal road passenger transport statistics, 1966 and 1967

Note : Eight municipalities did not provide data
as to whether or not they showed a
financial surplus/deficit in 1967

Number of municipalities		78
Number with net surplus :	1966	34
	1967	46
Number with net surplus in 1967 with deficit in 1966		9
Number with net deficit in 1967 with surplus in 1966		23
Number with increased total revenue in 1967 as compared		
	with 1966	59
Average total revenue :	1966	£1,404,692
	1967	£1,422,927
Average fleet mileage :	1966	6,811,140 miles
	1967	6,637,938 miles
Number with increased fleet mileage in 1967		15
Number with decreased fleet mileage in 1967		63
Average number of passengers carried :	1966	59,134,115
	1967	56,327,444
Number with increased number of passengers in 1967 as		
	compared with 1966	10
Number with decreased number of passengers in 1967 as		
	compared with 1966	68
Total (all towns) revenue :	1966	£109,566,102
	1967	£111,010,339 increased 1·3%
Total (all towns) fleet mileage :	1966	531,268,900 miles
	1967	517,759,221 miles decreased 2·5%
Total (all towns) number of		
passengers carried :	1966	4,612,460,941
	1967	4,393,540,633 decreased 4·7%

FIGURE 3. Municipal road passenger transport statistics for Great Britain, 1966 and 1967.

municipalities during the years 1966 and 1967. Overall, there is no doubt but that the trend exhibited by the 1967 data is that of decline as compared with 1966.

The data in Figures 2 and 3 suggest a historical repetition of familiar issues. Just as the development of the railways in the middle of the nineteenth century foresaw the end of stagecoach travel, and just as the electric tram swept away the horse-tram, it is probably true to say that the motor car is now threatening the railways and the bus services.

People want motor cars—there is plenty of evidence in support of this statement. For example, while recently there was 1 car for every 22 people in Britain, today the figure is approximately 1 car for every 5 people. By the turn of the century, the figure will probably be 1 car for every 2·25 people. This latter figure will vary according to locality. For example, the extreme possibilities which have been suggested by the Road Research Laboratory as likely to occur in various environmental locations in Great Britain are as follows:

Rural counties	1 car per 2 people
Typical counties	1 car per 2·0–2·2 people
Medium-sized towns	1 car per 2·2–2·5 people
Conurbations	1 car per 2·5–2·9 people
Inner London	1 car per 2·9–3·3 people

On a more local scale, it is interesting to note that, in the post-war years, the number of motor cars *registered* in Leeds rose from below 16,000 to its present figure of well above 70,000. In 1963, there was 1 car registered for every 9 people in Leeds; this ranged, however, from a highest district concentration of 1 car per 5·5 people in north Leeds to a lowest concentration of 1 in 20 in south Leeds.[6]

I have given the above statistics not only to show that the numbers of motor cars will grow in Great Britain but, also, that the rate of growth will vary from country to town, from town to town, and from place to place within a given town.

Another factor is that once people have got motor cars, they tend to use them. This is illustrated by the fact that although the number of motor cars in the country has increased tremendously over the past ten years, yet the average car mileage has remained just about constant at some 7400 miles. On a more local level, in the University of Leeds, a recent survey found that on a beautiful sunny Spring day, 80% of the staff members with cars used them to travel to work, while 61% of the students with cars used them to journey to the University.

The presence of a motor car in a household seems to release a latent desire for trip-making. This is quite dramatically illustrated in Figure 4, which is based on American data, and by the British data in Table 1.

Note that this British data also shows that the increase in travel is mostly for *non-work* purposes, which implies that these trips are made only because of the availability of the motor car, and would not have been made by any other means. Keeping in mind that standards of living are continually increasing, it should be noted that Table 1 also shows that the effect of increasing income is also to increase travel by all modes, particularly again for non-work purposes.

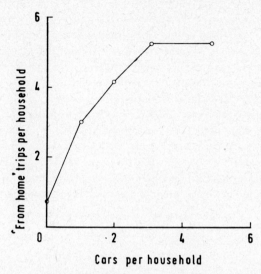

FIGURE 4. Relationship between the number of 'at-home' trips per household and the number of cars per household.[7]

TABLE 1

Trip generation, by mode and purpose, per household per day for households in London with one employed resident per household in an urban area of average rail and bus accessibility[8]

Purpose	Household income, £	Private transport			Public transport			All modes		
		0-car	1-car	Multi-car	0-car	1-car	Multi-car	0-car	1-car	Multi-car
Work	0–1000	0·2	1·2	—	0·9	0·4	—	1·1	1·6	—
	1000–2000	0·3	1·2	1·6	1·1	0·6	0·5	1·4	1·8	2·1
	>2000	—	1·0	1·5	—	0·5	0·2	—	1·5	1·7
Non-work	0–1000	0·2	2·0	—	0·8	0·4	—	1·0	2·4	—
	1000–2000	0·3	2·7	5·7	1·4	0·7	0·3	1·7	3·4	5·5
	>2000	—	3·9	8·4	—	1·1	0·9	—	5·0	9·3

The immediate availability of the motor car, its flexibility and its ability to provide direct door-to-door transport (in comparison with the public transport modes) is reflected in Figure 5. This figure shows how the growth in motor car travel has generally caused a decline in the trips made by public transport in towns.

THE TRANSPORT TASKS

The comments which I have made above about the growth of motor car travel, and the relative decline of public transport usage naturally raises the next question.

'Does this mean that public transport and, particularly, urban public transport is headed for the scrap-heap—that it is finished?'

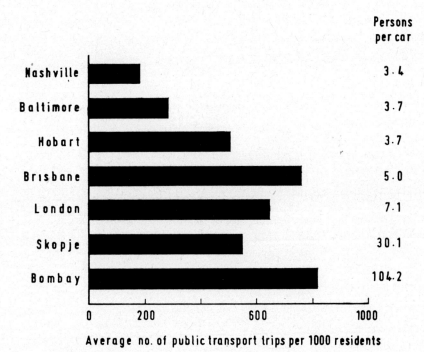

FIGURE 5. Daily public transport usage in selected cities.

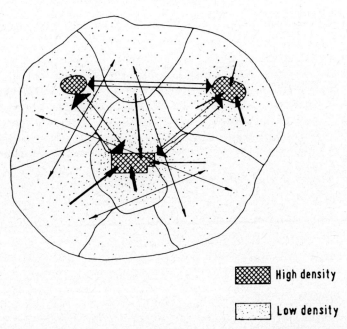

FIGURE 6. General pattern of transport desire lines arising from high and low density land uses.

Before attempting to answer this question it is useful to isolate the transport tasks which have to be met in this country. These are reflected in Figure 6. This figure is meant to illustrate how, from a land-use aspect, the nation is broadly composed of two types of housing concentration i.e. low density housing usage and high density housing usage. This pattern of land-use gives rise to three types of transport movement:

1. Inter-connection between and within low density zones e.g. rural area travel, village-to-village travel.
2. Inter-connection of high density zones e.g. inter-city travel.
3. Inter-connection of low density zones and high density ones e.g. suburban to central area travel.

A fourth transport task, not shown on this diagram, relates to travel within high density zones e.g. within central areas.

It is these two last situations which present the more obvious passenger transport tasks of today in this country. As Figure 1 illustrated, Britain is an urbanised nation and it is in towns that transport 'failures' appear most obvious to people. It must be remembered, however, that this country is physically rather small—and that it is not possible, from a national aspect, to consider its town problems in isolation from its other ones.

CARRYING OUT THE TRANSPORT TASKS

Now I would like to talk about the manner in which these transport tasks will be carried out within, say, the next 30 years. In this discussion, the emphasis will be on what I believe will happen, not on what should happen, and only a little on what could happen.

I should state, first of all, that my belief as to how passenger transport will develop in Great Britain is founded on a number of basic suppositions:

1. That people's standards of living will continue to rise, and that which is now regarded as satisfactory does not necessarily represent contentedness for the future.
2. That people now consider personal mobility—the ability to travel quickly, efficiently and conveniently as an integral part of a high standard of living.
3. That the numbers of people in this country will continue to grow (to, perhaps, 70 million by the year 2000).
4. That upwards of 90% of the population will live in towns by the turn of the century.
5. That personal transport—at present reflected in the motor car—has an assured future.
6. That the trend to lower urban density, far from reversing will increase.
7. That the emphasis in urban planning in this country will continue to dwell on the concept of maintaining the centrality of existing towns.

With these in mind it is now possible to consider how the above passenger transport tasks will be met.

Low Density to Low Density Transport

Into this category of travel falls the normal trips from rural area to rural area, from rural area to village, and from village to village. At the present time, this transport task is being met by the private car and the motor bus, with some little help from the railways.

It is relatively easy to predict what will happen in this situation—there is no doubt but that the motor car is and will continue to be the main passenger carrier. There are over 200,000 miles of road in this country, a very great number of which service these areas. Thus, while knots of congestion will occur on some of these roads, there are sufficient of them and they can be improved enough to meet all but the most extreme local conditions.

Railway services will practically disappear from routes in rural areas. There will also be a definite downward trend in the services provided by motor bus. Indeed, it is very likely that in many areas motor buses will be entirely uneconomical but that Local or National Authorities will maintain them for social reasons i.e. to cater for those who cannot or will not drive.

Overall, there is no doubt but that this transport task will be met by the motor car.

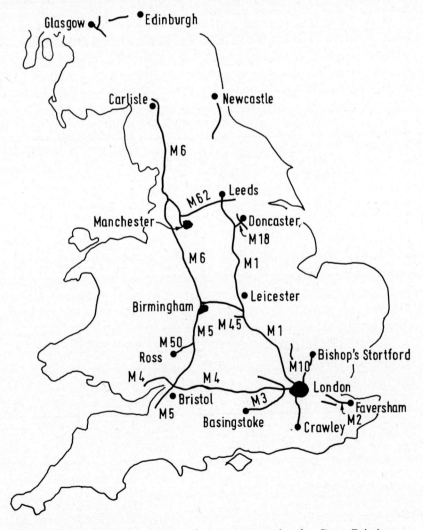

FIGURE 7. Present national (inter-city) motorway plan for Great Britain.

High Density to High Density Transport

At the present time this transport task e.g. providing for inter-city travel, is being met by the motor car, the motor bus, the conventional train and the aeroplane. From developments in high speed ground transport which are now taking place, it appears that this area will see the most exciting developments in future years.

On the conventional side, the 1000-mile motorway network (see Fig. 7) will be completed about the mid-1970's, and it is not at all unlikely that the turn of the century will show this motorway mileage to be increased to between two and three thousand. I am sure that 30 years from now all trunk roads connecting towns of, say, 75,000 and above will be of dual carriageway calibre, with all important intersections grade-separated. These roads will be heavily used for inter-city travel, especially when the trip lengths involved are less than about 100 miles and the destinations are not in the central area environment of towns of metropolitan size.

For transport between large towns when the travel distances are great and/or the destinations are within the central areas of these towns, it is likely that the 'ground' public transport carriers will be the primary choice of travellers—that is, of course, provided that the times required to get to and from the mass transport stations are not excessive. This suggests the very real requirement for the intra-urban and the inter-urban transport modes to be integrated e.g. if rapid interchange is to take place between inter-city trains and local buses, then the bus station and the railway station will have to be essentially one and the same.

Present trends relative to transport in Great Britain suggest very strongly that the conventional railway will be the prime carrier on the main inter-city routes. Future British rail plans aim at maximum train speeds, with 'conventional' trains, of up to 125 mile/h by 1973, and at a maximum speed of 150 mile/h with the Advanced Passenger Train (this is driven by gas turbine engines) in the latter part of the 1970's. This latter train could well initiate a new era in long distance rail travel in this country. An indication of what station to station journey times will be like with the advent of this new train service is given in Table 2.

The electrified and turbo-trains will make serious inroads on the inter-city traffic carried by the domestic airlines in this country. Domestic air travel will, I am sure,

TABLE 2

Some calculated performances for British Rail's turbo-trains[9]

Route	Intermediate stops	Estimated journey time	Overall average speed, mile/h
King's Cross–Newcastle	–	2 h 24 min	112
King's Cross–Edinburgh	1	3 h–37 min	109
King's Cross–Leeds	1	1 h–47 min	103
King's Cross–Bradford	2	2 h –	97
King's Cross–Hull	–	1 h–47 min	110
King's Cross–Sheffield	1	1 h 37 min	100
King's Cross–Nottingham	–	1 h 13 min	105
Paddington–Cardiff	1	1 h 29 min	98
Paddington–Swansea	2	2 h 05 min	92
Paddington–Bristol	–	1 h 11 min	100

survive, but it will be found to be most sustaining (until about 1980–85, at any rate) at distances above about 225 miles. Below this distance ground transport, particularly rail transport, will be supreme.

Any major development in commercial air transport beyond, say, 1985 is going to be heavily dependent upon use of VTOL (Vertical Take-Off and Landing) planes. These aircraft will be aimed at the short-haul market and as such will be in direct competition with high speed ground transport. For air transport to compete successfully with high speed ground transport, air travellers will have to be able to cut out the airport–town part of their journeys—in other words, they will have to be able to land *within* towns. If they are allowed to do this, then the European market alone for VTOL aircraft could well amount to about 500 by about 1985, while by the year 2000—which, after all, is only 30-odd years away—VTOL aircraft could carry anything up to 75% of intra-European air traffic.

From a transport efficiency aspect, there is a strong case for VTOL aircraft. Perhaps a more important factor, however, is whether or not towns will accept 'metroports'. I think that probably they will—but this will only be after much soul-searching and public enquiry—which is as it should be.

You will notice that I have not so far discussed the monorail. To the layman, the monorail has a great emotional appeal. He believes it can run above ground on relatively light supports, whereas he thinks that the conventional duorail (train) needs embankments, massive abutments, etc. This comparison is a fallacy—modern construction methods are now such that a conventional duorail carrying lightweight rolling stock needs no more massive supports than monorails.

It is interesting that of the seventeen monorails which have been put into commercial use, all but two have been considered commercial failures. The two successes have been the 9·75-mile Listowel and Ballybunion line which operated in Co. Kerry, Ireland between 1889 and 1924, and the suspended monorail in Wuppertal, Germany which, although constructed in 1901, is still in service today.

Low Density to High Density Transport

The most difficult transport task of all is undoubtedly that of moving people from low density housing (in suburbia) to high density destinations (in central areas) and vice versa. An appreciation of the existing situation in this respect may be gathered from Figure 8. The main features which I wish this figure to illustrate are:

—that omitting walking, the travel choice in smaller cities is essentially a bi-modal one i.e. between bus and car, whereas in the large cities it is tri-modal i.e. between bus, car and train
—that the larger the urban area, the smaller the percentage of trips made by private car
—that the smaller the urban area, the less the percentage of central area-destined trips that are made by public transport.

In other words, the smaller the town the greater the reliance placed on the private motor car for conveyance into the central area.

Thoughts as to how this transport task will be met in the future (up to about the year 2000 at any rate) inevitably lead to the conclusion that three general approaches will be

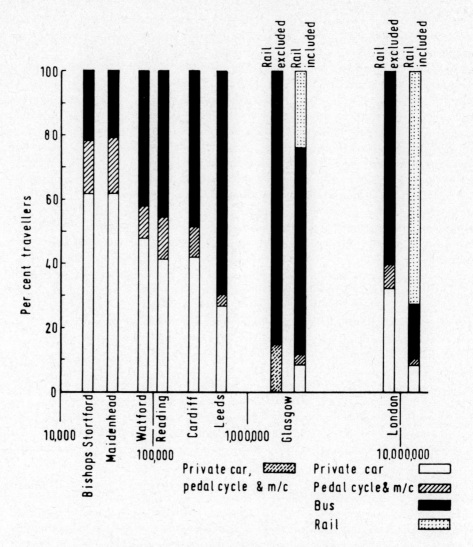

FIGURE 8. Percentages of persons entering central areas by road* in the period 7–10 a.m. and travelling by various forms of transport.

taken, depending upon the size of the city. Thus, for example, let us look at a metropolitan city e.g. London; a small city e.g. Bishops Stortford; and a medium-sized city e.g. Leeds. (I am not at all considering a historic town e.g. York, as I believe that transport developments in such towns must be heavily influenced by the need to conserve and preserve.)

Metropolitan city. I wonder whether the sheer magnitude of London's growing population, coupled with the inherent congestion created by and in this megalopolis of

* Note that for Glasgow and London, data are also given which include rail travel.

over ten million people, has produced a situation with respect to passenger transport which cannot be properly tackled at this time. At any rate, I wonder whether the scale effects rule out a solution in London which is based on preserving the centrality of the city and on using the presently-known modes of transport.

To try to tackle the situation in terms of the motor car is certainly not reasonable in London. The unsatisfied demand for road space in the city is so chronic, that additional and improved road facilities are immediately absorbed by the motor car once they are completed. To provide facilities which would not be so absorbed would not only entail tremendous financial considerations but, if implemented, would completely change the character and geography of the city. This I cannot see being accepted.

I am certain that the recommendations which will be implemented in London will involve a very great reliance on public transport. In particular, great emphasis will be placed upon the use of existing—and extended—fixed route (above and underground) facilities. I am not sure, however, that these will provide a level of service in London which will be acceptable.

Nevertheless, some practical developments which we, in our lifetimes, should certainly see in London are:

—Further extensions of the underground rail system.
—Complete integration of road and rail services so that passengers will be able to interchange transport modes under cover and without having to pay any fares in the process.
—The creation of large scale 'park-'n-ride' facilities at or adjacent to suburban railway stations.
—The deliberate creation of 'kiss-'n-ride' short-term parking facilities at suburban stations.
—An even stricter degree of restraint on the use of the private car in central London (possibly implemented with the aid of a 'Road Pricing'[10] mechanism).
—The creation of exclusive right-of-ways on all major city routes along which buses will be able to travel unhindered by other forms of traffic.
—Separate lanes for buses at all major street intersections. (These will, in each instance, stretch back at least from the intersection to the last bus stop.)
—In all instances, buses leaving the kerb will be given priority of movement over private vehicles already in the traffic stream.
—The creation and construction of an integrated major urban motorway and arterial street system.

As I have said already, I am not sure that these developments will be adequate for the future—at best, they can hope to keep pace with present levels of congestion. I do not think that these developments, combined with the present transport modes, are capable of meeting and overcoming the mobility demands of the twenty-first century—and still maintain our major cities as we know them. It seems to me that, given the maintenance of town centrality, the dominating desire for mobility (in comfort, of course) can only be met in the future by developments in transport technology.

Thus, for example, the twenty-first century could see the replacement of the conventional stop-start underground train with the non-stop, automatically controlled, Continuous Integrated Transporter.[11] The future bus transport system may involve the use of automatically-controlled and guided buses moving on reserved tracks in or above the roadway. A natural development of this is the suggestion for using 'bus trains' in metropolitan areas such as London. (The idea here is that several feeder-buses should be used to collect passengers in the suburbs; they would then come together to form trains with corridor connections, and travel under automatic control into the central area along reserved bus-ways. The corridor connections between the buses would enable passengers to move to the coaches appropriate to their destinations before the 'bus train' split again.)

Supplementing the mass public transport systems could be semi-personal transport modes e.g. the Automatic Rail Taxi.[12] The Rail Taxi is essentially an automatically controlled private train which a passenger would rent for the trip at the boarding station. Or then again, the supplementary transport may be something like the StaRRcar system[13] which would allow a passenger to drive his car, under manual control, from his home to a loading station; there the (same) car would come under automatic control for the rest of its trip into town.

I doubt whether any of these innovatory developments will be put into use in this country within the next 30 years.

Smaller cities. It is relatively easy to visualise the developments in passenger transport which will take place in the smaller urban areas e.g. Bishops Stortford (see Figure 8). As I have already said there is much evidence available to suggest that the people have already made up their minds on this issue. They have already opted for private transport and against public transport—and there is little to suggest that they will change in the future. This will mean that these smaller towns will contain highly developed road networks, with perhaps (out of proportion with their size) some motorway-type facilities on the outskirts. When travelling within these towns, motorists will be able to drive to the edges of the (small) central areas where they will leave their cars in parking facilities and then walk to their destinations within the (pedestrian precinct) central areas.

In these towns there will also be a need for public transport services, since there will always be people who cannot/will not drive. The extent to which a public transport service will be provided in any given town cannot be forecast at this time—but whatever it is in the year 2000, it will be severely curtailed as compared with what it is now.

Can I emphasise my belief that public transport in smaller cities cannot hope to be self-supporting in the future. Thus the quality of service provided in any given instance will not be dependent to any important extent upon financial support from the fare-paying passengers but, rather, will primarily be a function of what the community's transport governing body—whether it be local or national—are willing to sanction. In other words, public transport in small towns will simply be regarded as another social service.

Medium-sized towns. Having talked about the metropolitan city and the small city, there is really little extra that can be said about the towns in between them in size. The facts are that these cities are too large to rely upon the private car as the bulk carrier, and too small to support fixed tracked carrier systems such as the railway. Hence, the motor bus is and will continue to be the prime public transport carrier in these towns; it provides the only real alternative to the private car at this time—and in the immediate future.

In a given town whose size tends to be on the large side the policies and developments will tend towards those implemented in large towns, whereas those whose size tend to the small size will tend to be as in smaller towns. In either case, the future will see the creation of a formidable network of high quality roads in the outer parts of these towns.

There are two further points which I might add about these towns. Firstly, there will be a very definite policy of preventing the journey-to-work traveller from bringing his car into town. Secondly, there is relatively little point in suggesting major park-'n-ride and kiss-'n-ride schemes in these towns; in Leeds, for example, the public transport loading/unloading stations would have to be located so far within the city limits (to pick up enough passengers to make the scheme economically viable) that motorists just would not make the short trip on congested roads and then leave their cars voluntarily to change to public transport for the remainder of their journeys.

Transport Within Dense Land-use Areas

The first and most important consideration here is that there will continue to be a great acceptance of the concept of turning central areas into pedestrian precincts. This is the key development of the future.

In the smaller cities, this will mean that people will walk the relatively short distances from car parks at the outskirts of the central area to their destinations within. There will be no public transport services which will specifically service the central areas only in these towns.

In cities of medium and large size, the central areas will obviously be larger. People who wish to bring their cars close to the pedestrian precinct parts of these central areas will have to pay dearly for this 'privilege'. Many of the central areas will be sufficiently large to require transport facilities to distribute passengers coming in by public and private transport, and to act as links between shops, offices and the like. These requirements suggest the need for small, quick, easily manoeuvrable public transport vehicles able to make easy use of the central street network, yet capable of handling a large turnover of passengers—in other words, Minibuses. Services of this type are now in (successful) operation e.g. the Washington project.[14]

The larger and richer towns may possibly see some technical innovation aimed at providing adequate circulation within big central areas. Two systems which may well provide an indication of what future central area public transport will be like are the Pedestrian Conveyor and the Carveyor.

Over 80 years ago, the pedestrian conveyor was regarded as the transport mode of the future. However, for many years they were used only in exhibitions and world fairs. The best example of this usage is the system used in the 1900 Paris Exhibition; this was a 2·5-mile long elevated conveyor which carried 6·5 million people with a total of only forty minor accidents over an 8-month period. Since then pedestrian conveyors have become accepted as practical means of moving people over short distances along well established pedestrian routes. At these locations, their prime function is generally regarded as being to reduce the burden of walking rather than to speed up passenger movement. Current examples of this usage can be seen at airports, surface and underground railway stations, dock sites, supermarkets, pedestrian precincts and large car parks.

Whether the pedestrian conveyors of the future will extend beyond the above locations, I cannot definitely say at this time. If, however, the community is willing to pay for them, I see no technical reason why moving footpaths could not replace many existing footpaths in central areas. The main factor holding back their extension at this time is fear—fear of the consequences of innovation, fear of the consequences of accidents. In this latter respect, I cannot help but sometimes feel that the 'successful' pedestrian conveyor will be that which is designed for an 80-year old with one leg!

The Carveyor[15] is essentially an extension of the pedestrian conveyor. It consists of a system of small wheel-less cars which are carried on continuously moving conveyor belts. An intra-central area trip via this system would begin by the passenger stepping on to a horizontal moving platform whose motion would be at the rate of 1·5 mile/h. This platform would be moving in the same direction and at the same speed as the train of Carveyors being entered; thus boarding/unboarding would take place as if both systems were stationary. After the carveyors leave a station, they would pass over a bank of rubber-tyred insulating conveyor wheels which would move at increasing speeds until, after a few seconds, the individual cars would be moving at a cruising speed of about 15 mile/h, and spaced uniformly apart. When the cars approach another station, the procedure would be exactly the reverse of that described above.

In this paper so far, I have endeavoured to bring forth a number of points:

—that our present transport systems were never planned, they just 'developed'.
—that, historically, more efficient transport systems have tended to crush and displace less efficient ones.
—that public transport, as we know it today, on the whole, is losing ground to personal transport.
—that, nationally, there was a number of transport tasks to be tackled and that the successful handling of these tasks requires acceptance of the fact that particular transport modes are more appropriate to particular tasks.
—that the manner in which these transport tasks are likely to be dealt with during the next thirty years will not be so much different from the manner in which they are handled now.

I have not talked about 'solving' any of the transport problems. To explain why this is so, it is necessary to define what is meant by the 'transport problem'.

It is my belief that people now regard personal mobility, the ability to travel quickly, safely and conveniently, as an integral part of their standard of living. Thus, the 'transport problem' is the reflection of the apparent failure of the existing transport systems to provide them with this facility.

Looking into the future I cannot but foresee that this demand for personal mobility is going to increase and increase. I can also foresee that existing transport facilities, notwithstanding the large amount of money which will be spent on them, will not be adequate to meet and satisfy future demands at all locations. In large towns it is probable that events will be considered 'under control' if present levels of congestion are maintained.

Solving the transport problem in medium and large towns in a desirable way is not going to happen in this century. Indeed, I might go so far as to suggest that the solution is unobtainable as long as these towns maintain their centrality complex, and as long as the transport system as a whole is dependent only on *existing* transport modes.

I can but repeat that people want personal mobility. In general, people want to be able to get into some form of transport capsule at the home and then to travel in it to the required destination. This suggests the need for a vehicle which (on the principle of the StaRRcar) can be parked at the home and is capable of being driven to a road (or track) where it will come under automatic control for a major part of its journey. Because this vehicle will be parked at the home, it will satisfy people's need for convenience; because it will come under automatic control during its journey, it will enable high roadway capacity to be obtained.

Even though high roadway capacity can be obtained by automatic control, the volumes of vehicles to be moved and parked, and the congestion inherent in having very great numbers of people congregate in a small (central) area also suggest that it would be more efficient, from a mobility aspect, if the central areas of larger towns could be dispersed. If this could happen, then it is probable that the task of getting people from their origins to their destinations within towns would not be as difficult as it is today.

It is easy for me to say that solving the transport problem—in the sense of providing the people with the mobility they desire—requires the implementation of the above suggestions. But the question may rightfully be asked—at what cost, both socially and economically? I do not know the answers to this question—furthermore, I do not believe the question can be answered at this time. All I can say is that I believe this demand for personal mobility has set an inevitable trend in motion, and that developments in the twenty-first—perhaps the twenty-second—century will see the transport problem being solved along these lines.

SELECTED BIBLIOGRAPHY

1. BELLOC, H. (1923). *The Road*. Manchester: Hobson.
2. BRUCE, F. E. (1954). The evolution of public health engineering. *Journal of the Royal Society of Arts*. **102** (4925), 475–494.
3. JOYCE, J. (1967). *The Story of Passenger Transport in Great Britain*. London: Ian Allen.
4. MINISTRY OF TRANSPORT (1969). *Passenger Transport in Great Britain, 1967*. London: H.M.S.O.
5. ANON. (1968). *Passenger Transport Yearbook* (*1967*). Shepperton, Middlesex: Modern Transport Publishing Co.
6. LEEDS CITY COUNCIL (1967). Town and Country Planning Act, 1962: First Review of City Development Plan. Leeds: The Council.
7. OI, W. Y. & SHULDINER, P. W. (1962). *An Analysis of Urban Travel Demands*. Evanston, Illinois: Northwestern University Press.
8. SMITH, W. S. (1966). Urban transport co-ordination. *Traffic Engineering and Control*. **8** (5), 304–306.
9. CORNWELL, E. L. (1967). B.R.'s advanced turbo-train project. *Modern Railways*. **23** (224), 234–235.
10. SMEED, R., *et al.* (1964). *Road Pricing: The Economic and Technical Possibilities*. London: H.M.S.O.
11. BOULADON, G. (1967). The transport gaps. *Science Journal*. **3** (4), 41–46.
12. BLAKE, L. R. (1966/67). A public transport system using four passenger self-routing cars. Proceedings of the Convention on Guided Land Transport. Institution of Mechanical Engineers. Proceedings 181, pt. 30, 132–144.
13. ANON. (1966). Mass transportation on the move. *Industrial Design*. **13** (10), 28–47.
14. GOVERNMENT OF THE DISTRICT OF COLUMBIA (1965). The Minibus in Washington: Final Report on a Mass Demonstration Project. DC-MTD-2. Washington, D.C. U.S. Government Printing Office.
15. PASSENGER BELT CONVEYORS, INC. The Carveyor: Solution to City Traffic Snarls. Bulletin 256. Stephens-Adamson Manufacturing Co., Aurora, Illinois, and the Goodyear Tyre and Rubber Co., Akron, Ohio, U.S.A. Undated manufacturers literature.

Discussion

Burton: I would like to include in the cost that we have been discussing an additional cost which is that of re-building alongside these new forms of communication. Costs should include for the rehabilitation of those areas of living or working which are alongside new systems of communication. If we do not, we will be creating totally unacceptable environmental conditions for many of those areas.

Burberry: Professor O'Flaherty has been referring to central areas and the centrality of areas in existing towns. It is not at all clear to me why centrality should be preserved or what its virtues are. We seem to be struggling to maintain centrality by means of new transport applications and ingenious mechanical devices to fit in amongst the pattern of existing buildings.

O'Flaherty: I have lived in three American towns none of which was heavily centralised. In Los Angeles, which is the city at which everyone throws up their hands in horror, all the Los Angeleans are happy and are not worried one bit about centrality. I would hate to see the centre of London or York changed, but I doubt if there is anything to preserve in Leeds. One reason people want to go to central areas is because they have a choice of goods. There is of course tremendous investment in the central areas of towns.

Stone: When you put a modern highway through the centre of a town, you are concerned not with taking just enough land and just enough buildings to do the job but you must also acquire sufficient land on either side to enable you to build a new sort of urban form, which is compatible with having a high speed road system running through it. You might box the road system in, so that the noise and fumes inside would disappear, or you might build buildings backing on to it, or bridging over it, so you would lose the unpleasant part of the road system by building a new 'built-in' form. Obviously this would be very much more expensive, because the problem of putting a new road system in is not just the cost of putting the roads in but also of replacing what you have knocked down and in an acceptable way.

Bennett: In dealing with the highway problem, no highway authority in the past did the job in the way they might wish. They can carry out highway improvements, but they cannot carry out improvements in the sense that we are saying is important. We found, when working on the motorway project, that to do the work in a way that we thought acceptable would cost over one mile, only 6% more but we cannot get a grant for that 6%. To buy enough land in order to plan for the road in a comprehensive way may take away the homes of thousands of people, but this land can be re-developed in an acceptable way. As things stand today, we do not have the power to do the work in the way it should be done.

O'Flaherty: We are trying to develop the transport system and towns are being remodelled in certain ways, but there is no bringing together of all the relevant problems. What are the goals with respect to traffic movement? I am an Engineer and I very much value money, but I think it is important to keep in mind that economics are not everything; money is to spend.

Jones: It is money that is stopping Mr. Bennett from producing a proper environment. The environment loses every time; it is the chap with the motor car who always wins. If we can afford new roads we must afford not to wreck the environment.

Thomas: The point is to set your objectives and bring in the economist to see if these objectives can be met, but it seems that mobility has become the goal and the objective.

Nealon: The motor car, which is often only one-third filled, cannot be allowed to run about our towns only fractionally used.

The airport and the town

by

C. A. O'FLAHERTY

INTRODUCTION

WHEN THE PIONEER Orville Wright wobbled into the air for 12 seconds over the sands of Kill Devil Hills at Kittyhawk, North Carolina on 17 December 1903 there can have been no thought in his mind of the trends and developments which he was about to set in motion.

The Wrights' 'Flyer' achieved a maximum speed of 30 mile/h, when it flew on that fateful day in December; now commercial passenger planes are travelling in excess of 1400 mile/h—and it may not be very long, perhaps even in this century, when hypersonic transport planes will make it possible to fly from London to New York in 35 minutes. The Wrights' plane was barely able to carry its pilot on its first flight; today's 'Jumbo Jets' are capable of carrying between 360 and 490 passengers between continents. Unfortunately, however, the benefits gained from these tremendous achievements in the air are considered by many to be frustrated by the lack of developments on the ground with regard to the rest of the trip made by the air traveller. It is for this reason that very considerable interest is now being generated by what is popularly known as the 'ground access problem'.

Figure 1 shows that the air traveller's trip may be broken down into three main phases—the ground trips to and from the airport, the periods spent at the origin and

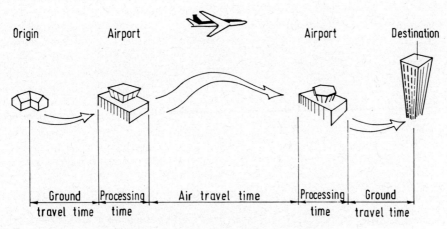

FIGURE 1. The air transport system.

destination airports, and the air trip itself. While the most spectacular developments in air travel have been concerned with the intermediate portion of the system (the air trip), the greatest number of complaints appear to be concerned with the other phases. In particular, the airline and airport executives appear to be continually worried about the ground phases.

It is the primary purpose of this paper to attempt to place these various phases of the air traveller's journey in perspective in relation to each other and in relation to the town. Before doing so, however, it is useful to briefly examine some basic trends with respect to the growth in the numbers of air passengers, the planes which transport them, and the airports which these planes service.

THE GROWTH OF AIR TRAVEL

The two most striking trends in the field of passenger transport at this time are the great increases in the number of private motor vehicles on the road, and the rapid growth rate of air passenger travel. Everybody is aware of the problems brought to the roadway by the private car, primarily because all experience them daily on the congested urban roads of this country. The general public is however, very much less aware of the problems associated with the growth of air travel, mainly because even now the numbers of people to travel by air are still fairly small in comparison with the total numbers who travel by the other transport modes; and road transport problems are just outside their doors.

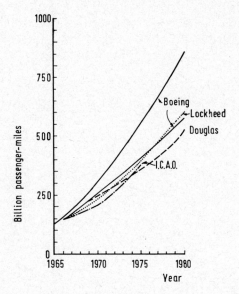

FIGURE 2. Some forecasts of scheduled passenger air traffic in the Western World.

The trends with respect to air travel are really quite staggering. Consider Figure 2 in which is shown the range of expected *scheduled* passenger traffic predicted by I.C.A.O.

and by a number of aircraft manufacturers.[1] Whichever of these forecasts is the correct one is incidental to this paper; what is more important here is the recognition that air travel by people using the scheduled air carriers is expected to more than double, and may possibly quadruple, *within the next 10 years*.

Since the end of the immediate post-World War II depression, scheduled air passenger travel development has been characterised by three main growth periods. First of all, there was the buoyant growth period which lasted until about 1957; during this period air traffic growth averaged about 16·5% per year. Between 1957 and 1962, there was a world-wide economic recession during which the growth rate dropped to about 10%. As a result of the world-wide economic prosperity which on the whole has been experienced since 1962—combined, of course, with the introduction into service of jet aircraft and an associated real reduction in air fares—the average growth rate per annum has been of the order of 16%. If world prosperity increases, and current trends towards the introduction into service of bigger and faster jet planes continue, then it is extremely likely that past history with regard to growth will be extended into the future—and that air passenger volumes of the order shown in Figure 2 will be achieved.

It is not entirely clear from the reference on which the data in Figure 2 are based whether or not the Boeing projections include only air passenger traffic via the scheduled flights. Since it appears that the other projections do not include any non-scheduled air traffic, then it is probable that the growths shown in this figure considerably underestimate what the actual increases in air travel will be like in the near future.

(It might also be emphasised here that no attempt is made in Figure 2—or elsewhere in this paper—to discuss the growth of travel associated with developments in regard to the general aviation fleet and the freight air traffic fleet).

The data in Figure 2 are expressed on a passenger-mile basis. It is of interest to note that the numbers of air passengers actually carried by the scheduled air carriers have been predicted by I.C.A.O. to increase from 200 million in 1966 to about 770 million by 1980.

International air passenger traffic is expected to increase at an even greater rate than world passenger traffic—but it will vary greatly from region to region. An illustration of the manner in which the Boeing organisation expect growth to take place is given in Figure 3.

On the most important intercontinental route, that across the North Atlantic, an average of I.C.A.O. and Lockheed forecasts indicate that the number of passengers carried should increase from the actual value of about 4 million in 1965 to over 8 million in 1970 and to about 17 million by 1975—in other words, a fourfold increase over the projected period of ten years. (In 1968, the actual North Atlantic traffic amounted to 5·26 million passengers.)

In 1965 the world's scheduled airlines carried about 177 million passengers, of whom 48% composed the U.S. domestic air passenger traffic. By 1980, the U.S. domestic market share of the total air passenger traffic is expected to be anywhere between 34 and 55%. The emphasis on the lower percentage suggests that more dramatic developments may be expected in the future outside the United States rather than within. Thus, for example the number of intra-Europe air passengers which will be carried by the scheduled air services between 1964 and 1980 is predicted by Lockheed to be as shown

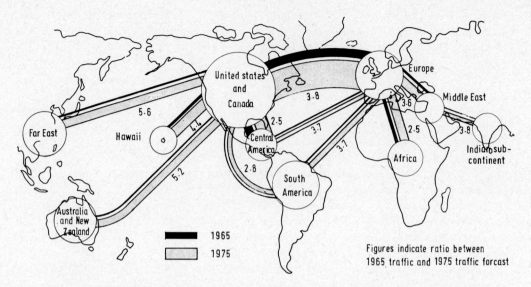

FIGURE 3. Intercontinental air passenger traffic predicted by Boeing, 1965 and 1975.

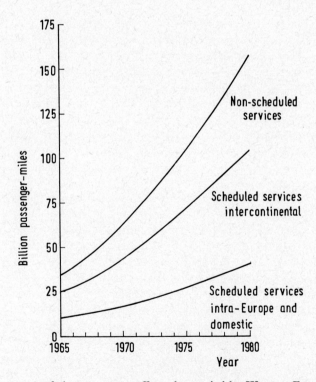

FIGURE 4. Forecasts of air passenger traffic to be carried by Western European airlines.

in Table 1. Also given in this table are some predictions of traffic along some other intercontinental routes involving Europe.

TABLE 1

European air passenger traffic growth, millions

Year Area pair	1964 (Actual)	1970	1975	1980
Intra-Europe	22·9	48·0	80·0	120·0
Europe–Africa	1·6	4·0	8·2	15·0
Europe–Middle East	0·9	2·6	4·5	8·5
Europe–South America	0·3	0·6	0·95	1·5

There is very little data available on which to base predictions of non-scheduled air passenger traffic growth. Historically, however, it is known that intra-Europe non-scheduled inclusive tour and other charter traffic have grown at an accelerated rate from what was essentially zero in 1960 to about 50% of the scheduled traffic in 1966. A prediction[2] of what may be expected in this respect in the future is given in Figure 4. This suggests that by 1980 the non-scheduled air traffic in Europe will be as great as the scheduled air traffic.

GROWTH OF THE AIR FLEETS

It is obvious that if the numbers of air passengers carried in future years are to increase to anywhere like the extent described above, then there will also have to be considerable changes in the characters of the airline fleets.

Using statistics such as those given above, and assuming that a typical 100-seat medium-haul subsonic aircraft has an output of $62·5 \times 10^6$ passenger-miles per year, it is possible to estimate the *equivalent* number of these 100-seat passenger aircraft which will need to be in service on scheduled and non-scheduled passenger operations at any time in the future. The real problem is to decide how this demand will be divided between aircraft categories ranging from small feeder aircraft to 'jumbo jets' and to the supersonic aircraft of the present and the future. One estimate[3] of how this demand may be split between the different existing and future aircraft is given in Figure 5.

While supersonic military aircraft have been flying for some time, it is only recently that the first commercial supersonic transport (SST) was put into the air; this was the Russian-built TU-144 which made its maiden test flight at the beginning of January, 1969. This aircraft (140 passengers); the Anglo-French Concorde (132–140 passengers) which flew on 2 March 1969; and the American Boeing 2707 (270 passengers) which is expected to fly in about 1976; are intended to operate on long-haul high density air routes i.e. at distances greater than about 2000 miles, at speeds in excess of twice the speed of sound. Because of the social nuisance of the sonic booms created by these aircraft they will operate primarily over water; when passing over land it is very likely that they will have to travel at subsonic speeds. Thus it is unlikely that supersonic aircraft will be used for long-haul intra-Europe flights. (It might also be noted that the TU-144 is not expected to penetrate the Western World travel market to any great extent.)

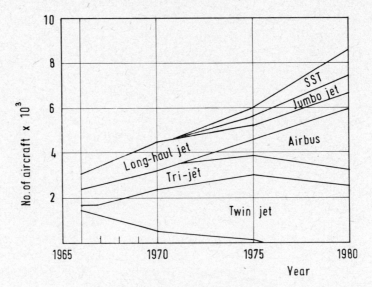

FIGURE 5. World airline fleet forecasts.

A major point to remember with regard to these long-haul supersonic aircraft is that because of their very high speeds each aircraft will be, on average, able to make two trips where hithertofore only one was possible with subsonic jet aircraft.

The family of subsonic aircraft which is most likely to cause problems at airports in the future is the 'jumbo jet'. The first of these planes, the 380–490 passenger Boeing 747 (see Figure 6) flew on 9 February 1969. Because of its great passenger carrying abilities this aircraft is also expected to serve the densely trafficked long-haul routes. I am conscious that airlines are in business not only to carry passengers but also to make money and, hence, I am quite confident that the 747 will also penetrate the high-density medium-haul (1000–2000 mile range) market; thus we could well see them in use on some heavily-trafficked intra-Europe routes, particularly during the busy summer months.

While discussing the jumbo jets, mention must be made of the maxi-jumbo of possibly the near future—the Lockheed Company's L-500 which is the civilian version of the military transport plane, the C-5A. The C-5A, which is now undergoing its test flight programme prior to delivery to the U.S. Military Airlift Command for use on intercontinental routes, is the biggest and heaviest aircraft yet built. It has a maximum gross weight of nearly 350 tons and is designed to carry 920 troops or 100,000 lb of cargo. Lockheed are now seeking firm orders for the civilian version of this aircraft, the three-decked L-500—it will be capable of carrying upwards of 750 air passengers and their baggage—and if sufficient interest is generated Lockheed say that deliveries of this aircraft to airlines could begin in 1972.

The conventional long-haul jets e.g. Boeing 707, stretched DC8, are currently flying the routes which the SST's and the jumbo jets are designed to serve. Thus the future of the conventional long-haul aircraft is obviously going to be affected by the degree of success of these future ones. On the assumption that the SST's and the jumbo aircraft

FIGURE 6. The Boeing 747 'jumbo jet'.

will be 'successful', then the long-haul jets are likely to be gradually retired because of their overlapping service role.

The mid-1970's should also see the introduction into service of the Airbus aircraft. (Nobody in the airline industry really likes the name 'airbus', because of its implications of a cut-rate approach to service and comfort—which, it is claimed, is the very opposite to what is intended.) Basically, the airbus reflects a flexibility concept which calls for applying new technology, especially new engines, to the development of an aircraft that can carry between 200 and 350 passengers over diverse routes ranging from as low as 200 miles to a maximum of 3500 miles. In other words, the airbus will simply be a new branch of the jumbo jet family which is intended to dominate the medium- and short-haul travel market. (The 747's and SST's will be principally aimed at the transcontinental and intercontinental travel market).

Virtually all major airlines believe that there is a need for the airbus but, as yet, nobody is quite sure as to which will be the accepted design forms.[4] Nevertheless, because of its expected ability to carry large numbers of people economically and comfortably over long distances, the airbus will no doubt further cut into the demand area which is within the province of the conventional long-haul jet—just as it will also cut into the short-and-medium haul markets served by conventional two- and three-jet aircraft. In fact, some of the airbuses may themselves be trijet planes e.g. Lockheed 1011 (see Figure 7) while others may be twinjet planes e.g. the French/German A-300B.

Figure 5 also shows that notwithstanding the fact that we are rapidly heading into an era of the high capacity aircraft, a significant number of aircraft with carrying capacities

FIGURE 7. The proposed Lockheed 1011 trijet airbus.

of between say 80 and 110 passengers e.g. BAC 1-11, will also be required in the future. These aircraft will be used on short-haul and some medium-haul routes. These routes will probably be mostly domestic feeder routes and the less densely trafficked international routes not serviced by the airbus.

In summary, there can be no doubt but that the data in Figure 5 also suggest very clearly that a new era is being entered upon with respect to air travel. Air transport is booming and, of necessity, the airlines are having to introduce new, bigger and more flexible aircraft in order to cope with the new traffic. Thus, the high capacity aircraft era, cannot but have dramatic effects with respect to airport development.

GROWTH OF AIRPORTS

From what has been said already with respect to air travel and the air fleets, it is clear that airports are also entering on an era of rapid expansion and change. This is well appreciated by the authorities administering both major or minor airports. Obviously, however, the impact will be most felt in the future at the major airports.

In order to appreciate how developments at large airports as a whole are likely to take place it is useful to refer to a study[1] published in 1968, which attempted to gauge the future of the world's 65 major airports i.e. those likely to handle the high capacity jumbo-jets and the supersonic transports of the next decade. In the study these airports were divided into two groups according to the number of passengers handled in 1965; the first group contained 25 airports which handled more than 2 million passengers in 1965, while the remaining 40 handled less than this volume. The main results of the study can be summarised in the two alternative sets of estimates (which were based on two different sets of assumptions), given in Table 2.

TABLE 2

Projections of air passenger growth at the world's 65 major airports

Estimate	Airports	Air passengers, millions			
		1965 actual	1970	1975	1980
No. 1	At first 25	163	325 (×2·0)	523 (×3·2)	703 (×4·3)
	At 40 other	36	Not given		
No. 2	At first 25	163	399 (×2·4)	796 (×4·9)	1335 (×8·2)
	At 40 other	36	75 (×2·1)	127 (×3·5)	180 (×5·0)

These projections of future air passenger traffic represent only a rough indication of future traffic volumes at the major airports as a group, and are not necessarily indicative of expected values at any particular airport. Even so, these values do suggest that by 1980 the first group of 25 airports will have to handle four to eight times as many passengers as in 1965. The study also showed that at least eight of these large airports will have to handle about 20 million passengers per year in 1980, while at least four may each have to deal with 45 million or more—which raises the question, of course, can these extremely large numbers be handled at single airports before their plane handling capacities are exceeded.

It might be noted that the only airport in Britain which fell into the top 25 category of airports is Heathrow. (Gatwick, the next largest in this country, did not handle 2 million passengers until 1968; it now expects to have to deal with over 20 million air passengers per year by 1980.)

If present-size aircraft only were to be employed to handle the predicted air passenger traffic volumes of the future, there is no doubt but that many major airports would become hopelessly congested during peak hours. By 1980, about 24 million departures of present-size aircraft would have to be scheduled each year to meet the predicted free world demand;[5] however, with Boeing 747-type jumbo aircraft handling long-haul routes, the annual departures may possibly be reduced by about 37% to 15 million (see Figure 8).

According to Boeing projections (see Table 3) there will be 16 passenger and 5 cargo flights of 747 aircraft departing from London's airports on a typical day in 1971; by 1976 daily departures of this aircraft from London will climb to 50 passenger and 19 cargo planes. Inevitably, this type of traffic is going to have a considerable effect upon passenger and baggage handling facilities not only at London's airports but also at those others which almost certainly will be handling at least the airbuses of the mid-1970's (e.g. Manchester, Dublin, Glasgow, Belfast, Jersey, Southend, Edinburgh, Birmingham).

13 UE

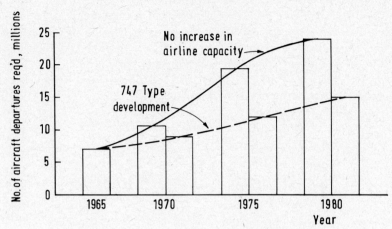

FIGURE 8. Aircraft departure requirements, 1980.

All in all, it is safe to say that airports are in for a sustained period of expansion. The biggest problems will, of course, have to be dealt with at the big airports. Even so, it must not be forgotten that what are now small airports will soon be big ones—that Luton Airport for example, is growing at such a rate that by 1975 it will be as big as Gatwick Airport is today, or that the Leeds/Bradford Airport of 1980 will be the same size as Belfast Airport is now.

TABLE 3

Predicted daily departures of Boeing 747's from airports at some of the world's cities in 1971 and 1976

City	1971		1976	
	Passenger	Cargo	Passenger	Cargo
New York	87	15	198	49
Los Angeles	35	7	96	33
Chicago	33	15	95	52
San Francisco	18	6	54	35
London	16	5	40	19
Honolulu	28	1	49	10
Paris	14	2	29	13
Montreal	10	0	28	15
Miami	14	0	28	7
San Juan	11	0	27	5
Seattle	6	1	25	5
Washington	7	0	25	5
Rome	5	3	23	11
Frankfurt	6	3	22	12
Tokyo	11	1	22	5

GROUND TRANSPORT TO AND FROM THE AIRPORT

The airport 'ground access problem' is a major consideration which is well to the fore in the minds of airline executives and airport planners and administrators today.

The extent to which it has registered in the mind of the average air traveller is, as yet, unknown—although it is well appreciated that most air travellers now allow themselves generous 'safety margins' with regard to the times which they allocate for getting to busy airports.

Within the communities serviced by airports it is probably true to say that at this time there is little major concern about ground access. Instead there is concern about the site of the airport—and the wish is often expressed that the airport could be farther away from the town. Indeed, from the newspapers one often gets the impression that the only suitable location for an airport is where nobody lives or wants to visit, preferably in a coastal area (deserted by native birds), so that the runways can be extended into the sea to avoid wastage of agricultural land! Unfortunately, these areas, when they can be found, are very poorly serviced by transport facilities.

Location of Airports

The majority of the world's larger airports—many of which were established during the early 1930's—are generally located at some distances from the central areas of the towns and cities which they serve. The main reasons for this were that the large land areas needed by the airports were usually cheaper at these distant locations; there were fewer buildings to obstruct the landing approaches; the aircraft noises caused less annoyance; and, when accidents occurred, they rarely involved people on the ground.

Since World War II, however, cities and towns have continually expanded and have spread out and out so that although airports are still far from city centres, they are no longer as isolated as they used to be. Also, airports themselves have attracted connected industries, while the availability of adjacent cheap land, serviced by air and other forms of transport, has attracted other industries as well as housing developments.

The result is that nowadays an airport, although once located away from a community, is no longer isolated from it.

Thus, ground travellers going to/from the airport are now experiencing the congestion and other movement difficulties which have for some time been more normally associated with transport and travel within towns themselves.

The Airport Population

From the ground access aspect all of the groups of people who comprise a given airport's population are of interest. The main population groups are as follows:

1. Air passengers with originating or terminating trips in the area serviced by the airport.
2. Visitors accompanying or meeting air passengers.
3. Other visitors e.g. sightseers, people on business, etc.
4. Airport employees.

From the limited statistics which are available regarding airport populations it would appear that no simple relationship exists between the size of a given airport's population and the proportions of air travellers, visitors, and employees comprising it.[6] In general, however, it is perhaps true to say that

—the ratio of employees to total airport users decreases as the airport population increases

—the constituent proportions of the airport population vary significantly not only according to the time of the year but also according to the day of the week.

The most complete published set of data available with regard to the population of an airport in Great Britain were collected relatively recently in the course of a survey at London (Heathrow) Airport.[7] This study showed that there were 37,350 people employed at Heathrow at the time of the survey, and that the great majority of these lived close to the airport. Limited data regarding air passengers are available from the Heathrow study in that only *departing* air passengers were interviewed in the course of the survey. Even so, it was found that the 15-hour totals of these passengers were approximately 21,000 on a peak season weekday and Sunday, and about 10,500 on an off-peak weekday and Sunday. A calculation of the numbers of people using Heathrow's central terminal area (C.T.A.) on a typical weekday during the busy season gave the following approximate figures:

Departing air passengers	17,500
Arriving air passengers	Not counted
Visitors meeting or seeing-off air passengers	22,000
Sightseeing visitors	12,500
Persons employed in the C.T.A.	6,500

It is also interesting to note that at Heathrow, departing air passengers on business trips form only 20–30% of the total during the peak-season days whereas they jump to 60–70% in the off-season. (It might be noted that the lower percentage in either case relates to Sundays.)

Origins and Destinations

The diversity of the origins and destinations of ground travellers to/from airports is illustrated in Figure 9. This figure is intended to show that the locations of the origins

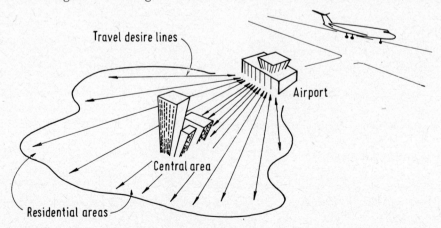

FIGURE 9. The origins and destinations of people who travel to and from airports.

and destinations are not grouped at any one point but rather are diffused throughout the community served by the airport.

On the whole, visitors who travel to an airport to sightsee or for entertainment or to patronise restaurants or to bring (or collect) air travellers, do not leave or return to a place of business; instead they come from and return to their homes which are scattered throughout the community.

For the majority of employees, the origins and destinations are also their homes; these will also be dispersed but, as mentioned already with respect to Heathrow, will typically be on the side of the community which is closest to the airport. The origins/destinations of air travellers obviously vary according to whether the airport being considered is at the home town or an 'away' town, and whether or not the trip is being made for business or personal reasons.

Business air travellers at the origin town travel to the airport either directly from their homes or from their offices which may or may not be near/in the town's central area. At the destination town, arriving business air travellers may go to a place of business or hotel, either in the central area or in a decentralised location. Upon returning to their home towns, these travellers may go to their offices, or probably more frequently, directly to their homes.

Air travellers who are journeying for personal reasons usually begin their trips at their homes, only a small number of which can be expected to be close to the central area. At the destination town this air traveller may go to a home or to a nearby recreational area—it is probably true to say that it is only in the largest cities, e.g. London, New York, that this type of traveller will want to go to a hotel in the central area.

It is important to appreciate that the origins and destinations of people travelling to/from an airport and the visitors accompanying/meeting them are, on the whole, spread throughout the area serviced by the airport. It is only a proportion of these trips which originate/terminate in the central area of the town close to the airport. Furthermore, the smaller the town, the smaller the proportion of trips which originate/terminate in the central area.

While few studies have been carried out into the origins and destinations of people using airports (and most of these have been at the very large airports), there is enough evidence available to substantiate the above deductions. For example, in the Heathrow Airport study[7] it was found that only 2·5% of the employed work trips originated in the central area of London, whereas about 60% came from within 5 miles of the airport. The very diversity of the origins of the ground trips to the airport is most dramatically reflected in Figure 10. (In relation to Figure 10 it might be noted that zones 21 and 23 are two of the three zones forming the central area of London. The remaining zone, number 23, is not outlined in this diagram.)

An analysis of air passenger data gathered at seven major airports in the United States in recent years[8] gave the origins and destinations for air travellers, which are listed in Table 4. In the Heathrow study it was found that about 40% of the outgoing air passengers travelling by ground to the airport had origins in the central area of London; a further 30% came from the rest of London, while the remaining 30% came from outside the boundaries of the area under the control of the Greater London Council. (It might also be mentioned here that approximately three-quarters of the outgoing air passengers with origins in the central area of London were non-residents of the United Kingdom.)

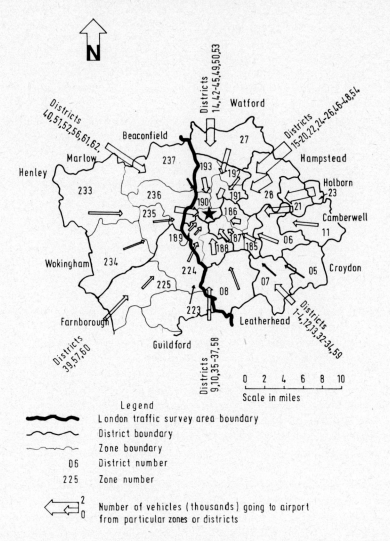

FIGURE 10. The origins of all vehicle trips inbound to London (Heathrow) Airport.

The data in Table 4 also illustrate a further important point. It is that even at large cities there is no 'fixed' percentage of air travellers with origins and destinations in the central area. The percentage can vary very much from city to city and even between two airports (see New York) in a given city. Undoubtedly the form and layout of a given town, its function and purpose, as well as the entertainment attraction of its central area, are major factors influencing the split in any given instance.

A search through the literature has failed to reveal any detailed data regarding the origins and destinations of air passengers using airports which service smaller communities. If such data were available I am sure that they would show that proportionately less air travellers originate/terminate their trips at the central areas of smaller towns as

TABLE 4

*Proportions of air passengers travelling to and from
the central areas of some American cities*

Airport	Per cent travelling to and from the central area
New York –J.F.K.	46
–La Guardia	60
Chicago –O'Hare	30
Washington–National	25
–Dulles	26
Los Angeles	11
Miami	59

compared with larger ones. This is certainly suggested by the data in Figure 11 in which is summarised information regarding the North of England origins and destinations of domestic air passengers using the Leeds/Bradford–London (Heathrow) air route. This figure shows that only 24% of these domestic trips started or ended in Leeds as a whole (*not* in the central area) and 12% had origins or destination in Bradford. No detailed data was collected in this study regarding the percentages with origins or destinations in the central areas of these towns but undoubtedly they are considerably less than the values obtained for the towns as wholes.

Choice of Ground Transport Mode

So far I have attempted to show that most airports are located well away from the central areas of towns, and that the desire lines for ground travel extend from the airport to all parts of the community. This inevitably suggests that the transport modes most used to transport people to and from airports are those which are best able to cope with this diffuse pattern i.e. private cars and taxis. The evidence which is available points up that this clearly is the case.

With few exceptions, access to world airports is by road only. The exceptions in Europe are London's Gatwick Airport which is serviced by the London–Brighton commuter railway lines, Vienna whose airport is also astride the regular commuter rail network, Berlin which has a special rail link from Templehof Airport to the city's central area (and is, anyway, a 'special case'), and Brussels which has a special link railway which connects the National Airport with the general rail network servicing the city. Table 5 gives some details regarding these rail links.

TABLE 5

Some details of Europe's rail links from central area to airport

Airport	Frequency of service, min	Duration of journey, min	Distance miles Total	Distance miles Over own track
Berlin–Templehof	5–10	20	2·5	2·5
Brussels–National	13–35	16	8·75	1·7
London–Gatwick	30	40	27	0
Vienna	—	40	15·5	0

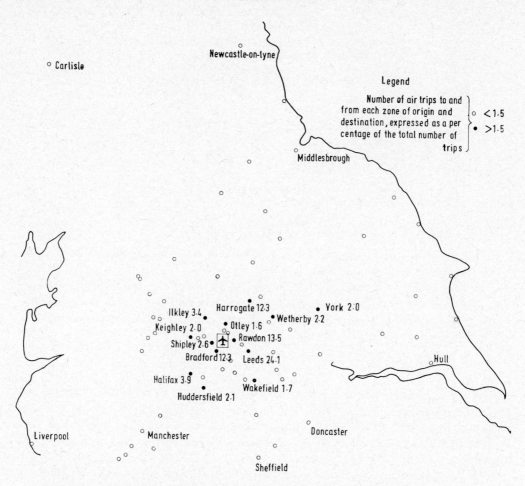

FIGURE 11. The North of England origins and destinations of domestic air passengers
using the Leeds/Bradford–London air route.

In Brussels, air passengers represent, on average, half of the rail link's users, the other half being visitors and airport employees. Overall, the air passengers using the rail link between National Airport and the city account for about 29% of all the air passengers handled by the airport.[9] Studies carried out by the Ministry of Aviation have shown[10] that of the air travellers arriving at Gatwick's landside to depart by air, 56% travel by rail (28% come by car and 15% by coach).

The only airport in North America which can claim to be serviced by a rail link is Boston's Logan Airport. This is an underground rail system which links downtown Boston with the edge of the airport from which point a bus, running on a continuous loop within the airport brings passengers to and from the various terminals. Although considered to be the fastest, most dependable and least aggravating route between the airport and the town, only about 5% of Logan's air passengers use the rail link.[11]

What is perhaps the newest as well as the most exciting fixed-rail airport-town link is the 8·2 mile long monorail connection between Tokyo's International Airport at Haneda and Hamamatsu Station which is six minutes by car from the central area. Opened in September, 1964, this monorail had been expected to carry 10–14 million passengers in its first year;[12] in fact, it carried just over 3 million.[13] Departures on this line—it has two tracks—take place every 7 or 10 minutes, and the trip takes about 15 minutes.

At all airports in the world other than those mentioned above, ground access is by rubber-tyred vehicles using roadways. Some of these are rubber-tyred vehicles which connect with rail vehicles whereas others are the prime movers. In either case, the carrying vehicles are private or self-drive hired cars, taxis, coaches or buses, and limousines i.e. vehicles capable of carrying six to eight people and their baggage which are used in North America. In any given town, the coaches, buses and limousines most usually ply between the airport and points of dense air traffic concentrations in the community e.g. air terminals—most often in the central area—or railway stations which may be located either in the central area or elsewhere. Buses may also, of course, form part of a town's public transport system.

As indicated by the data in Figure 12, which is based on relatively comparable data obtained from ten different major airports and partial data from at least two dozen others in the United States,[14] the private car accounts for the ground transport of between 37 and 74% of the airline passengers using major airports in America: taxis account for between 12 and 41%, limousines from between 18 and 38%, and public buses for not more than 4%. (Helicopters carry fewer than 5% of the airline passengers —data from 1955 to 1960—most of whom are connecting passengers between airports.)

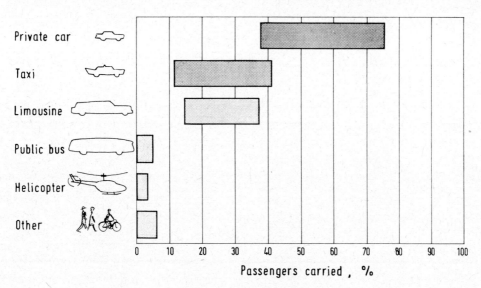

FIGURE 12. Airline passengers ground transport modes to/from some major airports in the United States.

By far the greatest number of airport employees at American airports travel to and from work by private car e.g. the figure is more than 90% for Washington's National Airport. At London's Heathrow Airport about 76% of the employees use private cars to journey to work; of those from car-owning households, 93% use cars and only 7%

use public transport, whereas of those from non-car-owning households 43% use private transport and the remaining 57% use public transport.

Published data regarding air passenger choice of ground transport mode to and from European airports are relatively meagre. However, some material which is available with regard to some European airports is given in Table 6.

It is difficult to draw firm conclusions from the data in Figure 12 and Table 6. First of all, it is important to appreciate that the data was collected under varying conditions and at different times of the year. Nevertheless, it is probably true to say that public transport i.e. bus or tram, plays a negligible part in bringing air travellers to either American or European airports. It may also possibly be true to say that the private car and taxi play a more dominant role in America than in Europe; the evidence supporting this conclusion is, however, very limited.

TABLE 6

Some various statistics regarding air passenger ground travel modes to European airports

Airport Trans- port mode	Per cent share by each mode						
	Amsterdam –Schipol	Paris –Orly	Brussels –National	Geneva	Zurich	London –Heathrow	London –Gatwick
*Special coach and/or train services	39	34	29	12	53	52	71
Taxis		25·5	30		15	8	
Private cars left in the car park	61	10	41	88	8	40	29
Private cars taking passengers		28·5			21		
Hired cars		2			1		
Public transport					2		

* Plus bus public transport for the London airports.

What is perhaps the most valid deduction which may be drawn from the above data is that there are some very significant variations regarding the percentages using particular ground travel modes to different airports. It is important to appreciate this since it infers that what occurs at one airport is not necessarily representative of what will happen at another if similar transport facilities are provided.

A further point which might also be made here is that most published data regarding transport modes and splits refer to larger airports and not to smaller ones. Even so, it is not illogical to assume that the smaller the airport, the greater the percentage of air travellers who will arrive at/depart from the airport by private car.

TABLE 7

Average maximum times taken for central area–airport journeys, in relation to distances

Distance, central area to airport	All N. American airports*			Thirty-two U.S. 'Large Hub' airports*			Thirty-nine U.S. 'Medium Hub' airports*			Fifty-one European International airports*			
miles	No.	%	Max. time, min	No.	%	Max. time, min	No.	%	Max. time, min	No.	%	Max. time, min	Min. time, min
3	174	22·8	18	2	6·3	23	1	2·6	17	4	7·8	10	6
3 – 6	259	33·9	26	3	9·4	28	16	41·0	31·5	19	37·2	27	14·5
6 – 9	129	16·9	32	6	18·8	38	12	30·7	36	11	21·6	32·5	20
9 –12·5	83	10·9	36·5	9	28·1	43	4	10·2	39	6	11·7	48	24
12·5–16	39	5·1	41	4	12·5	48	4	10·2	41	4	7·8	61	32
16 –19	32	4·2	43	4	12·5	55	1	2·6	39	1	2·0	42·5	35
19 –22	18	2·3	42	1	3·1	48	—	—	—	1	2·0	60	40
22 –25	9	1·2	42	1	3·1	⎫	1	2·6	40	1	2·0	60	40
25 –28	6	0·8	58	1	3·1	⎬ 49	—	—	—	3	5·9	50	29
28 –31	6	0·8	49	1	3·1	⎭	—	—	—	1	2·0	72·5	48
31 –34	—	—	—	—	—	—	—	—	—	—	—	—	—
34 –37·5	1	0·1	—	—	—	—	—	—	—	—	—	—	—
37·5–41	6	0·8	—	—	—	—	—	—	—	—	—	—	—
41 –44	—	—	⎫ 60	—	—	—	—	—	—	—	—	—	—
44 –47	2	0·2	⎭	—	—	—	—	—	—	—	—	—	—
Total	764	100·0	—	32	100·0	—	39	100·0	—	51	100·0	—	—

* Mainly by limousine and taxi
† Mainly by airport coach

Ground Travel Times and Distances

The time required to get to or from the airport is obviously a most important criterion to the airport user. Unfortunately, important though it may be, there is really relatively little known about it. What is known is primarily information obtained from airports and airport coach operators regarding times from the central areas of towns i.e. air terminals within the central areas, to the airport. Little or nothing is known about the times taken to travel between the airport and the origins/destinations of the airport users.

Some data which has been gathered regarding central area distances and times are summarised (9) in Table 7. Of the 764 North American airports mentioned in this table, 695 are in the United States and 69 in Canada. Of the 695 U.S. airports, data is also given separately for 32 'large hub' and 39 'medium hub' airports i.e. airports which *at the time of the survey* (prior to 1960) handled more than 0·5 million passengers per annum and 0·125 to 0·5 million passengers per annum respectively. The 51 European airports were all 'international' airports at the time of the survey (in the mid-nineteen sixties). In each instance maximum travel times were gathered as it is this time which is of greatest interest to the air traveller preparing for his trip.

The statistics shown in Table 7 enable the following facts to be established:

1. For North American airports.
   —the ground distances range between 0·5 and above 44 miles.
   —84·5% of the airports are located within 0·5 and 12·5 miles of the central area.
   —the maximum travel times vary between 5 and 90 minutes.
2. For the thirty-two 'large hub' airports in the U.S.
   —the ground distances vary between 1·5 and 31 miles.
   —72% of the airports are located within 6 and 19 miles of the central area.
   —the maximum travel times vary between 10 and 90 minutes.
3. For the thirty-nine 'medium hub' airports in the U.S.
   —the ground distances range between 1·5 and 23 miles.
   —92% of the airports are situated within 3 and 16 miles of the central area.
   —the maximum travel times vary between 10 and 60 minutes.
4. For the fifty-one international airports in Europe.
   —the ground distances vary between 1 and 30 miles.
   —86% of the airports are situated within 1 and 16 miles of the central area.
   —the maximum travel times vary between 3 and 90 minutes.

The above data is of interest in that it points out the 'status quo' at the times the information was gathered. Other than that, however, their value is limited. It is impossible, for example, to deduce from them what *should be* the airport distances and travel times. Some attempt at determining criteria for adequacy/inadequacy was made at the time that the European data were gathered (in a survey carried out in 1965 by the European Conference of Ministers of Transport). In this survey, the airports were asked to state whether or not their road links with their related central areas were satisfactory. Analysis of their replies provided some 'norms' of distance (minimum 4 miles, maximum 12·5 miles), as well as maximum and minimum journey times and maximum and minimum average journey speeds (see Table 8). It will be noted from this table, however, that opinions as to what is adequate and inadequate overlap to a considerable extent.

TABLE 8

'Typical' conditions for international airports in Europe, the adequacy of whose connections with the central areas of towns they service have been considered

Travel conditions	Criterion	Adequate		Inadequate	
		Minimum	Maximum	Minimum	Maximum
Least favourable	Journey time	15 min	40 min	21 min	60 min
e.g. peak hour	Ave. speed	37·5 mile/h	6·25 mile/h	20 mile/h	6·25 mile/h
Most favourable	Journey time	12 min	40 min	11 min	40 min
e.g. off-peak	Ave. speed	37·5 mile/h	12·5 mile/h	36·25 mile/h	12·5 mile/h

Further analysis of both the North American and European data in Table 8 shows that no close connection exists between the size of a town and the journey time from its central area to the airport. The average journey speed rarely exceeds 31 mile/h and is most usually between 9 and 22 mile/h; it tends to be higher when the airport distance is high, i.e. when that part of the journey accomplished outside the town boundaries tends to be long in comparison with the journey length within the town.

Comparison of the North American and European data shows that the average travel time tends to be, on the whole, higher for Europe when the travel distance is between 9 and 31 miles; this probably reflects the higher priority which is given to the construction of semi-rural airport links in America. The contrary is generally true with regard to travel distances below about 9 miles. It is difficult to explain why this should be so; perhaps it is that European towns are generally more compact and less subject to sprawl than their North American counterparts and, thus, that a relatively large proportion of each American trip of less than 9 miles is spent travelling within busy build-up areas.

AT THE AIRPORT

Once the air passenger has reached the airport he has yet to pass through a series of time-consuming, but necessary, procedures. The processing times involved can be separated into what are essentially two main time steps:

A. Time to transfer to/from the terminal building (landside).
B. Time to transfer to/from the terminal building (airside) and to get through the terminal building.

The times and procedures actually involved in either of these two steps varies with the size of the airport, whether or not the air trip is an international or domestic one, whether or not the air passenger is arriving or departing, and the ground transport mode used to get to/from the airport.

Transfer (landside)

The landside transfer process ends at the landside entrance to the terminal building for the embarking air passenger, and vice versa for the arriving air passenger. In the case of the person who is dropped/picked up at the entrance to the terminal building by coach, car, taxi or limousine, the procedure is very simple and the transfer time is negligible. In the case of the person who has to transfer between the building and the car park, the situation can be very different—and time-consuming.

In order of priority, the location of car parking facilities in relation to the terminal building can be tabulated as follows:[15,16]

1. Pick-up and discharge curb spaces for coaches, private cars and taxis.
2. Short-term parking for arriving and departing air passengers.
3. Long-term parking for departing air passengers.
4. Hired car stations.
5. Taxi 'hold' areas.
6. Employee parking.

Although there is obvious logic to the above listing, very few airports apply it in practice. The result is that air passengers only too often have to walk quite long distances (carrying luggage) between their cars and the terminal building, simply because of the very great land areas occupied by large surface car parks. For example, a recent survey of thirteen of the larger airports on the continent of Europe[17] showed that the *average* longest walking distance (from the farthest public parking space to the nearest check-in desk in the terminal building) is 1352 ft. At Chicago's O'Hare Airport, the distance from the farthest part of the car park to the terminal building entrance is 1800 ft.

The undesirability of these long walking distances—and the consequent waste times involved—is recognised and so nowadays the trend in airport design is to provide for vertical rather than horizontal parking. In other words, the trend is to construct parking garages as part of, or close to, the terminal building. At this time, however, only three British airports have multi-storey parking facilities. At London (Heathrow) Airport the longest walking distance is 500 ft. while at Glasgow Airport (1·5 million air passengers) —both of these airports have parking garages—the longest walking distance is a low 230 ft.

The importance of providing adequate car parking facilities at an airport cannot be over-emphasised. What happened recently at Los Angeles International Airport[14] may be considered by some to illustrate the 'ultimate' in this problem—but, to others, including myself, it is an example of what may become quite common in the future at the world's larger airports unless exit/entrance and parking facilities are considerably improved. One day in 1968, at an off-peak travel time when very few aircraft were lined up for take-off, all of the airport's parking spaces were occupied so that cars could only enter every three minutes, which is the rate at which other vehicles were exiting. The result was that the airport-bound traffic ground to a halt within the vicinity of the airport and jammed the main highways within a radius of several miles for the greater part of the day. It might be added that the airport had 7000 parking spaces at the time of the 'big jam'; it is now planning to have 30,000 parking spaces by about 1985.

In a study of parking requirements at U.S. airports which was published[18] in 1964, it is reported that airports handling more than 10 million air passengers per year had, on average, a total of just over 5000 public parking spaces, while airports handling about 5 million air passengers per annum had approximately 4000 public parking spaces. By comparison, it might be noted that Heathrow (12·6 million air passengers) and Orly

(6·9 million) have 3550 and 4440 public parking spaces, respectively, at this time. (At most large airports, the public parking facilities are available to anybody, but normally employees use separate facilities at which the charges are either non-existent or considerably lower than in the public car parks.)

IN THE TERMINAL BUILDING AND TRANSFER (AIRSIDE)

Obviously the procedures and times involved at this stage varies considerably according to whether the air passenger is arriving or departing, and whether or not the flight is an international or domestic one. In any instance, the basic procedure involved at the terminal building is outlined in Figure 13.

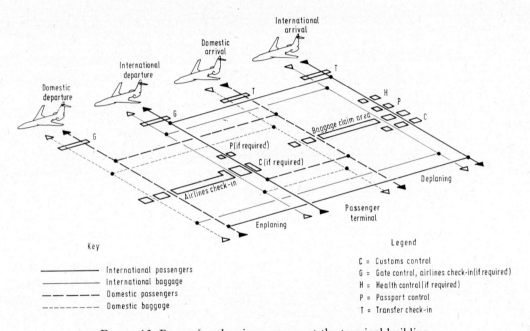

FIGURE 13. Processing the air passenger at the terminal building.

Embarking Air Passengers

The time required by a departing air passenger at the terminal building can generally be assumed to be about the same as the latest published time for checking-in for an air trip. This time, which is calculated on the basis of a countdown from the 'flight closed' deadline, is composed of the following:

1. Time required to check-in the last passenger.

2. Time required to get the last passenger from the check-in desk to the embarkation (exit) gate. If the flight is an international one, this may also involve the passenger going through customs and health formalities as well as passport control. With the growth of air travel and the consequent rapid expansion of airports, this time can be significant, particularly at major international airports. Simply walking to the embarkation gate can take a lengthy period of time, particularly at large airports which utilise

the finger system of aircraft parking e.g. see Table 9 which gives some comparative walking distances at ten major airports in the United States.[19]

TABLE 9

Walking distances at major U.S. airports

(Note: the 'originating' distances include the distance from the entrance to the check-in desk)

| Airport | No. of gates | Originating passengers | | Inter-line passengers |
		Min. distance to nearest gate, ft	Max. distance to farthest gate, ft	Max. distance ft
Chicago–O'Hare	72	580	1735	4720
New York–J.F.K.	104	200	1130	7780
Los Angeles International	64	836	1020	6640
Atalanta	56	630	1730	2680
San Francisco International	56	555	1300	3500
Dallas	26	730	1650	1990
Miami International	74	510	1120	3290
Philadelphia International	25	480	1240	1940
Detroit Metropolitan	47	560	1150	4280
Washington–Dulles	40	160	600	600

3. The time required to transfer the passenger from the departure gate to the aircraft. Nowadays it is a rare airport where the time required for this process is very significant.

4. The time required to start the plane's engines and clear away the starting generators following the closing of the cabin doors; start take-off procedure.

Table 10 summarises the published latest times for checking-in which were in use in 1967 (at the world's major airports.)[9] It is of interest to note that these times are shortest

TABLE 10

Latest times for checking in at the world's airports

| Airports | | Airport Extreme limits, min | Ave. for the airport, min | | | Ave. for the air terminal, min | |
Location	No.		International flights	Domestic flights	General	Extreme limits	Ave. limits
N. America	41	90–15	45	40	45	135–35	65–90
Europe	32	90–15	40	20	35	120–30	70–75
Central and S. America	12	100–30	62·5	58	60	—	—
Africa	14	90–15	55	35–40	45	120–60	86–90
Asia and Australia	13	90–15	52	30	42	130–40	85–90
All	112	100–15	45·5	30–35	40–45	135–130	80

for Europe—probably because most trips in Europe are made up of relatively short (city-to-city) flights, where reductions in ground delays assume key importance.

One further point which might be mentioned here is that whereas the average check-in time for international flights at European airports is now about 40 minutes, it used to be at least 60 minutes only a relatively few years ago.

Arriving Air Passengers

The processing of a passenger who has arrived at the terminal building on the airside and wishes to transfer to the landside is roughly the reverse of that described above for the embarking passenger. In this case, however, the hold-up is very often associated with the difficulty of uniting the passenger with his luggage. The time taken is usually longer for international flights than for domestic ones, and for large airports as compared with smaller ones.

Nowadays, the time required for customs has been cut drastically since the introduction of 'selective examining' by the Customs and Excise authorities. The processing of travel documents at international airports has also been very much speeded up in recent years compared with what it used to be.

Typical values for arrival passenger processing times for domestic and international flights probably range from about 10 to 15 and 25 to 35 minutes, respectively.

THE AIR TRIP

The air travel time or block-to-block time of the aircraft is composed of *ground time* and *air time*. In this case ground time is the time which the plane spends in taxiing prior to take-off and after landing plus the time spent waiting at the end of the runway prior to take-off. The air time is, as the name implies, the actual time spent by the aircraft in the air. As is reflected by the data in Figure 14[20] it is with respect to this latter time that the most dramatic developments have taken place in recent years.

Notwithstanding the impressive speed capabilities of the supersonic aircraft, it should be kept in mind that the great bulk of passenger-carrying over the next 10–15 years will be done by subsonic jet aircraft whose speeds will be very much as we know them today.

What is becoming of increasing concern to airlines and airports nowadays are the times which planes are having to spend in the air 'stacks' over major airports, both in this country and abroad, before they can be cleared to land. Similar concern is also being expressed with regard to the times spent by aircraft in long queues at the beginning of the runway while awaiting take-off. What is probably the most infamous airport in both of these respects is J.F.K. Airport in New York. Indeed, congestion at this airport is so severe that one airline official has predicted[21] that

'J.F.K. is going to become so notorious in a few years it wouldn't surprise me if the Kennedy family asked that the field be renamed Idlewild.'

'Stack' delays of between 15 and 30 minutes are now common at J.F.K. during the peak air traffic periods. The classic hold-up on the ground however, at this airport was recorded on Friday, 7 June 1963 when departure delays of up to nearly 2 hours were experienced.

A major cause of some of the ground and stack delays experienced by aircraft is the intense competition amongst airlines for the attractive peak periods. For example, the

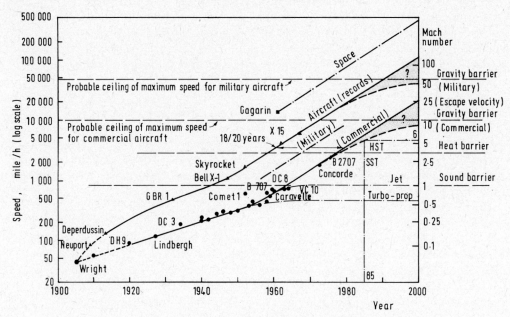

FIGURE 14. The past and future of aviation.

analysis of the 'Black Friday' incident at J.F.K. Airport showed[22] that 57·5% of the total weekly aircraft departure traffic was scheduled during 3·3% of the total time. In fact, on the day of the great hold-up the scheduling was so critical that at one minute of time, 18·00 hours, there were actually twelve aircraft scheduled for take-off at the airport.

There is no doubt but that stack and ground time delays form a greater proportion of the block-to-block trip, (the shorter air trip)—this, of course, is as might be expected. Ground time normally accounts for about 15 to 18% of the block-to-block time for short-haul trips, 10 to 15% for medium-haul trips, and 8 to 10% for long-haul flights.

SIGNIFICANCE OF GROUND TRAVEL TIMES

It is currently fashionable to bemoan that while airlines are steadily cutting down on actual travel times spent in the air, the times spent by the air traveller on the ground, particularly on the links going to and from airports, are getting longer and longer. I do not believe that this is necessarily so. For example, the data in Table 11—this is a compilation[23] of published times allowed by airline coach operators for travel between town centre and airport at twelve typical metropolitan airports in the United States at various intervals between 1941 and 1967—shows that with the exception of La Guardia, where the listed travel time has increased by 10 minutes in 26 years, and Cleveland, where the listed time is the same as it was in 1941, the travel time has in fact been reduced.

Moreover, the general overall trend exhibited by these data is not that of an ever-increasing rise in travel time followed by a sudden drop (as might happen when a new highway is opened) but rather that of an increase following World War II—resulting,

TABLE 11

Published city centre—airport travel times for some major airports in the U.S.

Airport	1941	1946	1951	1956	1961	1967
			Travel time, min			
New York–La Guardia	35	35	45	40	60	45
–Newark	55	50	55	40	45	45
Chicago–Midway	50	50	60	60	70	30
Dallas	30	40	40	40	40	25
Los Angeles	—	60	60	60	60	45
Washington–National	20	30	30	30	30	15
Boston	30	25	25	25	60	20
Cleveland	45	60	60	60	60	45
Buffalo	45	40	45	45	50	25
St. Louis	55	60	60	60	60	30
Cincinnati	—	—	50	50	50	25
San Francisco	45	50	60	60	60	30

The header "Year" spans the six year columns.

no doubt, from increased numbers of vehicles on the road—followed by a 'plateau' after which there was a decrease.

While I have not been able to obtain sufficient equivalent travel time statistics for this country, I venture to suggest that a similar trend is happening here. I think it most likely that we are now in the 'plateau' area with respect to travel time to the airport. I believe that improved traffic management and 'normal' road improvement programmes will be able to maintain ground travel times to most airports in this country at this plateau level for some time to come.

I do not think that the current disgruntlement with the quality of airport ground links is really very much concerned with the fear that current air travellers will be lost as a result of ground travel times being increased. More likely it is associated with airline and airport fears that predicted air passenger volumes and desired air travel standards may not be achieved unless ground travel times are *reduced*.

Table 12 summarises some recent data on average air and minimum ground travel times for the fifty most heavily trafficked city-to-city air routes in the United States. (The data shown in this table does not include any terminal building waiting/processing time, or delay of any other form.) This table clearly shows that the time spent travelling on the ground range from 22% of the total time spent 'on the move' for trips of over 1000 miles in length to 51% of the total time for trips of under 250 miles in length. In other words, a passenger making a trip of less than 250 miles currently can expect to spend *at least* half of his travelling time on ground transport, and when the trip is between 250 and 500 miles, the proportion spent on ground transport is still about two-fifths.

The situation becomes even more obvious when processing times at the airports are taken into account. In Table 13 I have built up a number of hypothetical trips, all

TABLE 12

Comparison of times spent in the air trip and the ground trip for some total trips between town pairs in the U.S.

Distance between airport pairs, mile	Number of airport pairs	Air link portion		Ground link portion			Ave. 'moving' speed, mile/h
		Ave. distance, mile	Ave. flight time, min	Ave. road distance, mile	Min. driving time, min	As % of total 'moving' time	
0–250	14	178	53	23	55	51	111
251–500	15	335	83	22	54	39	157
501–1000	12	709	119	27	63	35	243
1001 +	9	1742	246	28	68	22	338

originating at London, to illustrate what is involved. The data in this table is based on a number of assumptions.

—The time taken to travel to Heathrow Airport (54 minutes) is the average time (based on 552 interviews) taken by air passengers travelling north on the London–Leeds/Bradford air route.

—Stage 2 times include published times for checking-in at Heathrow (15 minutes for domestic flights, 25 minutes for international flights) plus car park to terminal building transfer times (assumed 5 minutes for domestic flights, and 10 minutes for international flights).

—Stage 3 times are those published by the airlines with the exception of the flights by the supersonic aircraft which are, of course, estimated.

—Stage 4 and Stage 5 times are based on a combination of personal experience and published data.

The practical implications of statistics such as those given for the short-haul flights in Tables 12 and 13 lie in the fact that:

1. The airlines consider the short-haul trip distance of less than 500–600 miles represent the most lucrative market yet to be tapped (see, for example, Figure 15).

2. The majority of city pairs in Europe and North America are separated by distances of less than about 750 miles (see Figure 16).

3. New and improved technology is making ground transport modes more competitive with air transport with respect to inter-city travel e.g. British Rail will have 150-mile/h turbo-jet trains in operation on main inter-city routes in this country by the late nineteen seventies.

In other words, the data in the above tables raise the whole question as to what extent the airlines can expect to penetrate the inter-city short-haul market. Clearly in the 0–250 mile range, and possibly in the 250–500 mile range, there exists an excellent opportunity for alternative (ground) travel modes to appear as attractive to potential air travellers.

One further point may be mentioned in relation to the data in Table 13. The supersonic aircraft, with their great speed capabilities can probably be expected to cross the

TABLE 13

Some examples of times spent on air journeys

Stage in the total air trip	Process involved	Lengths of time, min			
		200-mile trip		3500-mile trip e.g. London–New York	
		Domestic e.g. London–Leeds/Bradford	International e.g. London–Paris	Via current jet aircraft	Via supersonic aircraft
1. Origin to embarkation airport	Average travel time from home/hotel or office to airport	54	54	54	54
2. Embarkation at airport	Departure operations	20	35	35	35
3. Air trip	'Block-to-block' air trip	60	55	450	185
4. Arrival at destination airport	Arrival operations	10	30	35	35
5. Destination airport to trip destination	Coach from airport then taxi to destination near central area	31	45	65	65
	Total, min	175	219	639	374
	Ground time share of total, %	66	75	26	51
	Ave. journey speed, mile/h	69	55	329	561

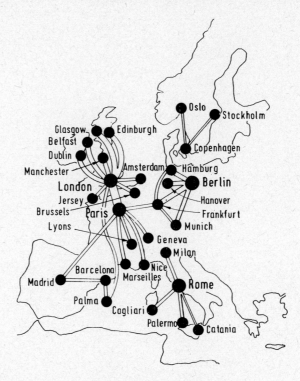

FIGURE 15. The 30 busiest scheduled air routes in Europe in 1975.[24]

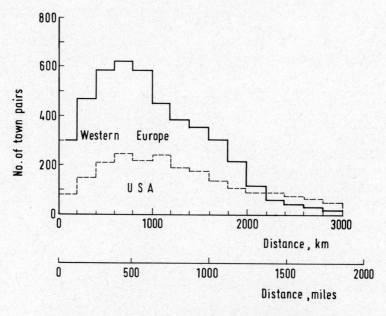

FIGURE 16. European and American inter-city distances.[25]

Atlantic four times each day. The users of these aircraft will mostly be business people who will be expected to pay higher fares in return for the high quality of service provided. Yet over half of their total trip times will be spent on the ground—a fact which does not lend itself to the image of supersonic travel.

SOME THOUGHTS ON FUTURE DEVELOPMENTS

It is a dangerous thing to speculate about the future—especially when one's speculations are put down on paper. Nevertheless I will attempt to do so, albeit with some hesitation. In so doing, however, I should state that the emphasis of my remarks will be on what I think will happen with respect to airports in the U.K. and not on what I believe should necessarily happen.

Any discussion about the future must be concerned with two time periods i.e. the immediate future (pre-1985) and the post-1985 future. The reason for this is that by about 1985, new generations of aircraft will probably be coming into service which may well cause a further major revolution with respect to air travel.

The Immediate Future

There are two aspects of the pre-1985 air transport era which are of particular interest.

1. How will airport development take place?
2. What is going to happen with regard to ground access?

The airport. The single greatest feature of airport development in this country is, of course, that whereas the airports handled about 25 million air passengers in 1967, they will have to deal with perhaps 100 million passengers per annum by 1980–85. Furthermore, while the major portion of this traffic will undoubtedly pass through the airports serving London, the rest will have to be dealt with by the remaining 26 or so airports from which scheduled flights are now flown every year.

It is probable that by 1985 four airports, (say Heathrow, Gatwick, Manchester and the new London airport) will handle about 75% of the air passengers moved in this country. This means, of course, that there is not going to be any sudden establishment of numbers of new large-scale intercontinental airports. I am quite sure that the next 15 years will see the establishment of only one completely new major airport in Britain, the so-called 'New London Airport'. The developments at Heathrow, Gatwick and Manchester, while very great in scope, will most likely take place within what are now these airports' limits.

I am not going to give any opinion as to where the new London airport will be— except to state the obvious which is that it will be outside the suburban boundaries of the Greater London catchment area. If the ground access to this airport is considered to be the major factor governing its location, then it is quite likely to be situated where there are existing excellent road and rail communications with London, the Midlands and the north of England. If environmental considerations are deemed to be the dominant ones, then a sea-coast site is not unlikely.

Nowadays, people are becoming much more aware of the cost of pleasant living and are questioning the intrusion of airports and their planes into the environment in which they live e.g. the Stansted affair. This is a phenomenon which is not unique to this country. As a result of this, for example, four planning studies are underway in the United States at this time which are examining the feasibility of constructing major airports either in or on water.

Two studies are being carried out in the New York area, one of which is contemplating a floating airport in Long Island Sound which would be connected to shore by a causeway; this airport would have a pivot which would enable it to swing to adapt to the prevailing wind conditions. The other New York airport contemplated would be a concrete multi-level 'aircraft carrier', each successive storey of which, in the process of construction, would cause the completed levels to sink further into the water until the structure attained a total of some ten storeys; aircraft would land on the surface and be carried by a lift system one level down for passenger service, then another level down for aircraft service, while offices and car parking would be in lower layers still.

Another project under examination in the United States is for an airport on Lake Michigan, six miles off shore from Chicago; land for this airport would be redeemed by dyking and pumping. The fourth American project being studied would involve the use of fill to create an additional international airport some two miles off the coast of California at Los Angeles.

Let me turn now from these fanciful airports for, as I have said before, only one new major airport of this type will be established in this country over the next 10–15 years. Hence, I think I am correct in saying that, on the whole, the form of airport in use in Great Britain over the next 10–15 years will not be very different from that which we know. In other words, the Heathrow Airport now is an indication of what Gatwick Airport will be like in the future, while the Manchester Airport now is not terribly different in form and operation from what, say, Leeds/Bradford Airport will be like in 1985.

At all airports, the next decade should see the development of new devices and procedures to aid and speed passenger movement into and through terminal buildings. There will be increased provision of parking facilities, particularly of multi-storey parking garages which will be close to or form integral parts of terminal buildings. Within the buildings themselves, the emphasis will be on using automated devices and procedures to cut down on both the check-in-time and the time required to reunite the air passenger with his luggage after his flight. Both of these latter aims will be critical with the introduction into service of the high-capacity jumbo aircraft. Let me say now, however, that I believe that the time savings which are likely to be made here will, on the whole, be relatively small—indeed, I think that airports and airlines will be content if present day processing times and standards are maintained during the peak periods.

The problem of the peak hour (aircraft) traffic is likely to get worse with the introduction into airports of more and more planes: particularly into those airports whose capacities are even now near being exceeded.

Ground access. The airport ground access problem will not be considered in the immediate future as one which must be tackled according to airport and airline requirements only. The airport is now generally considered to be an integral part of the community serviced, by the roads (or railways) of the community. Thus, any improvements in the ground links will generally occur as part of the overall improvements carried out to the community's communication network.

First of all, there is the question of the oft-proposed *exclusive* rail link connecting the airport either directly with the central area e.g. Berlin, or with a rail network servicing the central area e.g. Brussels. In both cases, the primary aim is to provide the air passenger with the facility to move between the central area and the airport in a special train, the trip to take a specified and short period of time at a relatively high speed.

I have already attempted to show that the diffuse origins and destinations of airline passengers, airport visitors and employees act against the concept of using any form of fixed rail system to service airports. Particularly, do they act against the provision of an exclusive central area–airport link. The best chance of success for a fixed-rail link is probably as an adjunct to an otherwise heavily used commuter rail system e.g. Brussels. Even then it must be recognised that the best chance for the financial success of the rail link is when it is used to service a very large airport which has a high percentage of its air travellers with origins/destinations in the central area of a metropolis, and which has a significant proportion of its employees living along the proposed route for the fixed rail system.

While it is not the intention here to go, in any real sense, into the economics involved it is still useful to consider the data in Table 14. This table summarises the U.S. cities in which it is proposed to build new or extended public transport rail systems which include links with airports. Without dwelling too much on this, it might be noted that under the assumptions used, only the Seattle, Baltimore and San Francisco airport links would ever pay their way because the number of passengers required to do so is in each instance in excess of the capacity of the airport concerned.

If Washington was to construct a public transport rail system, its present air passenger movements would be sufficient to enable a break-even operation—however, it is as yet very doubtful where Washington's system will ever be implemented, in which case the exclusive airport link would require a volume of passengers in excess of the airport capacity. A similar situation applies with respect to Los Angeles, while J.F.K. would, under one assumption, achieve the necessary flows to make the link economical by 1979. While Cleveland, Boston and Chicago could support an economical airport link, their systems, on the whole, are basically designed for the commuter market, and simultaneous operation of low-cost commuter service in combination with the more expensive and higher quality service required by air passengers is considered to be impractical.[11]

London's Heathrow Airport, which handled 12·6 million passengers in 1967, is probably the only airport in Great Britain which might economically justify a new airport link within the next 10–15 years—that is, of course, provided that its capacity is not exceeded beforehand. As is well known, the British Airports Authority plan for Heathrow Airport to be serviced by a conventional duorail link (from Victoria Station) by about 1972. This project will require the building of 2·5 miles of new track and the expenditure of relatively small amounts of money on the remainder of the route to ensure a frequency of service of one train every 10 minutes in each direction; the entire trip should take under 25 minutes even during the peak commuter hours.

At all other British airports, with the possible exception of Gatwick because of its peculiar position, I am sure that ground access will continue to be by road. I have no doubt but that a number of these airports will be serviced by motorway links. It is

TABLE 14

Economics of rail transport to airports in the U.S.[11]

Airport	Airport link, miles	Vehicle and track investment required, dollars $\times 10^6$	Break-even no. of users		Earliest date when break-even no. will be reached	
			Air passengers only, millions	Employees plus air passengers, millions	Air passengers only	Employees plus air passengers
Seattle	10	85	6·5	19·0	Exceeds airport capacity	Exceeds airport capacity
Baltimore	12	120	7·8	23·2	Exceeds airport capacity	Exceeds airport capacity
San Francisco	7	112	8·6	25·0	Exceeds airport capacity	Exceeds airport capacity
Washington National	1(5)	17(85)	0·9(4·2)	2·6(12·9)	1962 (Capacity exceeded)	1967 (Capacity exceeded)
Los Angeles	4(16)	62(260)	5·4(26·4)	15·0(60·0)	1970 (Capacity exceeded)	1975 (Capacity exceeded)
Cleveland	4	14	0·95	2·7	1969	1972
J.F.K.	3	125	11·7	33·0	1979	(Capacity exceeded)
Boston	1	10	0·48	1·4	1962	1968
Chicago	7	38	6·4	13·8	1968	1972

Assumptions	*Fare, dollars*	*Usage, %*	*Operating cost, c/mile*
System designed for air passengers only	1·5	20	4·9
System designed for employees and air passengers	0·5	25 Employees 5 Passengers	2·2

Note: The numbers in brackets represent the case where a city-wide rapid transit rail system is not implemented.

extremely doubtful whether these motorways will provide direct connection between the central area and the airport for the exclusive use of the airport population and, particularly, air travellers. Unless financed by a toll method of operation, I do not believe that this could be justified even for Heathrow. More likely, however, is the development whereby relatively high quality airport links will be constructed as an integral part of each community's normal road system development. It is difficult to see how, in the light of the many and diverse origins and destinations which have to be served, any other outcome can be expected.

Post-1985 Developments

It is notable that all current published projections regarding air travel for the future stop short at about 1980. The reason for this is that the end of the nineteen seventies should see the introduction into service of a new type of commercial air passenger transporter, the Vertical Take-Off and Landing (VTOL) aircraft, and nobody is quite sure what is going to happen then. The general feeling appears to be, however, that its introduction will herald a new era in air travel.

Present-day helicopters are well known for their limitations as regards being commercial passenger transport vehicles. These limitations are related to the restricted speed, payload and range of which the conventional helicopter is capable, to vibration and noise problems, and to high operating costs. Now, however, following considerable research and development, it appears that a commercially viable passenger-carrying VTOL plane is not just a possibility for the 1980's. Add to this the fact that aeroplane researchers now believe that it may be possible for the noise created by these aircraft to be reduced to an acceptable level i.e. 95 PNdB at a distance of about 160 yards,[2] and the introduction into service of VTOL aircraft tends to become a probability rather than just a possibility.

Over the past 15 years, industry, government and the military services have expended considerable effort on VTOL designs. The result is that there are now three main design concepts which are regarded as contenders in this field. First, there is the design which makes use of direct-lift jet engines; secondly, an aircraft using a circulation controlled rotor which can be retracted in cruising flight; thirdly, there is the convertible rotor aircraft. On the basis of the available evidence, it is not possible yet to say which is the more likely to be chosen—all that can be said is that at least one will be chosen.

As mentioned previously there is a large potential market for short-haul (less than, say, 750 miles) airline operation in the future, provided that ground access times can be greatly reduced and air transport passenger fares can be held close to equivalent fares on the ground. It might also be mentioned here that some aircraft manufacturers see these aircraft as operating over distances which are normally within the realm of the rubber-tyred vehicle. Thus, for example, the concept of the Hughes Tool Company's 'Helibus' is based on the assumption that it will be competitive with ground transport at distances of 10 miles and over.[14]

Unless ground access times can be reduced, however, the airlines invasion of the short-haul high density travel market may not be a success. It is here that the VTOL aircraft is seen to play a vital role in the post-1980's. The extent to which it will be a successful invasion may be gauged from the fact that published estimates by some authorities have suggested that the European market alone for VTOL aircraft will amount to about 500 aircraft by 1985.

It is generally recognised, however, that the success or failure of VTOL aircraft will be associated with the extent to which they can use airport sites within towns themselves, so that the ground transport times and costs incurred by the air traveller are considerably reduced. Preliminary studies made in the U.K. with respect to this have been fairly encouraging from a purely technical point of view. There will obviously be very formidable obstacles to overcome before this happens, not the least of which will be the task of persuading communities to accept 'metroports' within their midst—and the consequent intrusion of airports within the 'normal' living environment (see Figure 17). Whether or not the towns will accept these intrusions is, of course, the big question.

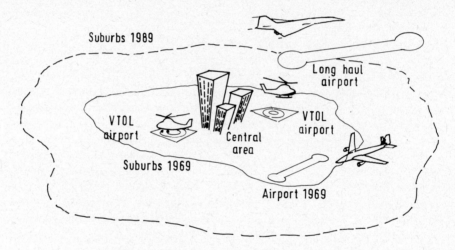

FIGURE 17. A large town and its airports, 1989.

Some time ago I would have said without any hesitation that the answer is 'Yes'— that towns would accept metroports. Now, however, I wonder. It seems to me that people as a whole are becoming more and more conscious of enjoying the quality of life in cities and are now willing to resist developments which they consider may be detrimental to this quality. Thus I believe that when firm proposals for metroport sites are put forward, there will be a very vocal group in each locality which will resist them strongly. Whereas in the past I would have thought the objections of the vocal minority would have been treated with respect but probably eventually overcome, I am not so sure that this will be the case in the future. This is a good thing, at the very least it should ensure that the engineers and planners of metroports will have to be sure of their facts before bringing forward definite proposals. This is as it should be. Only too often in the past have important events with regard to transport got out of control, simply because of important decisions being taken without sufficient thought being given to their possible consequences.

Nevertheless, it must be emphasised that from a transport efficiency aspect, a strong case can be made VTOL aircraft using aircraft within towns. It would, for example, bring all towns and cities in Western Europe within two to three hours travel of the centre of London. What it could mean in terms of the London–Paris or London–Leeds air trips can be quickly—and very *conservatively*—estimated by simply reducing the times taken in stages 1 and 5 of the hypothetical trips shown in Table 13 to, say, 15 minutes each in the case of London and Paris, and to 7 minutes in the case of Leeds. This would then give the comparisons shown in Table 15 via conventional take-off and landing (CTOL) aircraft and via VTOL ones.

TABLE 15

Comparison of hypothetical trips by CTOL and VTOL aircraft

	London–Paris		London–Leeds	
	CTOL	VTOL	CTOL	VTOL
Total time, min	219	150	175	112
Air trip share of total, %	25	37	34	54
Ave. journey speed, mile/h	55	80	69	107

If VTOL aircraft are accepted within towns then it is probable that every town of the size of Leeds would have one metroport within its boundaries. London would probably have four;[26] the use of this number of stations would not only relieve congestion by avoiding too much concentration at one site, but would also mean that at least one metroport would be within easy access of the great majority of Londoners.

While it is difficult to say what exactly would be the land requirements of a metroport it is logical that their size should be of the order of present-day terminal areas, and that they should contain terminal building(s), parking facilities, standing areas for aircraft and two pads, one for take-off, the other for landing. Thus, for example, London's main terminal at say, the Port of London, might require as much land as London (Heathrow) Airport's central terminal area i.e. about 160 acres. This is quite a modest land demand as compared with the needs of CTOL airports. (The total size of Heathrow airport is 2700 acres at present.)

Let me add one further point about VTOL aircraft and their potential with regard to air travel in the future. It is my belief that if metroports are accepted and if VTOL services are introduced by, say, 1985, then it is not unlikely that by the turn of the century —which, after all, is only 30 or so years away—they could well carry something like three quarters of the total air passenger traffic in Europe.

SELECTED BIBLIOGRAPHY

1. HEITMEYER, R. (1968). Future air traffic and implications for airports. In Vol. 2 of the Selected Working Papers on Major Airport and Terminal Area Problems presented at the 17th Technical Conference of the International Air Transport Association held at Lucerne, Switzerland, Oct. 9–14, 1967. Montreal, Canada I.A.T.A.
2. DAVIES, H. (1968). Some thoughts about the future of European aeronautics. *Journal of the Royal Aeronautical Society*. **72** (689), 385–395.

3. EDWARDS, G. (1969). Things are looking up. *Flight International.* **95** (3127), 247, 261.

4. ULSAMER, E. E. (1968). Who will build the first airbus? *Aerospace International.* **4** (1) 15–28.

5. HORAN, J. F. (1967). The Boeing 747. In *Airports for the future*, pp. 15–23. London: The Institution of Civil Engineers.

6. VOORHEES, A. M. (1966). Airport access, circulation and parking. Proceedings of the American Society of Civil Engineers: *Journal of the Air Transport Division.* **92** (AT1), 63–75.

7. FOX, FREEMAN, SMITH, WILBUR & ASSOCIATES. (June, 1967). London Airports Traffic Study: Heathrow Airport. Pt. 1 : *Traffic Characteristics.* London: The British Airport Authority.

8. MILLER, D. N. (September 1968). In Proceedings of the 6th Congress of the International Council of the Aeronautical Sciences. Hamburg, Germany. To be published.

9. MAURER, R. & PELADAN, R. (1967). *Terminal Transport and Other Reasons for Ground Delays in Air Transport.* Paris: O.T.A.

10. RODGERS J. L. (1966). London (Gatwick) Airport. In *Engineering the World's Airport Passenger Terminals.* London: The Institution of Civil Engineers. pp. 113–119.

11. PEARLMAN, C. (1968). Airport access—1980, a VTOL approach. In Proceedings of the 6th Congress of the International Council of the Aeronautical Sciences. September. To be published.

12. ANON. (1965). Monorails: where do they stand to-day? *International Railway Journal.* **5** (3), 32–37.

13. ANON. (1967). Why the latest monorail fell flat on its face. *Business Week.* pp. 118–124. February 18.

14. ULSAMER, E. A. (1967). Planning tomorrow's total air transportation. *Aerospace International.* **3** (3), 27–29, 32–36.

15. STEWART, C. D. (1966). Planning parking and movement for an airport of tomorrow. *Public Works.* **97** (7), 109–111.

16. ANON. (1960). Architectural Record. *Jet airports—passenger terminal design principles.* **127** (3), 167–174.

17. O'FLAHERTY, C. A. & RUSSEL, A. J. (1969). Motor vehicles at European airports. *Traffic Engineering and control.* To be published.

18. HOMBURGER, W. S. & EAGER, W. R. (1964). Automobile parking requirements at airports. Proceedings of the American Society of Civil Engineers. *Journal of the Aero-Space Transport Division.* **90** (AT2), 141–159.

19. HOBAN, J. L. (1966). Design of passenger terminals for American airports. In *Engineering of the World's Airport Passenger Terminals*, pp. 49–53. London: The Institution of Civil Engineers.

20. BOULADON, G. (1969). Aviation's role in future transportation: A technological forecast. In Proceedings of a Symposium on the Future of World Air Transport held at the 24th Annual General Meeting of the International Air Transport Association Munich, October 1968. pp. 7–25. Montreal, Canada. The Air Transport Association.

21. ANON. (1967). Can airports cope with the jet age? *Business Week.* pp. 54–73. July 22.

22. WILEY, J. (1968). Sorting out New York. *Aeroplane.* **116** (2966), 22–25.

23. SPATER, G. A. (1967). Airports and the community: an airline view. Paper No. 67–871 presented at the American Institute of Aeronautics and Astronautics 4th Annual Meeting and Technical Display. Anaheim, California. October 23–27.

24. ANON. (1968). The short-haul market. *Aeroplane.* **116** (2963), 4–8.

25. LEGG, K. (1968). The influence of aerospace on future transport systems. *Journal of the Royal Aeronautical Society.* **72** (693), 771–792.

26. CHICHESTER-MILES, I. (1965). The impact of VTOL on the air transport system. *Journal of the Royal Aeronautical Society.* **69** (652), 233–240.

Discussion

Jones: A new way of transport may be underground by vacuum tube using the earth's gravity as power. What is essential is to drop a vacuum shaft which goes from starting point to destination and which you enter at say New York and come out in say London about 90 minutes later having used no power at all. In the vacuum shaft are passenger carrying capsules which provide a rapid sort of bus service. There is no power required and of course you get right into the town centres.

You do not have the problems of London Airport and airport connections, nor do you have the problem of sonic bangs. The minimum distance for which this system is possible is 100 miles so that it can be used not only between countries but also within them. It is envisaged that this will happen in the foreseeable future.

O'Flaherty: What a marvellous idea. I do not think I will live to see it.

The sonic bang is over emphasised. West Germany has just passed an Act prohibiting overflying and other countries are examining the problem. These supersonic planes will be confined mainly to travel over water because they leave a continuous boom behind them which would be intolerable over land, so they will go to subsonic speeds once they approach land. As to the vacuum shaft; I try to look at the near future and the far future, but this idea is so far in the future that I am happy to let people in 100 years' time worry about it.

Jones: I do not wish to contest what you are saying, but I cannot help remembering what the Astronomer Royal said about space travel! 'Balderdash'.—And the headlines the following week were 'Sputnik 1 launched'.

Grey: Suppose the ambitious plans of British Rail come about and they have a train service running at 150 mph in the 70's in competition with VTOL aircraft, what effect would this have on London?

O'Flaherty: British Rail plan to have the turbo jet prototype ready in 1972 and the main trains in service in about 1975. They were bogged down about a year ago when the design team were going to emigrate to America owing to lack of financial support, and then the Government stepped in and provided the necessary funds. Definitely the turbo trains will be in by 1980. They are already in service between Toronto and Montreal.

There is going to be very stiff competition between the VTOL planes and ground transport. I think that you will see the introduction of VTOL aircraft and metro airports in towns. VTOL aircraft will compete with the turbo trains at distances over about 200 miles. The channel tunnel is going to reduce ground times initially, but the speed at which the train will move through the tunnel will be relatively low, so VTOL aircraft to and from the Continent will compete successfully with the rail times particularly at distances beyond Paris. They may well handle 60–70% or even all the traffic between the Continent and Britain by the year 2000.

Bennett: Do you think we have made a great mistake in the London region in allowing, owing to pressure of residential building, the whole of Croydon to be redeveloped for residential use and we are just beginning to cover the whole of Hendon. There are no other areas in the London region on that scale remaining to be developed. That is the predicament we are in.

Lawson: I am convinced that civil VTOL aircraft will not come about for two reasons. The first one is that the cost of VTOL aircraft is going to be high, and there will have to be a speed of something like 500 mph to get the pence per seat mile at a cost people will buy. The other thing is that the VTOL aircraft are all military and the serviceability of military aircraft is frighteningly low, because a civil aircraft flies something like 3000 hours a year whereas the military aircraft if it flies 600 hours in the year has really been flogged, so the services and the maintenance of these aircraft will again put up the cost per seat mile.

O'Flaherty: I am not an aircraft expert, but the Ministry of Technology, the airline manufacturers, and the airline people will not agree with you.

Burberry: Professor O'Flaherty has talked about the competition he envisages between turbo jet rail and VTOL aircraft. Should we allow competition of that sort to develop or would it be more economical to make some sort of decision in advance?

O'Flaherty: I think we must take great care because we are entering on a new era in travel. What is going to be the effect on the town? People are becoming more and more conscious about the quality of life, I think the Stansted affair was an example of this. Will people object to bringing these VTOL planes into towns? I do not know. I asked someone if they would object to putting a metroport in a town and he said 'no'. When I mentioned Stansted he said that it was in the stockbroker belt. These metroports are not going to go into the areas where the money is, they are going to go into the areas where the slums are, or into the industrial areas. In this way we may get rid of some of the slums. People will not object unless it interferes with them but a lot of people will think it is a good idea to have this convenience. There will be an outcry if a metroport is put into a residential area but if it is put into an industrial area or into an old slum area there will not be.

Jones: I speak as someone who has a house in the so called Stansted 'stockbroker' belt; it is true that it was the better paid people who campaigned to stop the airport. The trade unions however, were asking that the airport should be at Stansted in order to provide more work. So this appears to confirm what you said.

Stone: Are we paying sufficient attention to the problem of passengers getting to the airport? You can get to your train a couple of minutes before it goes out. It would be very much easier if the airports could do the same.

O'Flaherty: VTOL aircraft could reduce this tedious time factor. The airports themselves cannot cut time much. The check times for domestic flights is about 20 minutes and for international flights about 40 minutes. Baggage handling methods can be improved, they will have to be. Imagine ten jumbo jets coming into Heathrow, each disgorging about 400 people and their luggage at one time. The maximum that can possibly be cut on this phase of the operation is about 10 minutes. In other words on a domestic flight the 20 minutes check time might be cut to about 10 minutes. The international flight might be cut to 20 minutes. But owing to the increase in the volume of traffic I think the status quo will be just about maintained.

Lawson: There are about 35,000 people working at Heathrow and they deal with something like 12 million people a year. The underground station at Charing Cross copes with something like 35 million people a year and they are handled by twenty-five people. Engineers should be very much more cost conscious. If you divide the passengers using Heathrow by the cost of Heathrow it works out at £2 per passenger movement, so every time you take off and land £4 of your ticket goes to the Airports Authority, this is quite a sizeable sum.

The changing of cities

by

ROGER GILL

DURING THE symposium many current and potential developments in communications and transport have been described which will bring about other changes in their wake. Unless redevelopment keeps pace there is the possibility of our cities becoming increasingly out of step with technology in the foreseeable future. At the same time new technologies may offer a wider range of solutions to urban problems and as the range extends planning will become harder, if planning is to be a process directed to making the best use of resources to achieve social objectives. It is not difficult to find a feasible plan, it is perhaps well beyond our intelligence to get near an optimal one in a rapidly changing situation. If we cannot plan well the potential of our technology will be wasted and, even worse, used harmfully. This final paper in the symposium therefore moves on from questions of what is happening and what may happen, to the problem of determining what should happen. In particular to explore whether technology itself can help to improve the decisions we must take.

To any one planning problem, there may be innumerable feasible solutions from which a handful needs to be drawn out for detailed examination and evaluation. Common sense suggests that the more static and constrained the situation the more likely is it that the chosen solution will be near the optimal, and that in less constrained and altering situations the reverse will occur. Today technology is breaking down the constraints which determined the existing patterns of our cities, and the predictions made during the symposium do not suggest any slackening in the pace of change. If we have to rely on traditional approaches to planning the prospect would not be encouraging. The first approach, adaptive planning, has been used throughout recorded history and most settlements have evolved, many of them to a high degree of subtlety, through this process of trial and error. Successful ideas being copied and developed, the unsuccessful being rejected. Whenever constraints have kept experiment within a limited range there has been no need to plan a city as a whole, each new part has been added to the existing structure and every good adaptation embodied in craft traditions. Adaptation has given a wide variety of settlement and building patterns. All these settlements have features in common, but all have developed particular features suited to particular environments and functions. When conditions remain more or less stable adaptation will lead gradually to a point of equilibrium where no further improvements are possible.

However, conditions rarely remain stable, and with the growth of industrialised societies learning by trial and error became inadequate. Early in the nineteenth century more deliberate action had to be taken which in retrospect has been termed remedial planning. Essentially this type of planning involves the identification of a problem, an enquiry to establish the facts and to make recommendations, and administrative action. This approach is little more than an extreme form of adaptation, and permits a problem to get to a critical state before counter measures begin. Often the cure has to be tough with the attendant risk of upsetting the rest of the system. This disability naturally led to predictive planning and the attempt to forecast the probable future state of a system, thus enabling appropriate measures to be taken in advance.

Prediction and remedial action are the basic tools of planning today, but man has never been satisfied with the slow processes of evolution and every so often he has tried to impose utopian solutions. Thomas More and many followers have described new social and physical environments designed to cure the ills of society, and since 1700 there have been numerous practical experiments with small communities, model industrial villages and new colonies, culminating in the nineteenth century with the fascinating attempt to re-create a mediaeval inspired See of the Church of England at Canterbury in New Zealand, and the building of Port Sunlight, Bournville, and the first Garden City at Letchworth. Although many of the experiments failed to achieve all the expected goals, the idea of optimal planning of aiming at the best possible solution has gradually gained credence, but the static solutions of the utopists have been forgotten as rigorous studies of the city have grown more numerous and the decision process itself has become a fruitful field for scientific investigation.

The various stages of the decision process have been isolated and although authors differ in detail and terminology the following structure brings together the main common features:

1. Goal formulation.
2. Analysis of the system and the prediction of future states.
3. Formulation of strategies.
4. Evaluation of strategies and final selection of a solution.
5. Implementation.

With simple problems these steps can be taken in sequence and the conclusions at each step can be drawn with a reasonable degree of accuracy, but as problems become more complex the framework tends to fall apart. Methods available for implementing a plan effect the previous stage, goals become less clear and may be too numerous to define and order, and above all a large gap appears between analysis and plan formulation. In the end all pretence at a logical move from one to the other disappears and attention is riveted on methods of evaluating plans produced by the human brain unaided. How do we produce plans, create designs? How can we achieve optimum solutions? Wherever possible set procedures, or algorithms, are used which inevitably arrive at the best answer. The classic examples being the calculus and mathematical programming. A procedure for not losing at noughts and crosses and winning if an opponent makes a mistake, is another example of an algorithm. Very large scale problems can be reduced for solution by these methods, but once the complexity of a situation is reduced there is a risk that the 'model' will not react in the same way as the real life situation, and all mathematical procedures optimise with respect to one objective—least cost, or maximum growth rate, or minimum accident rate, being feasible objectives provided only one of these objectives is sought at any one time. Highway engineers could however be concerned with all three of these objectives and be seeking a compromise or acceptable balance between them, thus the search for an optimum solution moves beyond the reach of the algorithm.

For example there is no known rule for winning at chess, which is conceptually simple compared with planning problems; although theoretically it would be possible to evaluate every possible set of moves the time cost would be formidable. In playing chess we have to use strategies and tactics whose only justification is past success. Such methods are known as heuristic, a heuristic procedure being defined as a narrowing down of the field of search for a solution by inductive reasoning from past experience of similar problems.[1] The noun form of the word heuristic, is similarly defined as any rule, trick or device used in decision taking that has been derived from experience.

In a paper on the planning of the cities in the hot and dry region of northern India, Viren Sahai has given a fascinating account of the use of heuristics in ancient times.[2] In these cities the general layout and the house plans became standardised as the builders learned how to control the stringent climatic conditions and reached, taking into account the available materials, what must have been near optimal solutions. The orientation of the houses was naturally of critical importance and Viren Sahai quotes the heuristic from an old Hindu text (approximately 300 B.C.), which was used for this purpose. '. . . let a Sanchu be erected, of twelve angulas in height and of the same diameter: mark points where the shadow falls before and after noon on the east and west of the circumference: then, having computed the sines of the declination three ghaticas after sunrise and three ghaticas before sunset, multiply the difference between these two sines by the hypotenuse of the shadow at the third ghatica after sunrise, and the product being divided by the cosine of the latitude of the place, the quotient will give the angulas or their integral parts'.

It is interesting to compare this thoroughly worked out heuristic with some of the more extreme rules of thumb propounded earlier in this century which were based more on wishful thinking than experience, and might therefore be called quasi-heuristics. The writings of Le Corbusier who has had much influence on architect planners are rich with examples of the quasi-heuristic. 'A level site is the ideal site for a city', and 'The river should flow far away for a city', and again 'The city of today is a dying thing because it is not geometrical. The result of a true geometric layout is repetition. The result of repetition is a standard the perfect form'.[3] We must be thankful that the builders of London, Bristol, and Norwich, or York, Edinburgh and Plymouth, had not been taught to obey such rules. Looking back with our new found understanding of the complexity of the city it is difficult to understand how such unfounded generalisations ever gained credence.

Today we use heuristics for determining land use patterns, the densities and forms of housing layouts, car parking provision, the floor area for shopping, road layouts and so on. Without them we could not start to plan, and they have become so embedded into our thinking that they are applied without conscious thought, and often we fail to realise how suspect they are. In the design of the New Towns after the war some of the more important heuristics were:

1. An optimum population figure between thirty-five and fifty thousand.
2. The division of the town into neighbourhood units of approximately five thousand people.

3. The separation of the neighbourhood units by collector roads and open space to emphasise the integrity of the basic communities.
4. The self sufficiency of the towns for employment and shopping.

These rules were only partially derived from experience, and their main inspiration came directly from the utopian tradition. In practice the anticipated improvements in the social environments did not materialise to any marked extent, and many of the ideas have since been dropped or modified.

Is the planning process any better today? It is of course now possible to use more precise forecasting models and optimising techniques, and to simulate simple systems to get a better understanding of their operation. We can therefore take decisions with more confidence about some of the sub-systems of the city, provided the limitations and disadvantages of these methods are appreciated. To bring a problem within the compass of a particular technique it is generally necessary to over-simplify and to make assumptions about the linearity of the relationship between the variables which may not be justifiable. Attention may also be concentrated on those aspects of a problem which can be tackled with a degree of respectability, and other not less important aspects for which techniques are not available may, as a result, be forgotten to the detriment of the whole. So although algorithms will be extended and used whenever possible in planning, heuristics will always be necessary for the major decisions in multi-goal situations; they are the only tool for formulating plans and strategies on the city scale.

To improve these heuristics information will be needed and this will undoubtedly flow through communication networks in ever increasing volumes, but can it be assimilated by the human brain?

The answer to this question must be no, the human brain can only absorb a small part of the available information about the city, and the future is bleak unless technology can be brought in to help with the task of learning from experience. Computers can of course record experience directly, and they have been taught to play noughts and crosses by updating a file of results until inevitably in this restricted problem field it finds the most successful move. But rote learning is too clumsy for more complex problems which do not recur in precisely the same form, and to achieve greater sophistication the computer will have to be programmed to draw inferences from its records.

The ability to draw inferences, to generalise, is an essential attribute of intelligent behaviour and if it can be synthesised on a computer able to handle far more information than the human brain (that is data about problems), there is a good prospect that one day there will be an efficient tool for sharpening planning and decision taking.[4]

It is helpful to see the process of arriving at a solution as a narrowing down of a field of search by successive applications of constraints. This may not be the manner in which the human brain acts but it is a routine process well suited to the computer. The constraints arise first of all from the requirements of the problem, a plan must provide for a population within specified brackets—thus excluding from consideration all solutions for a population outside the brackets. Other constraints are implied by the basic constraints, for example people must have dwellings, schools, and hospitals. However these required constraints are unlikely to produce a solution by themselves except in very restricted circumstances, so additional heuristic constraints will have to be superimposed, that is constraints which in the past have produced good results.

Thus the outline of a general decision model emerges with two distinct processes. An On-Line process to apply from an ordered list the required and heuristic constraints until the search provides a solution (assuming a solution is possible), and an Off-Line process to make generalisations from previous problems and solutions, in order to update and modify existing heuristics and perhaps in time manufacture new ones. An On-Line process has already been written and tested; it remains to be seen whether an Off-Line process can be produced.[5] Essentially it involves the preparation of a package of pattern recognition routines so that features common to a number of solutions can be isolated, and an evaluation routine to assess the effectiveness of these common features or properties. There are many possible approaches and there can be little doubt that the task is feasible in theory. Whether it can be made to work in practice is another matter, and perhaps irrelevant in the immediate future. For if an effective Off-Line process is beyond the present horizon man and machine working in harness today could arrive at better generalisations than man on his own.

The use of experience in the formulation of decision rules is not the whole story, for obviously planning must be directed at the right goals. The determination and clarification of goals will not be easy. A meta-goal in city planning might be the creation of a good environment. But what makes a good environment? What are the sub-goals? How do they rank in importance? In what way does the ranking differ from one situation to another, from one culture to another and from one time interval to another? Are long term goals more important than short term ones? Are we right in accepting money as the most useful measure and therefore by implication equate the rich man's pound with the poor man's? Question after question can be framed about goals until it becomes clear that goals themselves change and must be learned. Furthermore it is impossible to learn without feed-back, and at the moment available statistics cover only a small part of the city environment. Consequently there is over reliance on personal opinion and the ever present danger of change being brought about by the biased attitudes of organised pressure groups. An unbiased monitoring system will take a long time to develop and will be costly; the first step is to recognise the need for one. There is another complication. Feed-back from actual experience takes time and it may be years before the long-term implications of a particular policy become manifest. It would be helpful to get an indication before irreversible measures are made, but computer technology is not sufficiently advanced to simulate systems as broad in scope and as complex as a city. For this task new hardware will be necessary with facilities for simultaneous operations and better input and output devices.[6] It should be noted that a simulation model of a city system would itself be heuristic as the relationships between the variables could only be established by experience, and it would also be adaptive as such a model would be ever subject to change.

SUMMARY

In this paper it is argued that precise analytical techniques can never entirely replace heuristic decision taking in city planning, and that the assimilation of the necessary information to keep the heuristics up to date is, and will be, a task beyond the capacity of the human brain—if we aim at optimal instead of merely feasible solutions. In consequence technology must be harnessed to help the planner.

One possible method of constructing an adaptive decision model is briefly described, but it is also pointed out that any decision process which relies on experience must have an adequate flow of information about the changes and behaviour of the system being controlled.

REFERENCES

1. To be found in *A Dictionary of Science*. Penguin Reference Book.
2. Lessons from tradition. *RIBA Journal*. March 1967.
3. RODKER. (1929). *The City of Tomorrow*. Translated from Urbanisme. Reprinted 1948.
4. The main references which have been used in the research on machine learning described in this paper are:
    (a). ASHBY, W. ROSS. (1964). *An Introduction to Cybernetics*. Methuen.
    (b). FIEGENBAUM, E. A. & FELDMAN, J. (editors). (1963). *Computers and Thought*. New York: McGraw-Hill.
    (c). GEORGE, F. H. (1960). *Automation Cybernetics and Society*. Hill.
    (d). GEORGE, F. H. (1962). *Semantic Machines*. Antorga.
    (e). SHANNON, C. E. (1960). Programming a computer to play chess. *Philosophical Magazine*.
5. The structure of the decision model has been fabricated by S. BERGER, Department of Architecture, University of Bristol. A full account has not yet been published, but a more detailed description can be found in *Computer Aided Architectural Design*, Part 1. Reports of three Working Groups, pp. 64–66 and appendix 16. R. & D. Paper: Ministry of Public Building & Works. London. (1969).
6. KAUFMANN, ARNOLD. (1968). *The Science of Decision Making*. World University Library, pp. 223–224.

Discussion

Jones: Dr. Gill told me that he gave up planning some ten years ago when he had to sit down with his seniors to design a town in a day! This comment may give even greater relevance to his paper in which three things have been stressed: the need for research and study as a basis for decision taking; the use of electronic devices as an aid to decision taking; and to avoid making unnecessary decisions.

Parsons: Are we going to eliminate mental activities and prevent people from making decisions, even bad ones? In a sub-normal hospital I visited recently, inmates were putting ball point caps on pens. A psychologist there told me that 40 years ago these people would have been in the fields muck-spreading or cleaning hedges and ditches and being otherwise employed. Are we eliminating the need for people to do both useful employment *and* to enjoy their work?

Gill: If we go on taking decisions in the present way, as more and more information becomes available, and the amount of information is going to explode in the next 20 years, the human brain cannot assimilate it. But I am not suggesting that the human brain will be replaced in decision taking; what I am suggesting is that there is some promise of helping people to take *better* decisions, to explore more possible solutions, and to assimilate much more detail than they could unaided. I see this sort of model as enabling us to amplify our own intelligence, just in the same way as the machine amplified our muscle power during the last century.

Parsons: I would suggest that this method enables a very few people to make decisions.

Gill: It would tend to alter the nature of the planning team. Some people will be moved away from taking decisions which they cannot take sensibly, into fields in which they can do more useful work.

Parsons: People are continually making decisions which, though on occasion may be wrong, give them a lot of satisfaction. Are we going to take the excitement of decision making away from everybody?

Jones: I do not see why it is desirable for people to make decisions based on inadequate information at other people's expense.

Gill: We have done a pilot study and looked at the problem of stress when people are re-housed, we cannot draw any firm conclusion about it because the sample is too small, the results we have at present indicate that people who live in rented accommodation and who do relatively simple work and who take relatively simple decisions have got a clean bill of health. The people in our sample who own cars and houses and who are in positions where they have to take more important decisions suffer from just about every mental illness known. Now, are they really happier making decisions, or are they not?

Stone: In taking decisions we are really doing two things. We are trying to collect together the facts in order to take a decision and we are doing various calculations in order to bring these facts together to get an overall indicator of the order of preference. I think there is a similar situation in stock control where every fact and every piece of information is measured and a mechanical decision is reached. But, certainly in design work and in planning, this is not true. There are an enormous number of facts to be taken into account as well as a large number of assumptions. The first thing in good decision taking is to bring all these decisions and assumptions out so we can see exactly where we start. This is where the computer comes in. It is only an extension of our mind and we are still making the final decisions. What the computer can do is to bring in a very large complex of characters, much larger than we can ever cope with in our minds, and it can enable us to analyse these. In other words we first of all try to measure, and a computer programme forces us to measure otherwise there is nothing to put into the machine, so we have to do research in order to find out what are the basic facts. But we still end up with a large number of assumptions, for instance we do not know what human behaviour is going to be like, nor how we are going to change, but we try to take account of these things. But what we want to find out is whether there is a solution which is still better. The decision we are making is an evaluation of a particular assumption. This is where the computer can help, it can do all the variation analysis in a few seconds, where it would take us hours, or perhaps be even impossible to do. What we should not do is to feed information into the machine and then take the answer as a decision. That is only the beginning of it. We have got to evaluate the answers and to decide what weight to put on the assumptions, what the probabilities are and whether this rather than that is likely to happen. What the computer can do is to evaluate information in much more detail so that we have a better basis on which to take a final decision.

Gill: In a space capsule I would prefer the computer rather than the human brain to take over when I started to glide down to earth. Where speed is essential the computer should be used.

Ireland: I would like to go back on Mr. Parson's point because decision taking and the improvement of decision taking has certain dangers which are already evident in industry.

Gill: Fifteen years ago I did not directly control anything but I was influencing several million pounds worth of investment a year preparing development maps for various towns and in the end I got pretty miserable. I suppose the economic resource I directly influence in my work today is about £25 and I am very happy!

Redfern: If information is fed into the system which is incorrect information it will become enlarged and assume a much more important role.

Gill: I would anticipate a whole hierarchical series of models, not just one large model, from an international economic model, to a national economic model, down to a regional model, and down again to a sort of sub-model for particular towns, and there will be a continual interaction between them. The important thing about the decisions that are taken is that the effects must be measured as quickly as possible.

Dakin: Richard Meier suggests that information is the basis of society and that therefore a simulation model could not be built without the use of adequate data. I suppose a lot of planners would agree with the conceptualisation of the Universe which is some kind of a system. But the question is what kind of system is one talking about? A growth system, or is it an echo system, in which one is thinking about drive towards equilibrium or balance, or are we thinking about some other kind of system?

Gill: We must inch forward because if we are going to design for people on a large scale, we must have some sort of sociological input, but this is one of the glaring gaps in our present knowledge. So we have first to find out what is happening, and then build up a model of what we should be doing. I think this is the direction in which progress lies.

Simulation as a design tool in
urban planning

by

M. G. HARTLEY

WE ARE A small group of people in the Digital Process Laboratory of the Electrical Engineering Department in the University of Manchester Institute of Science and Technology and we have been engaged in simulation work for some years. We have carried out software simulation, that is using computer programmes alone and also hardware simulations, building special purpose equipment.

The emphasis has been on the provision of a special purpose digital simulator which can be used by Traffic Engineers and city designers as a design tool, and it seems to us that the techniques we have been employing might be extended to a wide variety of situations which occur frequently in the field of environment. So I would like to say something about our approach so that members of the Symposium can see if any of the techniques might apply in their own circumstances.

If we are working in the city environment as it is at the moment, or as it may be in the future, we have many cases where we have to operate with what we might describe loosely as multiple queuing situations. For example, we have various types of road traffic intersections, we have the conventional intersection with four lanes with possibly a single stream of traffic in each lane, T junctions, round-about systems, and so on, and if we consider these situations in detail we see that each one has a typical pattern including random arrival of vehicles, vehicles waiting for service, and then intermittent service depending on the traffic signal situation, and the effect between streams of vehicles in opposing directions. This last would apply particularly to turning traffic, right turning in the United Kingdom and left turning in North America. We have the same sort of situation at the T junction, and when we come to a giratory system of the conventional sort the vehicles fight it out. We may have the situation where the vehicles obey the priority from the right rule and then we have the ultimate where they decide that the giratory system is ineffective above all at rush hours resulting in the installation of traffic lights. These are the sort of areas we have been interested in, but if you extend the idea a little further, you get similar possibilities of conflict when you have the pedestrian situation in the shopping precinct or the supermarket where people come along wheeling their trolleys and conflict with each other. You certainly have the queuing situation as the people leave the supermarket, endeavouring to pay for their goods. You have the conflict situation in the hospital environment where in the corridors you have a variety of traffic, pedestrian traffic, trolleys with patients, trucks with goods, and so on. Again, you have this conflict situation with a high speed transit system.

225

These systems have been described during the course of this Symposium, both for the movement of goods and people. In some of them one has a situation where the vehicles will proceed at exactly the same speed and then maybe, queuing is absent on the main highways, but there is certainly a queuing situation as the vehicles on the subsidiary routes endeavour to enter the main highway. Moving a little further to the future we have the vertical take off and landing situation for aircraft.

Now I am going to describe the steps in design procedure for a multiple queuing situation. The first stage requires a certain amount of field work to discover something about the basic parameters. As in the road traffic situation you send out observers on to the road to determine something about the mean velocity of the vehicles, the headway distributions, and so on, and you do the same sort of thing as if you were plotting the supermarket situation.

If you want to modify an existing situation or build a new one, you then consider how you are going to set about the design. I think that in all but the very simple situations the mathematical analysis breaks down almost immediately. You can do a mathematical analysis for the single observer dealing with a single queue, you can extend it to the case of several arrivals shared between various queues, but when you have a conflict at a single traffic intersection of, shall we say, eight conflicting streams of traffic, late arrivals, changing situations, right turning, and so on, even the analysis for a single intersection is very difficult, and almost impossible when you then consider the diffusion of traffic from departure to intersection and its arrival at the next intersection net-work, and you extend the net-work over a large area. Mathematical treatments of a formal kind fail completely.

So, we then come back to the possibility of modelling. As I see it there are three main ways of modelling and the individual investigators may choose one or another, or a combination of the three types. The first way is to take something which looks very much like an existing situation and perform experiments. For example, the Road Research Laboratories have done track experiments in which they bring people in with cars, they hire local taxi cabs, buses, and so on, and they all drive round while the observers see what happens as they change the geometry of the individual intersection under consideration. This sort of approach though it may sound rather naïve is in fact very effective in practice, though it is an expensive technique in terms of manpower and in terms of equipment required.

The next approach is the so-called software approach, where you take a carefully prepared computer programme, which models in some sense or other the attributes of the situation. This is used nowadays at both macroscopic level for surveys of a complete region (this is widely adopted in North America for areas which cover a large number of square miles) and also for the microscopic level where one models the behaviour of the wheeling section in a giratory system. Here you apply a great deal of detail, you move the vehicles, accelerate, decelerate, you allow a certain probability for driver behaviour to do something rash, you allow another probability for the cautious driver, and so on.

The third possibility, just beginning to get consideration, is the use of hardware simulation. The analogue, as we know, has been used for some time. You set up on your analogue machine the differential equation which represents the behaviour of the vehicle system under consideration, you run the simulator fairly quickly, perhaps ten times real time, and you plot out the performance of this system on cathode ray tubes, pen recorders, and so on. The analogue computer, using first of all valve operational amplifiers and now transistorised equipment, has been with us for some years. The digital type of hardware simulator is just beginning to come into operation and this is the technique I want to describe in rather more detail. Before I do that, however, for those who are not familiar with the modelling techniques I want to say a little bit about the softwear approach to simulation using five diagrams.

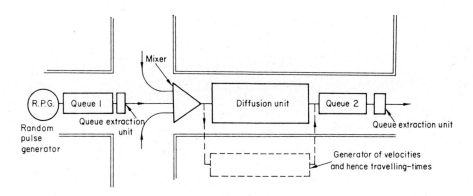

DIAGRAM 1.

This particular piece of work is one we have done ourselves. It illustrates the approach and gives some idea of the complexity of modelling the behaviour of traffic at a pair of intersections. The traffic is generated on the left-hand side and passes into a queue extraction unit, then to mixing diffusion units to allow distribution of velocities of the vehicles to the second queue.

Diagrams 1 and 2 show the concepts on which the computer programme is based.

Typically, you can start off the programme by setting an initial state and then up-dating the situation at frequent intervals, perhaps once a second. Every second you see whether another vehicle has been generated, you then up-date the flow and ebb between the intersections.

This sort of approach is fairly straight forward, the programme writing is not particularly difficult, but it does take time and you need a fairly large computer for a fair amount of time. This modelling which we did ourselves is running at about thirty times real time on the computer and it costs us about £375 per hour in terms of computer time. So, it is quite an expensive undertaking.

Several situations have been investigated, including early morning, theatre and football rush hours. The computer output can be by line printer and graph plotter. The information obtained predicts average delay and the number of vehicles queueing.

Diagram 3 shows a theatre rush hour which is not too severe and indicates waiting queue length and delay and so on.

The advantages of the softwear approach are fairly obvious and you programme the large general purpose machine which might be fairly readily available in a University, or in a computer bureau. You can re-run a situation with a wide variety of data and many people these days have access to machines and have knowledge of auto code programming.

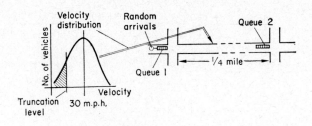

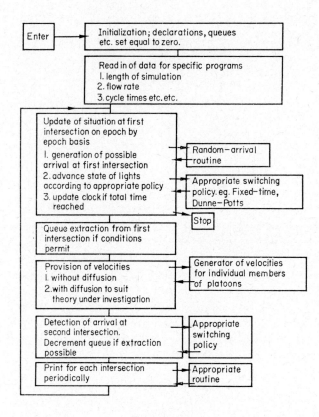

DIAGRAM 2.

The disadvantages might be summarised as follows: you have to write the programme; you have the turn round time while you wait for your results to return, and our own experience is that we often have to wait two or three days for a large programme to come back; the work can, of course, be expensive in terms of running time on the machine; and the interpretation of the results is tedious. You plot your results and you say, well I do not like that sort of single changing policy let us see what happens if we change the green time, or the red time. You have to go back to the computer before the results appear and by the time you have modified your policy you have got tired of the problem.

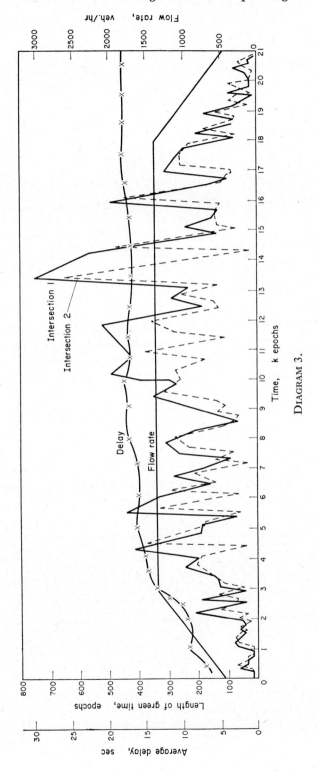

DIAGRAM 3.

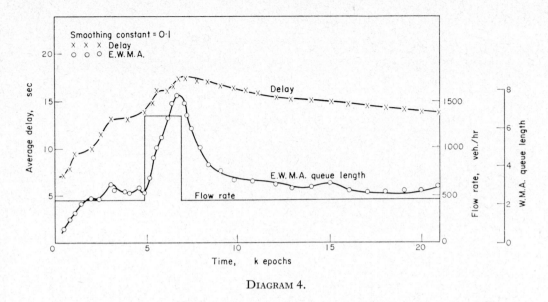

DIAGRAM 4.

This approach has been used by various people in the United Kingdom, particularly the Road Research Laboratories and the Transportation Group in Birmingham. You do, of course, also require a fair amount of engineering skill to determine the level of detail to put into the programme which will vary from time to time.

In the hardware approach you build a special purpose digital equipment which you interconnect in a variety of configurations in order to model different types of traffic situation. In this way you have a problem which can be set up fairly readily; you can plug up with an intersection to represent a T junction, roundabout, Y junction, and so on, and a situation which has the benefit of traffic signals, or not, and you have the possibility of building in various types of switching policy, fixed time, fluctuation, and so on. A further advantage is that you can use a small process control computer to control the model, so the computer thought it was controlling the signals at the intersection and the intersection was under the impression that there was a computer helping it. You have to have data links, we used telephone cables by courtesy of the G.P.O. who were extremely helpful, and we tried out things like fixed time working in fluctuation and various other types of control policy of a more sophisticated sort. We have obtained experience of using data links and the effect of information down the data links. We have been able to get an experience of error correction codes, the unscrambling of information out of the computer, programming in machine language, and so on.

I will list the advantages we claim for this hardware approach: we have instant availability; ease to set up; fast operation; repeatability of experiments; variety of upward displays; and the possibility of using computer control.

Now I want to indicate where we are going now.

We are considering using a single hardware model on a time sharing basis to review behaviour of a complete net-work of city streets. Again, you plug in your configuration to suit yourself, this takes only a few minutes. The hardware equipment now can simulate on a time change basis, the behaviour of all the intersections in the town using core storage to

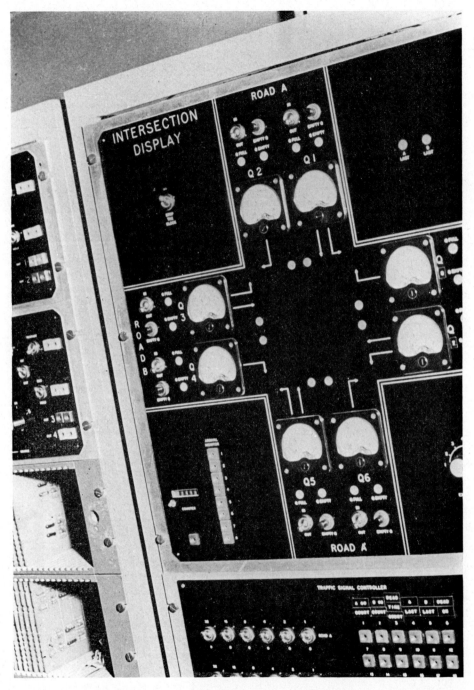

FIGURE 1. This model will handle any sort of traffic intersection up to the complexity of eight lanes, with or without right turning traffic. It was a mistake to draw it up as an actual cross roads.

FIGURE 2. This shows rather more of the equipment. The inter-connection panel and the traffic signal controller is in the centre. This equipment provides the diffusion of traffic between one intersection and the next. Taking into account distribution of velocities.
This equipment has been used now for some years and we have gone as far as we can with a single intersection. We are now going to on the consideration of multiple inter-sections.

dump into the core store the information for the other N minus one intersections when it is considering the Nth intersection. The question of outward display is very important and we are lucky to have people who are experienced in display. With a situation of the kind under consideration there is a great deal of outward information and you want all that in graphic form, if possible. So our job is to arrange things with a special cathode ray tube for the outward display. To display a particular net-work of intersections we prepare an ordinary 2×2 in. slide and we have a lamp to illuminate the screen from the back showing the configuration of streets. Diagram 5 shows the arrangement. You then have your model of the net-work, process control computer, and you can see on this display something like curved lines of varying length which indicate queue length from second to second. So you have a long one there perhaps, a long one here and when this one here going in that direction, backs up to the previous one, you realise that that particular configuration and that particular traffic flow just is not on.

This instant output arrangement enables the operator to communicate directly with the equipment from second to second and to modify his designs as he is going along. This is an important inter-change between the man and the machine which we feel has very useful opportunities for the future.

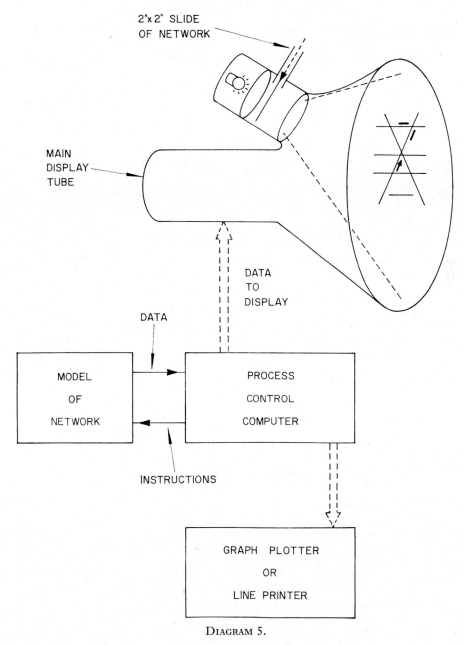

DIAGRAM 5.

The laboratory we are setting up, and on which work has begun is a three storey building, the main floor is on ground level which has cubicles for taking in equipment, a large general purpose computer. Or the main machine before we put our simulation models, such as the ones I have been describing, data in between them and we have a floor below for the cathode ray tubes, and so on, with physical data links between them to minimise the very complexity of the equipment.

Discussion

Burberry: As designers we have in the past concentrated on the visual aspects of things, but the problems that we have heard about during the course of this Symposium, though they may have had visual implications, have not been visual ones. Although the electronics that Dr. Hartley has been talking about are fairly fearsome, nevertheless a designer can go along and manipulate them. He does not have to build the electronics. We do this in the Department of Architecture here and although the sophistication of the equipment is small in comparison with Dr. Hartley's, nevertheless useful results can be achieved in fields that would be unpredictable otherwise. So I would consider important the means of attempting to appraise the consequences of our decisions and also, as Architects, to develop some sophisticated concepts and postulations to match those of the Engineers.

Floyd: We analyse the human being and we find that his reactions are rather random and in many cases he responds as he would have done in the jungle to what he considers to be a hostile environment. He may feel that he has no control over many aspects of his life but if he does feel put upon he will want to do something about it. I suppose that this comes with education, knowledge and freedom of movement and of communication. People increasingly question everything and want more control over their own immediate environment, which is I think a good thing, and while local environments may be controlled more by local people, the problem becomes more abstract as the scale gets bigger and as more help is needed from mechanical and electronic aids. At the city scale participation will be more difficult. Because communication in cities is giving greater flexibility space requirement may become less important in terms of physical planning. But the line, pipe, track, rail, route, road, air corridor is much more flexible than individual buildings. I have always been brought up to think of individual buildings as being the most flexible of things because they are solid, but because they are such tiny units they are much more flexible than are the lines of communication. This suggests to me that the lines of communication will come first and we will get systems of corridors of movement for all means of transport and communication with the points where people are working and living off these corridors.

When we come to existing cities which today's planners are mostly concerned with, it seems to become increasingly important that the corridors of movement should not be plugged into the middle where they get snarled up with all the old problems, but are taken alongside.

Ireland: This is fine, you can plug into the socket alongside the city, but remember that there must still be an inter-connecting lead between the plug and what you want to use at the other end.

Dakin: One of the things that comes through to me from listening to the telecommunications experts is that there is a clear absence of research in the comparative cost of telecommunications over distance, and the effects of these comparative costs on our activity patterns. The location of industry in relation to railway tariffs, railway rating, and electricity rating for distance indicates to me that there is a possible range of constraints about the physical arrangements of human activity patterns which arise from the way in which tariffs are organised. In my own area of Canada to change the method of tariff charges for telephone cables would make a considerable difference to the location of industry. I would like to hear Mr. Whyte on this subject because as far as I am concerned I now have a new line of thinking on it.

Whyte: I agree with Professor Dakin that there is substantial scope for research of the type he has mentioned and I hope during this year to be able to initiate one or two studies relating to cost benefit analysis of the users of the telecommunications service, under various alternative postulates about different tariff structures. At the moment I am trying to get a suitable economist to join the staff to undertake such studies. In the United Kingdom over the past 30 years the cost of long distance telephone traffic has been falling in real money terms throughout that period and there has been a progressive reduction of the distance element in the tariff and we are now in a situation where we have only four bands to cover total distance in the country. It is my personal opinion that this process has not yet stopped and that we are going to see it continue towards the ultimate in which there is only a single fee for any distance within the United Kingdom, though this is not in prospect in the foreseeable future.